Local Religion in Sixteenth-Century Spain

Local Religion in Sixteenth-Century Spain

William A. Christian, Jr.

PRINCETON UNIVERSITY PRESS

Princeton, New Jersey

Publication of this book has been aided by a grant from the
Paul Mellon Fund at Princeton University Press

This book has been composed in Linotype Janson

Contents

List of Tables

List of Illustrations

Acknowledgments

I thank the Del Amo and the Tinker Foundations for their financial aid; the Marian Library of the University of Dayton; the Biblioteca del Escorial; the archivist of the diocese of Toledo, Don Ignacio Gallego Peñalver; the archivist of the diocese of Cuenca, Don Dimas Pérez Ramírez; and the following friends for providing criticisms of an earlier draft: Q. Aldea, S. Arrom, L. W. Bonbrake, P. Brown, R. Christian, N. Davis, S. Tax Freeman, N. Galpern, C. Gibson, J. and R. Gimeno, R. Harding, M. Jiménez, T. Kaplan, T. Kselman, J. Lang, J. and R. Linz, C. Lisón, M. O'Neil, S. Ozment, S. Sharbrough, K. Sklar, and Bruco Storchovsky. In particular I thank Donald Moore for his intelligent, painstaking editing, Cristina García Rodero for generously sharing her archive of photographs, and Natalie Zemon Davis for her example and her encouragement.

Local Religion in Sixteenth-Century Spain

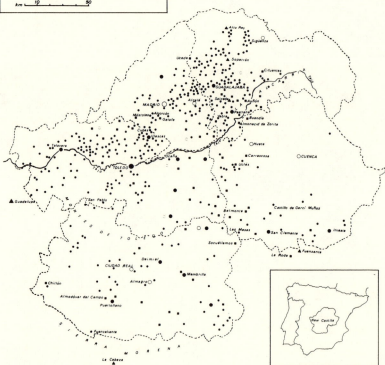

Map of New Castile.

ONE

Introduction

PHILIP II's chroniclers sent a printed questionnaire to the towns and villages of New Castile in the years 1575–1580. This study of religious belief and practice is based on the responses to that questionnaire.

In the villages, towns, and cities of Central Spain (and, I suspect, in most other nuclear settlements of Catholic Europe) there were two levels of Catholicism—that of the Church Universal, based on the sacraments, the Roman liturgy, and the Roman calendar; and a local one based on particular sacred places, images, and relics, locally chosen patron saints, idiosyncratic ceremonies, and a unique calendar built up from the settlement's own sacred history. The responses to the royal questionnaire are particularly useful for understanding this local level of religion.

Although I have arranged the information in what seems a logical order, I have tried to stand back and let the people of New Castile speak in their own terms. They tell how they make contacts with saints and how the saints help them in such basic matters as avoiding plagues of insects, healing the body, and obtaining rain. But we must listen if we want to hear. If we impose modern categories and issues, we learn—perhaps—more about ourselves, but miss much about them. Social class, sexual division of labor, intellectual freedom, or the growth of the state, for instance, do not appear to be the questions central for understanding the religious experience of these people.

Historians of sixteenth-century Spain have been more concerned with the notions of clergy about religion than its practice by lay people. Marcel Bataillon, Agustin Redondo, and other scholars have made careful appraisals of humanists, leading bishops, and spiritual figures in the different religious orders.[1] To many Spanish reformers, lay religion was ignorant, pagan, and lax. They caricatured, ignored, or refined to the point of unrecognizability the kind of raw theology described and quoted in this book. Appreciating localistic lay devotion was as difficult for the humanists of the Renaissance as it has been for modern historians, who too often adopt the humanists' facile dismissal of local religious practice as "magical" or "superstitious."[2]

Other strategies and other points of view are needed to understand the devotion of persons whose lives did not center professionally on religion. Inquisition records are better sources for Italian sects, the Albigensians of the Pyrenees, Spanish alumbrados, and Jewish conversos than Catholic peasants.[3] For aside from minor cases like blasphemy and superstition, the Inquisitors did not usually investigate everyday Catholics and everyday behavior. Building a picture of rural Catholicism from their archives would be like trying to get a sense of everyday American political life from FBI files.

While historians of Spain have preferred the intellectuals to the populace and the heterodox to the orthodox as subjects of study, historians of France have used infinite ingenuity in uncovering measures of lay religiosity. For the early modern period, Michel Vovelle has approached the subject through the formulae of wills, the composition of fêtes, and changes in iconography. Jeanne Ferté and Louis Pérouas have analyzed the reports of diocesan visitors to parishes and the books of brotherhoods. And others have scientifically examined miracles, farces, and Christmas plays.[4] These approaches are complementary in building an idea of lay practice. But sometimes in the search for indices of change and proofs of cause and effect, one loses sight of experience itself.

Emanuel Le Roy Ladurie's *Montaillou* and Richard Trexler's work on civic religion in Renaissance Florence are models for a more ethnographic approach.[5] The village reports used as sources for this study also tell about civic religion—how entire communities communicated with saints and God. They have the advantage of being from hundreds of different places, both small and large, and they address the matter of religion directly in an expository, narrative form. They are particularly unusual in that many if not most of the responses were given orally by unlettered persons in dictation to notaries public.

The royal chroniclers who drew up the questions (fifty-seven in a 1575 version, forty-five in a 1578 version) wanted to know about each town's history (how the town got its name, how it was founded, notable events, famous citizens); the jurisdictions in which it fell (in what kingdom, under what lord, in which judicial district, in what diocese); its location (neighboring towns, highways, mountains, rivers, ports); its resources (soil, flora and fauna, crops, sources of water and firewood, pasture land, minerals, salt, and stone); its physical characteristics (houses, castles, and notable buildings); its social composition (population, number of nobles, occupations); how it was administered and over what territory; and finally, its churches, benefices, relics, hermitages, miracles, feasts, monasteries, and hospitals. Only relevant questions were to be answered, and the responses were supposed to be brief and clear, "characterizing as certain what is certain and doubtful what is not known for sure." Respondents were asked to return the printed questions so they could be used again elsewhere.

The chroniclers' intention was to construct a history of the kingdom in aggregate from the history of the individual towns.

There exists no description or history of individual places; these studies will be the best basis for the description and general history of the monarchy. It is important to get under way with the former, so that the latter can eventually be concluded in an authoritative and complete way commensurate with the authority and greatness of Spain, and for the honor and ennoblement of these kingdoms.[6]

The village reports were not used for this purpose until the twentieth century. As far as we know, when they arrived from the villages and towns they were simply filed away. Today they are in the library of the Escorial.

The answers to the questionnaires, transcribed by a notary, were to be provided, according to the instructions accompanying the questions of 1575, by "two or more of the most intelligent or alert (*curiosas*) persons in the town . . . two or more persons who know most about the town and its district. . . ." Those chosen, whether by town meetings or town officials, were men selected above all for advanced age and local knowledge, rather than social station. About a third of them could not sign their names; many more must have been functionally illiterate. Occasionally a priest, notary, or doctor was chosen (especially in the larger towns), but by and large the respondents seem to have been older labradores, peasants with access to land. When ages are given they are often in the seventies and eighties. To be sure, the respondents were men, not women, farmers, not day laborers, and adults, not children; but they were nonetheless lost voices, speaking to their king for over five hundred thousand lost voices in their settlements.

Most of this study is based on the answer to two questions:

> 51. The notable relics that the churches and towns possess; and the well-known chapels and oratories in its territory and the miracles that have taken place there.
> 52. The holy days on which work cannot be done, and the fast days and the days on which meat cannot be eaten that are observed in the town by a special vow, in addition to those of the Church, and the reasons for them and their origin.[7]

The answers to these particular questions may be the strangest and the most curious to modern readers. That this should be so is due to our ignorance, not only of the culture of the sixteenth century, but also that of modern Europe. For much of Catholicism in peasant Europe remains unchanged. Of all the responses, the religious ones may be the most ancient and the most modern.

I began to study the patterns of rural religious belief in 1966, with a survey of Spanish shrines; subsequently I studied present-day religion for two years in villages of the province of Santander. The village reports to Philip II provide perspective on the beliefs and practices of the twentieth-century villagers I lived with.

The perspective cannot be complete. The foremost limitation of the 1575–1580 reports for the study of devotions is the corporate voice of the respondents. The questions seek and provide group sentiment and group devotions. One learns little of individual nuance, intensity, or doubt.

Second, not all important manifestations of piety are discussed. The universal, sacramental aspects of religion are taken for granted. Lent and Holy Week were deeply experienced in these villages and towns as a reliving of Christ's passion. This kind of calendrical concentration of devotion one sees only indirectly in the reports, as in the occasional mention of penitential brotherhoods.

Some kinds of devotions are not mentioned at all—those that took place in the *capillas* of the parish churches or convents, or lesser devotions to nontitular saints in the banks of images known as *retablos* above the altars of churches, convents, and chapels.

One suspects that out of local pride the respondents occasionally exaggerated the efficacy of their saints or the size of the hinterlands of their shrines. But on economic matters there was an opposite bias. The people of New Castile doubtless wondered if their answers would be used to raise new taxes; a Toledo priest raised this question explicitly.[8] It is hard to see how this suspicion would have affected their responses to the questions on religion, however.

And finally, not all of the towns paid the same level of attention to the questions. A few did not answer at all, others dismissed them with "nada de eso," and more gave them short shrift, naming only the most important *ermitas* and vows. Fortunately the distribution of these nonresponses and partial responses seems to have been fairly random.

In spite of these limitations one can glean enough from the replies to gain a fuller sense of the religion of rural people than is known for any Western country of the time. Some matters, like the causes for collective vows, the saints invoked, and the shrines frequented, are documented with the scientific certainty of sample surveys. More important, perhaps, the reports of legends, miracles, and vows reveal a rich sense of the villagers' philosophy of divine behavior.

Because of the predominance of small settlements in the responses, this is perforce a study of rural religiosity. But all evidence indicates that the kind of local religion described was shared by most of the people of Madrid and Toledo (and, for that matter, of Seville, Barcelona, and Florence) and was as characteristic of the royal family as it was of unlettered peasants. One is therefore led to question the idea of "popular religion," as distinct from some other kind.

One of the sources for this conceptual error may be an exaggerated distinction between city and country, with cities representing civilization and culture in the face of rural—"popular"—ignorance. Such a distinction is particularly inappropriate for central Spain, where, except for Toledo and Madrid, most of the urban-sized settlements were predominantly agricultural, and where even small villages were urban in design and orientation.[9]

Toledo was the great exception, both in terms of size (eleven thousand households) and composition. The priest who composed its report declared with pride, "Toledo is not agricultural, but rather industrial and commercial; indeed, as a measure of its nobility and urbanity, it can be said that no plough or pair of yoked mules will be seen within its gates or on its bridges."[10]

Because Toledo was a textile city, specializing in the

weaving of silk from Granada, Valencia, and Murcia, it had a large population of artisans. In addition to a colony of Moriscos, who were quartered throughout New Castile in 1569 after their revolt in the mountains of Granada, Toledo had immigrants from Galicia and Asturias. And inevitably it attracted the poor of the countryside. "When the farmers of nearby villages and even those farther away can no longer live honorably among their neighbors because of poverty, they come to Toledo to one of these small cellars (*sotanillos*) and live in secret want, knowing that because the people of this town are charitable and there are so many brotherhoods they will be provided for. . . ." In 1575 there were 1,240 households living in cellars or caves in the city.[11]

As a commercial center Toledo provided services to the countryside, but even more it was a consumer of rural goods: woolen cloth from Alcarria; wheat from the Sagra region to the north and La Mancha to the south; and firewood and charcoal from the mountains nearby.

Toledo had jurisdiction over all settlements under royal possession within five leagues, was capital of an even larger ecclesiastical seignorial domain, and had offices for the highway patrols of the Santa Hermandad and the patrols of the sheep routes of the Mesta.

But what distinguished Toledo most from other Castilian cities was its role as a religious center. It was the capital of the largest and wealthiest diocese in the peninsula, location of the archdiocesan appeals court, and headquarters of the Spanish Inquisition; its thirty-six convents and monasteries held about fourteen hundred religious, and it was served by four or five hundred secular priests.

In 1575 Madrid was still only half the size of Toledo (about six thousand households). A fertile hinterland to the south and east supported a population of artisans, diplomats, and bureaucrats that gathered around the court of Europe's largest empire. Like Toledo, Madrid exercised seignorial jurisdiction over numerous villages, and the towns around it were prospering and increasing in population.

Talavera and Guadalajara also had substantial numbers of subject towns (*aldeas*), claiming twenty-eight and twenty-six, respectively. Both had about two thousand households, seven or eight convents, and were the seats of landed nobility. Alcalá de Henares, with about twenty-five hundred households, was an educational center with more than two dozen convents and colleges. All three of these large towns had corregidors. Those of Alcalá and Talavera were appointed by the archbishop; that of Guadalajara by the king.

Other towns north of the Tagus (or Tajo) river also had some nonagricultural functions. Illescas, with a thousand households, was the seat of a *corregidoría* and a market town. Pastrana (twelve hundred households) had been the administrative capital for nearby towns belonging to the Order of Calatrava before it was sold by Charles V. In 1575 it was the prosperous headquarters of a duke, where Moriscos and Milaneses produced silk and cloth of gold, and three-quarters of the houses were of cut stone, not the more plebean adobe. It had three convents and produced exceptional amounts of oil and wine. Similarly, if smaller, Escalona, Cifuentes, and Torrijos (of an unknown number, seven hundred, and seven hundred and fifty households, respectively) were headquarters of large patrimonies, and the site of monasteries endowed by local nobility. It was around independent noble courts like these that religious innovators found favor and protection. Both Escalona and Pastrana had been centers of alumbrados earlier in the century. (See Table 1.1.)

The Tagus serves as a useful dividing line for the purpose of this study. North of the Tagus (the present provinces of Madrid, Guadalajara, and the northern part of Toledo) were compact nuclear settlements, small and close together, with a median village size about a hundred and thirty households. The eastern part of this zone, then a fertile region producing olive oil and fruit, is known as Alcarria. South of the Tagus the towns of La Mancha (the plains of Ciudad Real, Cuenca, and southern Toledo) were larger and more

Table 1.1. Mean and Median Sizes of Towns and Villages
Responding to the Questionnaires
(Excluding the City of Toledo)

Present province	Number of places that replied	Mean number of house- holds	Median number of house- holds	Towns with 1,000+ households
Guadalajara	145	179	100	Guadalajara, Pastrana
Madrid	91	194	150	Colmenar Viejo, Madrid,* Alcalá*
Toledo	162	260	130	Ocaña, Sta Cruz/ Zarza, Illescas, Talavera, Tembleque, Madridejos
Ciudad Real	67	369	200	Daimiel, Campo/ Criptana, Puertollano, Membrilla, Villanueva/Infantes, Ciudad Real*
Cuenca	48	350	230	Iniesta, San Clemente, Huete*

* Responses not available. Demographers estimate about 4.5 persons per household for Castile at this time, but there was considerable variation.

widely separated. Most of them were under the seignorial and religious jurisdiction of the military orders. The median settlement size in this area was over two hundred households. To the south of Toledo and Talavera was the Montes de Toledo, a poor mountainous region of small and isolated settlements, largely subject to urban jurisdictions.[12]

In New Castile south of the Tagus, administrative centers had a high proportion of merchants, artisans, and monastics, but they were not necessarily the largest towns. They included Huete (a textile town, capital of a district, with nine convents and a school); Belmonte (one of the headquarters of the marquis of Villena, with three convents and a Jesuit college); Uclés and Alcázar de San Juan, capitals in the region for the orders of Santiago and San Juan, respectively; Almagro, site of a Dominican university; and Ciudad Real, center of a small royal hinterland.

Uclés, Huete, and Ciudad Real once had substantial Jewish populations. The Uclés report gives a glimpse of past harmony. "Uclés has been Christian for many years, and Moors and Jews lived there, each according to his laws, and had their synagogues and mosques and churches; and each had a slaughterhouse until the Jews were expelled from Spain and the Moors were baptized. . . . They were baptized November 22, 1501. They have been and are very good Christians."[13]

South of the Tagus ten towns had a thousand or more households (over four thousand persons) and would have been considered good-sized cities in northern Europe at the time. Indeed many of them, far larger today, remain agro-towns. On any evening from spring to autumn the roads going into them are clogged with lines of tractors, mule carts, and workers on bicycles.

While some people lived in peasant cities, most lived in urbanlike villages. Most settlements in the region were both agricultural and small, with fewer than a hundred and fifty households. Yet all but the smallest strangely resembled cities. They are now tightly nucleated settlements centering on squares, and the most prized locations are in their centers, not on their outskirts. (For an American looking for scenery, it is disconcerting to find that houses with a view of the countryside are virtually nonexistent.) Most of these villages were not egalitarian, but reflected in miniature the extremes of wealth of the cities.

A French scholar, Noël Salomon, has carefully examined the responses to the questionnaire about social and economic matters. The main agricultural products of the region were wine, wheat, olive oil, and wool. The majority of the population (overall from 60 to 70 percent) were landless laborers; most of the remainder (about 20 or 30 percent, more in some of the smaller villages) were labradores, peasants with draft animals or land, some of whom could be quite well off. Even in the smaller towns there were a few artisans, and in the market towns there was a thin stratum of leisured landowners and professionals, perhaps 10 percent of the population.

Many peasants and laborers also worked part time or seasonally at other professions. Some were weavers of rough woolen cloth, working in weaving shops or in their homes; others, especially in mountain settlements, produced charcoal or firewood; and women spun wool and made lace and pottery.[14]

Salomon found that by 1580 these peasants were beginning to feel new burdens. On the one hand much of the market for their artisanal production, especially of cloth, was declining. And fewer agricultural products were needed in the New World. On the other hand they suffered from a disproportionate burden of taxation, the forced sale of produce to cities, and encroachment on communal lands.[15] Nevertheless, 1575–1580 was a time of prosperity for New Castile, a prosperity reflected in a dramatic increase in population over the century and a very large and still growing religious establishment.

The region studied fell within five dioceses. The present provinces of Madrid, Toledo, Ciudad Real, and western Guadalajara were in the archdiocese of Toledo; central Guadalajara was in the diocese of Sigüenza; southwest Guadalajara, easternmost Toledo, and Cuenca were in the diocese of Cuenca; a few villages north of Talavera were in the diocese of Avila; and the town of Chillón in western Ciudad Real was in the diocese of Córdoba. Overlapping the diocesan jurisdiction was that of the military orders of Santiago, San Juan, Alcántara, and Calatrava, which supplied priests and collected tithes from towns in their domains. Toledo was the only cathedral city that fell in the area studied; its enormous archdiocese was divided into the archdeaconries of Talavera, Guadalajara, Madrid, Calatrava, and Alcaraz, each an important administrative center.

The number of clergy was far greater than that of today. As is true now, priests were more concentrated in the north of Castile than in the south. According to a tax survey of 1591, there was 1 priest for every 42 households for the kingdom as a whole. The number of households served by a priest in New Castile varied from about 38 in the district of Toledo to 77 in the southeast of Ciudad Real.[16] In 1964 for the same region, depending on the diocese, there were from one-third to one-tenth as many priests relative to the population.[17] (See Table 1.2.)

Table 1.2. Priests in New Castile, 1591

Number of priests	Administrative district	Approximate number of households per priest
1403	Toledo	38
770	Guadalajara	45
333	Huete	56
529	Mesa Arzobispal de Toledo	63
432	Order of Santiago, Castile	63
294	Campo de Calatrava	71
96	Campo de Montiel	77
(347)	Madrid (without the city)	(71)

These figures mask a very uneven distribution of clergy, which was heavily concentrated in Toledo, Madrid, Alcalá, and certain market towns with collegiate churches or multiple endowed chaplaincies. The number of priests in the town was not requested in the questionnaires, but a few towns reported it anyway. Generally speaking, the poorer the town was, the fewer priests it had. (See Table 1.3.)

Even where there were relatively few priests, priests were numerous by today's standards. Their massive presence should alert us to the probability that most of the public religious activity described in the reports was observed, if

Table 1.3. Priests in New Castile, 1575–1580

Town	Number of households	Number of priests	Households/ priest
Belmonte (had *colegiata*)	600	26	23
Toledo City	11,000	400–500	22–27
Madridejos (T)	1,600	15	106
Carrascosa del Campo (Cu)	676	6	112
San Agustín (M)	140	1	140
Pedrezuela (M)	150	1	150
Miguelturra (CR)	400	2	200
Chillón (CR)	800	4	200

not supervised by the clergy. Although not all clerics were well trained, they were probably better trained than ever before. By no means were these villages and towns backwaters of neopagan "popular" religiosity, abandoned by the Church.

In addition to having an ample supply of secular priests, the region was studded with monasteries, in small towns as well as cities. In the 530 places in the survey in New Castile, there were at least 61 monasteries and colleges of male religious as well as 66 convents and *beaterías* of female religious. These 127 establishments were located in 48 places, with over 1,500 male religious and 1,900 nuns and beatas. If core area towns not covered by the survey are included (among them Madrid, Alcalá, and Huete), there were perhaps 100 male monasteries and 90 female convents, with 3,000 male and 3,000 female religious. Almost half of these convents and religious were concentrated in Toledo, Madrid, and Alcalá. With 7 or 10 convents each, Talavera, Ocaña, Guadalajara, and Huete accounted for an additional sixth of the total. Pastrana, Belmonte, Cifuentes, Almagro, and Yepes had 3 or 4 convents each.[18] The rest were dispersed, primarily in market towns of from 400 to 800 households.

Rural Iberian monasticism in the early modern period was predominantly Franciscan.[19] In New Castile about a quarter of all monasteries of male religious were Franciscan, and in the countryside the proportion was much greater. In towns of fewer than fifteen hundred households in this survey, twenty-one out of thirty-five monasteries of male religious were Franciscan, either Observant or Discalced. The Franciscan influence, still growing in 1575, partly explains the intense devotion of the period to the crucifix and the Passion.

Other orders had only a small number of monasteries outside of the eight major centers. Augustinians had five, and Dominicans, Hieronymites, and the new Discalced Carmelites had two or three monasteries each. To my knowledge, Benedictines, Cistercians, and Trinitarians each had only one rural monastery in the region. Jesuits and Minims were just beginning to penetrate the countryside from urban bases.

Nunneries were more likely to be in cities than towns, and when they were in towns, it was mainly in those that had monasteries of male religious. Especially after Trent, nuns were not allowed to support themselves by begging. Nunneries were more likely than male monasteries to be endowed; those that were not made a precarious livelihood by teaching young ladies or doing artisanal piecework. The city of Toledo had a thousand nuns and beatas compared with only four hundred male religious, but there were fewer convents than monasteries in the countryside. Of the convents under the aegis of orders, the three most common were Franciscan, Conceptionist, and Dominican.

The word *beata* is frequently misinterpreted because it could mean many things. In sixteenth-century Castile a beata usually was a woman who had made a simple (that is, private) vow of chastity, wore a habit, and observed a religious rule of some kind, whether temporarily or permanently, cloistered or in society, or alone or in company of others. Beatas were usually under diocesan supervision and not subject to an order, even if they adopted its habit and rule. Many were simply devout single or widowed women who lived in their own houses with habits they made for themselves. In Villarrubia de los Ajos (Ciudad Real) "there is no monastery of monks, nuns, or beatas. There are some women who call themselves beatas, who live discreetly (*recogidamente*) in their own houses. They call these women beatas because some of them do not marry; but although they call themselves beatas they belong to no religious order (*no estan en religion*)."[20]

In 1575 there were at least eight communities of beatas in the city of Toledo (as opposed to four in 1544), several in Madrid, and at least twelve communities in as many other towns. The *beaterías* ranged in size from four to forty beatas; some were cloistered, others were not.[21]

Permanent members of formal communities of third-order Franciscan women were also called beatas. Girls (*doncellas*) might live in these communities for a given number of years learning artisanal skills and then might marry (sometimes with a dowry from the community) or become permanent beatas.[22] Aside from a few communities of beatas who provided social services for the sick and poor, most women religious were cloistered.[23]

What kinds of services did the friars provide the general population? Most monasteries in the countryside had little endowment, forbidden in the constitutions of the Observant and Discalced Franciscans and the Discalced Carmelites. Sometimes when one of these monasteries was set up, it would be with the assurance of regular alms from a wealthy founder. But most mendicant monasteries were just that—mendicant. Monks went out in search of alms and in turn provided auxiliary pastoral services, confessing and preaching. The people of Getafe, fifteen kilometers from Madrid, reported that eight different orders regularly came to beg in their town "for new wine at grape harvests, for grain in August, and other things during the year, and these orders come sometimes to preach, and hear confessions in Lent and during jubilees." Carrascosa del Campo (670 households) had no monastery, but was served by Dominicans and Franciscans from Huete, fourteen kilometers to the north. The village of Fuentelaencina "se provee de sermones y confessiones" from the Hieronymite monastery of Santa Ana of Tendilla nearby.[24]

The monks, then, supplemented the parish priest, especially in the towns around Madrid that had fast-growing populations. One of these, Getafe, had only one parish church, badly located, for nine hundred households; there were no monasteries. When in 1574 some of its citizens invited Carmelites from Madrid to found a monastery, others invited the Discalced Carmelites, and both orders came the same night. The next morning "both kinds of friars said masses and gave sermons, and the townspeople went from one to the other like the Stations of the Cross on Holy Thursday." An ecclesiastical judge sent by the diocese settled the matter by sending both orders out of town and establishing a second parish church.[25]

As this example shows, in the 1570s monasticism was in an expansive phase, the orders competing for choice locations. No fewer than a dozen convents of Franciscans were founded in the region between 1564 and 1575, in La Mancha as well as in towns near Madrid and Toledo. The new foundations represented a fourth of the monasteries of the order in the region under study.[26] (See Table 1.4.) The older orders that depended on entailed lands were not flourishing, and, with the exception of the Hieronymites at

Table 1.4. Observant and Discalced Franciscan Convents
Founded by 1575
(Within 25 Kilometers of Towns under Study)

Date founded	Number
Unknown	3
Before 1400	8
1400–1499	12
1500–1557	13
1564–1575	12

the Escorial, not building new monasteries. The mendicant orders were those most favored with invitations from towns to establish new convents and provide spiritual services.

Of the 530 communities that replied to the questionnaire in New Castile, all but about 30 were within a day's walk (twenty-five kilometers) of a convent of monks. There were fewest monasteries in the southern area, dominated by the military orders, which for centuries did not allow other orders to found monasteries in their domains. But by 1575 there were only three districts in which at least one monastery was not close: the hamlets in the Montes de Toledo to the northwest of Ciudad Real and the southeast of Talavera; a strip of western Ciudad Real from Valdepeñas to Tomelloso; and a few towns belonging to the Order of Santiago around Corral de Almaguer in southwest Toledo. The majority of settlements, virtually all those north of the Tagus and in Alcarria, were within twenty-five kilometers of five or more monasteries.

New Castile was divided between two jurisdictions of the Inquisition: that of Toledo, which corresponded to the archdiocese of Toledo, and that of Cuenca, for the dioceses of Cuenca and Sigüenza. For over fifty years, since about 1520, the Inquisition had been directing its attention to Catholics as well as converted Jews.[27] The annual reading of its edicts in parish churches, the presence of its representatives in market towns, and the periodic visits of its commissioners to take denunciations (even for chance remarks) assured a fundamental orthodoxy in public statements on religious matters.

One may ask whether, given the saturation of the region by clergy and religious, such a monitoring of lay religion was necessary. In fact the Inquisition was as concerned with clergy as with laity, for the lesson of Martin Luther and other northern European reformers who were priests and monks had not been lost. Indeed, the archbishop of Toledo, Bartolomé Carranza, was indicted in 1559 and was perse-

cuted for Lutheranism until shortly before his death in
1576. One should therefore not be surprised at the orthodoxy of the practices described in the reports to Philip II.

I lived in the village of Alhambra in the province of
Ciudad Real from 1976 to 1977 and visited many other of
these villages, surveying shrines and looking in parish archives for documents mentioned in the reports. Even now
the fierce pride with which some brotherhoods or town
authorities guard the books of miraculous images, even from
the priest, leaves no doubt that whatever canon law may
say, local religion is theirs. The priests are usually from different villages. They often speak of local devotions with a
bemused tolerance, occasionally wondering out loud about
"pagan superstition." But when asked about the shrines of
their home villages, the same priests speak with tenderness,
excitement, and pride. For them the religion learned at
home, embedded in the home landscape, transcends the doc-
trinal attitudes learned in the seminary, which they may
apply elsewhere.

The reports to the chroniclers of Philip II are exceptional
sources for this local, or localistic, religiosity for the sixteenth century. We are taken out of the institutional church
into a sphere of direct contact between communities and
their saints, in which specific saints serve as helpers at critical times. The villagers describe in a matter-of-fact way
spiritual aspects of their civic lives and a landscape overlaid
with sacred significance. Note that these answers are from
laymen to laymen: the people, not the clergy, speak, and
speak with authority. It is definitely their religion, their
contract, their friendship with a saint. The clergy may provide a necessary link in this system, but in the eyes of the
villagers they are not principals in the age-old, continuing
negotiations between saints and towns.

Faced with serious threats to their collective well-being
from the environment, both peasants and townspeople
wanted to know who would help them and what they
should do in return. These questions had most probably

been asked a thousand years before and are still asked today. The kinds of promises and offerings they reported continued until the nineteenth century. But the specific subjects of their requests—the saints—had been constantly changing. It may be useful to see the repertoire of divinities used in the sixteenth century in a broader historical context.[28]

Prior to the eleventh century, lay votive devotion was directed to saints almost exclusively through their relics, and in countries like Spain was concentrated on local martyr, hermit, or bishop saints. With the introduction of images in the eleventh and twelfth centuries, this votive devotion was freed from the cathedrals, monasteries, and parish churches; holy sites in the countryside could be sacralized with images. Previously, Mary could not be a major factor in the veneration of relics because of popular belief in her Assumption. But as the Mother of God she was an ideal successor to pre-Christian mother goddesses in the landscape. Starting in the twelfth century Marian shrines gradually won preeminence over the bodies of local saints as important sources for practical divine help.

The use of images also permitted, in the face of epidemics like the Black Death, the importation of specialized "international" saints like Sebastian, and these too found their place in the community pantheons, more often than not as local, rather than district or regional, helpers. This was the kind of saint most often approached with vows. Because of their specialized nature, however, these latter saints were vulnerable to failure or obsolescence. Divine nonspecialists like Mary can balance out failures in some problems with successes in others, and can deal with new kinds of problems as they arise. The difference is akin to that of the economic vulnerability of single-crop farms as opposed to polyculture. As a result, the specialist saints tended to turn over more rapidly and were eventually supplanted by generalists like Mary.

In 1575 in New Castile there were thus three layers of devotion: the oldest stratum of local saints, their relics and bodies, primarily in the north of the region, whose southern portion was not reconquered until the thirteenth century; the second layer of Marian devotions, some of them powerful shrines, often localized in dramatic sites in the landscape; and the additional presence of images of specialist saints, whether in chapels or in parish churches. A fourth element, miraculous images of Christ, especially crucifixes, was just gaining popularity. Like Mary, Christ was consulted as a divine generalist, and he took over a combination of problems from the specialist saints.

The village reports of 1575 show a host of small changes and rearrangements in human-divine relations that were part of the larger shifts sketched above. The reason for the shifts was the desperation of people seeking help. Because they needed help so badly, they were relatively flexible and open to new options. New Castile in 1575 was not the forgotten, depopulated region of today. Then it was the heartland of the most powerful nation in Europe. Its wealthier citizens had a better chance for advanced schooling than ever before. Its villagers were tested in the ways of the most bureaucratized European state, fighting usurpations of land and nobles' dubious claims to exemption from taxes in lengthy suits in the distant courts of Valladolid and Granada. Its nobility was fighting in Flanders; its priests were traveling to Rome; and its citizens were coming and going from the New World. Laymen, priests, religious, and nobility were always on the lookout for holy objects that could help, or at least embellish, their hometowns. The reports provide a way of studying systematically these imports and local changes in devotion. But above all they show us a religion in which the local was of primary significance.

Vows

The holy days on which work cannot be done, and the
fast days on which meat cannot be eaten that are observed in the town by a special vow, in addition to those
of the Church, and the reasons for them and their origin.

A Response to Disaster

A STRONG central government had eliminated one kind of
insecurity mentioned by peasants in the past: the raids on
villages by bandits, rebels, and competing barons.[1] But other
insecurities of medieval peasant life persisted in the sixteenth
century, and with them their religious remedies. Plagues and
other epidemics, locusts, hail, or drought could mean that
entire communities could be decimated or forced to move.
In Atanzón (Guadalajara) villagers remembered a plague
around 1465 in which more than 400 persons died (the town
population in 1580 was 260 households, or about 1,200 persons). In Valdeavellano (Guadalajara) an epidemic reduced
the population from 80 to 13 households. In the village of
Cabañas de la Sagra (Toledo) there was a *gran mortandad*
(great mortality) that only one woman ("who was called
la Paxarera") and two or three men survived. In 1507 half
of the village of Meco (Madrid) died of the plague. And in
Puebla de Almoradiel in 1544, more than 600 persons were
sick at once, and 200 infants and 50 adults perished. In some
villages, like Arenas (Ciudad Real) it is stated that infants
normally died, because the land was "unhealthy." All of this
information on the effects of epidemics was offered by the
villagers (there was no direct question on the subject);
hence these dramatic cases doubtless stand for many, many
others.[2]

Particularly in La Mancha, the mass of landless laborers appears to have been relatively mobile, quick to abandon a town for work elsewhere. Some dramatic declines and increases the villagers reported in their populations were due to substantial population movement in hard times. Whole districts were thinned out after bad harvests because there was no food, with the larger towns and cities as destinations. Fifty out of three hundred households of Bolaños (Ciudad Real) moved to Almagro in 1577 because of taxes, because the town territory was small, and because it was a dry year, according to the village report. The villagers of Manzanares (Ciudad Real) similarly attributed fluctuations in their population to drought. Half the population of the small village of Camarma (Madrid), fifty-five households, was said to have left for Segovia to escape the taxes.[3] The widespread presence of hospitals for the vagrant poor in these villages (Question 54, 1575; 39, 1578) also testifies to the frequent circulation of the landless and those who could no longer depend on their families for support. Writing about 1580, Juan de Pineda condemned the exploitation of these poor in times of hunger.

> Some perpetrate another kind of misdeed against those who work on their lands at times when the poor cannot find work and there is hunger in the land. For when the poor ask for alms, they put them to work in their houses or property and give them only the most miserable food in recompense. And for that they say they gave alms to the poor and paid their workers. But because for the work alone much pay is lacking, they lie when they say they gave alms as well; because wages are a matter of justice and must be completely paid, and alms are voluntary and a work of mercy. He who does not even give what is just can make no claim of charity.[4]

Harder times were yet to come for these people. But even during what was in fact a period of relative prosperity, the

lives of individuals, families, and communities were fragile
and insecure.

For the community an abandoned village site nearby was
usually present as mute testimony of bad times in the past
(Question 56, 1575; 43, 1578). And older villagers could
themselves well remember the bad years in their lifetimes.
The most complete description of an epidemic is that of
Alcorcón, on the outskirts of Madrid. The plague, preceded
as it often was by a famine, occurred about 1496.

> About eighty years ago, more or less, there was a great
> epidemic like the plague. They have not been able to as-
> certain what disease it was, except that when a person in
> one house began to get it he or she gave it to everyone
> else so that all in the house died. Many people had to go
> outside the village, and they put up shacks a little way
> off where they stayed until the fury of the disease had
> passed. It is not known how long it lasted, but the village
> was decimated, with much want. Some hold that the want
> and the hunger came even before the epidemic. Because
> they were so hungry they made bread from grama grass
> that they dried in ovens and then broke up into small bits
> and took to be ground, out of the flour making bread
> that they ate. Others made bread from broad beans or
> chick peas, each with what he had. [They hold] that the
> epidemic came because the people were weak and with-
> out sustenance. This is what they have been able to find
> out from other old people.[5]

The epidemic remembered best was that of 1506–1507,
when plague struck the entire region, again after a year of
famine. Fifteen villages scattered throughout New Castile
mentioned that plague, which was also severe in points as
distant as Cadiz and Barcelona.[6] A writer at the beginning
of the seventeenth century claimed that the effects of this
epidemic could still be seen in abandoned villages and un-
tilled fields.[7] Villagers fled infected towns, hastening the
spread of the disease. Totanés (Toledo) was a refugee cen-

ter, and it was considered remarkable that only three persons died there.[8]

In 1527 there was a severe epidemic in the towns to the north of Guadalajara. One village, Robledillo, described it as a *pestilencia de secas*.[9] Other towns affected were Cerezo, Iriépal, Lupiana, Atanzón, and Santorcaz.

The next major epidemic was in the years 1545-1546, apparently centered in the southernmost portion of the present province of Guadalajara. The villagers of Hueva reported that more than 300 persons died (their population in 1575 was 135 households, around 500 persons) of *pestilencia y mortandad*. Other villages reporting disease in the area were Alvares and Santorcaz.[10]

In these same years the peninsula experienced a massive invasion of grasshoppers.[11] Grasshoppers affected New Castile in the years 1545–1549 from Yebra (Guadalajara) in the north (1545) to Almodóvar del Campo and Calzada de Calatrava, in southernmost Ciudad Real (1545–1546 and 1547, respectively). This invasion seems to have been particularly severe in La Mancha. Other towns reporting grasshoppers at this time included Villamiel (Toledo), El Provencio and Castillo de Garci Muñoz (Cuenca), Piedrabuena, Arenas, Cabezarados and Socuéllamos (Ciudad Real).

At Yebra the grasshoppers arrived during harvest.[12] "When many people went to cut the grain there came great bands of grasshoppers, and in front of their eyes, without being able to stop them [the grasshoppers] cut the grain and ate it and cut the clothes and garments of the laborers and pierced their wineskins and got into the pots in which they carried cooked food in such numbers that the food stunk too much to eat. . . ." To the south in El Provencio two years later, "in the year of forty-seven came flying to this town and district so many grasshoppers that they shuttered the sun and settled on the land fifteen leagues wide and twenty-two long; and in the years forty-eight and forty-nine no grain or wine was harvested." The locusts

were in nearby Castillo de Garci Muñoz in the years 1548–
1549.[13]

It was thought that grasshoppers multiplied especially in
pastureland, and this argument was used to bring pastureland under cultivation. Normal procedure for dealing with
serious concentrations of grasshoppers was the appointment
of a judge or commissioner with special powers, who would
supervise a mass assault on the insects before they were mature enough to fly. This procedure was supplemented by a
number of religious remedies.[14]

Is there a connection between the epidemic of 1545–1546
and the invasion of locusts of 1545–1549? With the loss of
food, the people would have been more susceptible to disease. There may have been another such conjuncture in
1556–1557. Grasshoppers were reported then in two villages
of Toledo, Gamonal and Villaminaya; three towns in Ciudad
Real, Piedrabuena, Arenas, and Socuéllamos, told of epidemics.

The epidemic of 1556–1557 may not have been the
plague, but rather typhus (*tabardillo*), brought on by a
very wet year with much standing water. Juan de Villalba,
author of *Epidemiología Española*, basing his information
on two sixteenth-century writers, Luis de Toro and Luis de
Corella, says that typhus was particularly severe from 1557
to 1570. There was definitely typhus in the area, as it is
mentioned in the report of Chiloeches (Guadalajara).[15] The
people refer to any epidemic, including the plague, as a
pestilencia. Occasionally they mention an *enfermedad*,
which seems to have been any lesser disease.

Finally another epidemic, of *catarro* (influenza?) struck
the region in 1580. "On August 31, 1580, the contagious
disease of the *catarro* took hold in Spain, almost depopulat-
ing Madrid and many other towns and cities." All of the
monks at the Escorial were bedridden at the same time. The
Barcelona city council's chronicler claimed that twenty
thousand persons were sick of the disease in August of that

year, and that infants, the elderly, and pregnant women died from it. Only a few of the village reports date from 1580; that of Talamanca (Madrid) stated that many had died that year from *catarro*.[16]

In addition to disease and grasshoppers, the northern part of New Castile was threatened by a host of insect pests that attacked vines and forests. Such attacks were by nature less dramatic and memorable, for they did not cause population loss. The earliest vow recalled for help against pests was in 1546—as opposed to attacks of grasshoppers, remembered from the mid-fifteenth century, and plagues, from the late fifteenth century.

The farmers used many names for these pests, most of them still in use today. The most common appears to have been the vine beetle (*Altica amphelophaga*), which is called *escarabajuelo*, and its larvae, known in an early stage as *queresa*, and in the mature phase as *pulgón, coco*, or *cuquillo*. The two other most common pests are the *arrevolvedor*, a caterpillar of the butterfly *Sparganothis pilleriana* that twists up and eventually breaks off tender vine leaves; and *rosquilla* ("grub"), a moth larva that attacks plants by the roots, occasionally in numbers large enough to be considered a plague. The villagers referred to the various larvae with the general terms *oruga* and *gusano* ("worm") and subsumed all insect and other pests (including lizards) under the general term *sabandijas*. The use of these terms was not scientifically precise but generally agreed with the standard agricultural treatise of the time, Gabriel Alonso de Herrera's *Libro de agricultura*.[17]

These tribulations were the major reasons for the collective vows made by the villages to the saints. For the area now comprising Guadalajara, Madrid, Toledo, Ciudad Real, and Cuenca, the occasions reported for collective vows to saints give an idea of the relative frequency of the various forms of natural disaster faced by communities. (See Table 2.1.)

Table 2.1. Reasons for Vows

Reason	Number of vows	Percentage of all vows with reason given
Plague, disease*	272	37
Vine pests	127	17
Grasshoppers	116	16
Hail	40	5
Drought	28	4
Rabies	17	2
Storm	15	2
Brotherhood	27	4
Devotion	51	7
Other	52	7
Subtotal	745	
Not given or unknown	679	
Total	1424	

* "Pestilencia, mortandad, enfermedad."

The depositions sent to Philip II give the orthodox religious response to these disasters: the saints appealed to, the procedures employed, and, by implication, the notions of divine intervention in daily life. Individuals and communities patiently searched for divine helpers and set up contracts with saints to ward off present and future dangers.

It should be emphasized that the people of New Castile had additional, less orthodox methods for dealing with disaster. At that time lay professionals circulated through the Castilian countryside selling their services to individuals or communities to ward off disease, locusts, other insect pests, or hailstorms by magical methods. Known variously as necromancers, enpsalmers, or conjurers of clouds, they competed directly with the priests of the parishes. Indeed, from Inquisition records it would appear that many of them were clergy or religious.[18] One of their methods for dealing with locusts or vine pests was to hold them up for trial and excommunicate them.[19] Similarly, the cloud chasers were hired by communities to conjure hail-bearing storm clouds away, or make the hail dissolve into rain. The clerical writers who reported these matters considered the magicians to be somewhat effective and attributed what power they possessed to pacts with the devil. In some places the wizards would hold matches with the local clergy to see who could best deal with the clouds.[20]

The clergy had their own "legal" prayers and exorcisms to chase the clouds. After prohibiting "enchanters, fortune-tellers, bewitchers, magicians, and enpsalmers," the Synodal Constitutions of Toledo of 1566 continue, "and for this reason we do not prohibit, but on the contrary we order and exhort all the clergy of this archdiocese who are responsible for souls: that decently and without scandal for those cases in the form that is in the manuals, they employ the exorcisms approved by the Church."[21]

Even locust trials, although generally condemned by theologians, were not entirely unacceptable. One trial was held as late as 1650 in the Hieronymite monastery of Santa María de Párraces, near Segovia. The witnesses for the prosecution were the patron saints of a number of villages and the souls in purgatory of one village, all represented by villagers; the prosecutors, spoken by a friar, were three different Saint Gregories (see below); and the judge who pronounced the excommunication on the grasshoppers was Our Lady Saint Mary, "constant advocate of men, particularly those in anguish and need," speaking through her lieutenant, the prior of the monastery. Her sentence, after consultation with her advisors Saint Jerome, Saint Francis, Saint Lawrence, and Saint Michael the Archangel, was that the insects would automatically fall under excommunication if they did not leave the territory. The trial was held only after all other remedies over the space of two years had failed, including exorcisms, the sprinkling of special water from Navarre, processions, novenas, and even the reform of public sinners. In his justification for the trial, which he held was really just a

severe form of exorcism, the prior cited similar excommunications of locusts in Avila and Valladolid, of rats in Osma,
and of swallows that dirtied a shrine on the outskirts of
Córdoba.[22] But of these less orthodox activities the reports
tell us little, aside from the description of two competing
necromancers, a friar and a priest, in Viso de Illescas, a village between Madrid and Toledo.[23]

THE VOW

In the reports we read of more orthodox practices—the establishment of long-term *votos* (vows) between the villages
and the saints. According to Martín de Azpilcueta ("Doctor
Navarro"), a Spanish canonist whose *Manual de confessores
y penitentes* was a standard reference work for priests in
the latter half of the century, "A vow is a deliberate promise
made (at least in one's mind) to God for some greater good
that has not been annulled by the superior."[24] Canonically
speaking, a vow to God for a good purpose, whether of
chastity, to take orders, to go to a shrine, to fast, or whatever, must be fulfilled under penalty of falling into mortal
sin.

The importance of vows in the daily life of the Catholic
laity has been insufficiently appreciated, perhaps precisely
because most personal vows were made and fulfilled without clerical intervention. Vows largely built and almost
completely maintained most shrines and chapels, and still do.
The Church and the Spanish state made a flourishing business out of the commutation of vows. Still in some parts of
Spain today, lay persons make vows for the most minor
problems, on virtually a daily basis.[25] Only when a vow
could not be fulfilled was the priest called on to intervene,
either to commute the vow or pardon the penitent for non-
fulfillment. Theoretically only bishops could commute
vows, and certain vows, those of pilgrimages to Rome, Jerusalem, and Compostela, that of chastity and membership in
a religious order, were reserved for the pope alone to com-

mute. But in the sixteenth century one could easily purchase Bulls of the Crusade, special papal indulgences originally intended to raise money for the Reconquest, which gave the buyer the right to have most vows commuted by any priest.[26]

The vow and similar prayers to the saints were forms of direct engagement between the Christian and the divine, with no inquisitive or costly middleman. Surely this universal and constant practice must in other countries have provided some of the groundwork for the popular appreciation of the more institutionally unmediated form of Christianity proposed in the Reformation. Reformed churches removed the images of saints and largely eliminated their cults, but in practice this may simply have meant shifting the same personal devotion formerly directed to the saints and Mary to Christ. In fact the same process was to a certain extent happening in the Catholic Reformation, for in the last years of the sixteenth century throughout Catholic Europe there was a major shift toward Christ-centered devotion.

Vows of a personal devotional nature were not binding on heirs.[27] That is, a son whose deceased mother had promised to go to Compostela did not himself have to go. (He probably would have. Still today such vows are commonly fulfilled.) But vows made by a corporation like a village were contracts with the divine that theoretically had to be fulfilled, even if a hundred years had passed and all the villagers who had made the original vow had died.[28] Such vows could be modified or eliminated only by decision of the bishop or the pope. They were the corporate obligations of the community to the divine, and were legally binding, usually drawn up officially as an act of government. In this sense it is not surprising that Philip II asked about community vows to the saints; he had inquired about obligations to temporal lords, and wanted to know of relations with spiritual lords.

Of the 745 vows for which a reason was given in the reports, about 9 out of 10 were in response to a natural disaster. Many of the remaining 10 percent were made out of a more diffuse sense of patronage, without a specific stimulus in the form of some danger to the community. Vows were made before a natural disaster struck, to ward it off; during a natural disaster, to halt it; or after it, in thanks for its cessation and as a protection for the future. The vow itself was to observe certain stated acts of devotion, usually annually and generally on the saint's day and the day before.

Such vows promised devotion and obeisance in exchange for the saint's intercession with God. The people saw God as actively intervening in human affairs when he was angered; their role was to figure out from his actions the reasons for his anger. Thus many vows were made as a result of what were seen as signs to the village from God. Although most vows seemed to approach the saints as advocates for the community, some reports indicate a belief that the saints themselves were capable of inflicting harm on communities.[29] For either purpose the vows involved a propitiation of the saints.

How Saints Were Chosen for Vows

SIGNS

The villagers saw the coincidence of a natural disaster with a certain saint's days as a clear sign. Hail, still a scourge of wheat and vine on the meseta, was particularly seen as a sign that devotion was not being accorded where it was due. Thus when the villagers of Brea (Madrid), ever attentive to signals from on high, noted that it hailed several years in a row on Saint Anne's Day, they instituted a vow to observe her vigil. ("Saint Anne's Eve is observed because two or three years consecutively hail fell on the vines on Our Lady Saint Anne's Day.") Conceivably suffering from the very same storms, the nearby village of Buges (Madrid) set up the custom of giving a public dinner, called a *caridad*, on Saint Anne's Day.[30]

Other villages, because of hail on particular days, instituted vows to Saint Athanasius, Saint Bartholomew, Saint Benedict, Saint John the Evangelist (at the Latin Gate), Saint Pantaleon, Saint Peter, Saints Quiley and Julita, the Finding of the True Cross, and the Cross of September.[31] By the same token, the lack of a hailstorm when it might have been expected was also seen as a sign. While in Cerralbo (Toledo), the Feast of Saint John at the Latin Gate was observed, "because on his day our grain fields were hailed on two or three years," not far away in Mesegar the same day was observed "because on that day the neighboring towns were hailed on, and by the mercy of God this place was spared."[32] Similarly, whereas in Valdelloso (Guadalajara) Saint Athanasius' Day was observed because it hailed on his day five years in a row, in Iriépal, not far away, the same day was kept because on that day a hailstorm did no damage to the crops while the villagers were returning in procession from a monastery in Lupiana.[33]

Other sudden disasters besides hail were seen as punishments and signs calling for public vows:

Fires: In Auñón (Guadalajara) Saint Benedict's Day was observed "because on that day ten [olive] oil mills belonging to the township burned down." Saint Peter's Day was observed in Fuentes (Guadalajara) because of a fire in the wheat fields.[34]

Floods: San Martín de Valdepusa (Toledo) observed the Feast of the Visitation (July 2) because more than sixty years earlier a flash flood drowned a farmer in his fields. Similarly Getafe (Madrid) observed the day of Saints Cosmas and Damian because of a flood that carried away a shepherd and two lambs.[35]

Earthquake: The village of Romanones (Guadalajara) observed May 10 because of an earthquake. They do not even mention a saint; the earthquake was a clear sign to observe that day.[36]

Lightning: In Usanos (Guadalajara) Saint Barbara's Day was observed and a *caridad* distributed because "this same day in the afternoon a lightning bolt hit the tower of this church and burned three or four people, and ever since they always distribute it and observe it."[37] The sign was all the more clear, since Saint Barbara was a protector from lightning.

Pestilence: Generally pestilence did not begin dramatically enough for a vow to the saint on whose day it began. However, in the town of Fuente de Pedro Naharro (Cuenca), where it struck very suddenly, "they observe the Feast of Our Lady Saint Agatha and fast on her eve, and began to do so because when the sun rose on Our Lady Saint Agatha's Day there were thirteen dead from the pestilence, and it was decided from devotion to observe said holy day and fast on her eve, and give *caridad* her day."[38]

In the above cases the people seem to have considered the saint on whose day a disaster occurred in some way the source of their misfortune; the saint was thought to be angry and to need placation, or else the saint was perceived as seeking devotion. Orthodox doctrine would have it otherwise: chastisement comes only from God, and saints intercede for people, not against them. Perhaps for this reason the implicit role of the saints as negative interveners in village fortunes was never explicitly stated in the reports.

Some vows were made as a result of less painful, more enigmatic signs. Around 1515 in Uceda, a town of five hundred households between Guadalajara and Madrid, a man butchered a sheep on December 7, and the sheep did not bleed—a sign that meat should not be eaten on that day, the eve of the Immaculate Conception.

In this town the Feast of the Conception of the Virgin Saint Mary, which falls on December 8, is observed by local vow; meat is not eaten on its eve, also by vow. This latter vow was promised about sixty years ago, its reason being that on one eve of this holy day, when it was the custom to eat meat, a butcher named Juan Díaz, while killing a ram in the town slaughterhouse, inserted a knife in the neck to cut its throat, as is done with other kinds of animals, beheading them. But no matter how hard he worked at it, or how far in he put the knife, not a drop of blood came out, even though he broke the throat and cut the head off and completely killed it. This was seen to be worthy of admiration and was taken down in a deposition. From that day it was vowed not to eat meat on that eve, and so it was observed and still is observed. And we Isidro de Lureña and Bachiller Ramírez certify that on the day of Saint John of June [June 24] of last year 1573, entering the main slaughterhouses of Toledo, we saw this same Juan Díaz weighing meat. The older of us thought he recognized him and asked if he had ever been in Uceda, and he said that he had. And without our asking him he told how he had been a butcher here, and how the aforementioned event befell him and that depositions had been taken. By then he was very old and gray. It is general knowledge in this town that it happened thus.[39]

I have quoted this case at length to show the wonder still felt about the incident by the villagers. Such an anomaly, occurring when it did, must have had a meaning, carrying a message to the village. Community vows to observe the Immaculate Conception for devotional reasons swept across Castile in the last quarter of the fifteenth century, and the feast was obligatory in all the dioceses whose sixteenth-century constitutions I could check.[40] So it is not surprising that by 1515 Uceda was already observing the day. However, before major holy days it was obligatory to fast the eve, or at least to abstain from eating meat. Although some bishops encouraged fasting on the eve of the Immaculate Conception by granting indulgences of forty days to those who fasted, fasting was not obligatory. Since it was not clear how important a day the Conception of Mary was, the townspeople were naturally receptive to a sign.

A sign takes on meaning in context. The doctrine of the Immaculate Conception of Mary conferred on Saint Anne a status like that of Mary herself. The apocryphal Gospels popular in the fifteenth century contributed to this enhancement of Saint Anne, filling in details about her life and virtues. Thus the Feast of Saint Anne came to be considered a holy day on the popular level before it was made obligatory by the Church.[41] In fact, in the sixteenth century Saint Anne was observed in several dioceses, including Sigüenza, but not in Cuenca or Toledo.[42] Hence the villagers were prepared to attribute signs like hail to a need for devotion to Saint Anne. It hailed seven years in a row on Saint Benedict's Day in Negredo (Gaudalajara) before the villagers vowed the day, but only two or three years on Saint Anne's Day in Brea (Madrid). Of course, the more dramatic the sign—earthquake, flood, or disastrous fire—the less important the context. But hail is something that happens a good deal, and apparently the villagers did not rule out the possibility of chance.

Several of the signs seemed to require that no work be done on a given day. Not working, especially at harvest time, was a major sacrifice in the observance of a saint's day. This was especially true for the majority of landless laborers, who depended on fixed daily wages for survival. Here again the villagers' uncertainty about their obligations to Saint Anne is clear. On Saint Anne's Day loggers sending timber from the mountains of Cuenca down the Guadiela River were amazed to see a log stand upright and burst into flame. As a result of their request, supported by the other citizens of the town, the mayors of Castejón (Cuenca) and those of other surrounding villages vowed the observance of the day, the burning log being held a sign that the loggers should not have been at work.[43] Their receptiveness to a sign must have been increased because the feast was kept in the neighboring diocese of Sigüenza and because there were shrines to Saint Anne in nearby Tendilla and Carrascosa. Less cryptic was the sign in Argamasilla de Alba (Ciudad Real): "It was vowed to observe Saint Anne's Day because in this town people used to work on that day, and it came to pass that several of those who worked on that day died."[44]

For carters and long-distance freight haulers, there were no holy days. They worked seven days a week, which led Juan de Avila, when proposing reforms for the Council of Trent, to suggest that carters be permitted to work on holy days, since they did anyway.[45] In his *Miscelánea*, written about 1590, Luis de Zapata averred that "in Castile and the kingdom of Toledo, where there is much carting, it is known and said to be certain that no carters have died, or broken arms or legs, or had their mules strangled, nor did they or their mules drown crossing fords, except and because of its being on a holy day."[46]

Saint Lawrence, whose popularity at the time is attested by the dedication of the Escorial, was one of the few non-biblical saints whose feast day was universally obligatory in central Spain. Particularly dire consequences were supposed to befall persons who worked on his day. Is hunting working? In Belmonte (Cuenca) three notables hunting on Saint Lawrence's Day were unable to hit captive targets, the strings of their crossbows snapped, and when they blasphemed one of the bows spontaneously broke. Zapata gives a number of instances of divine retribution visited upon those who worked or even lighted fires on that day.[47]

Saint Blaise was another saint for whom devotion on a local level in Madrid and Guadalajara had outstripped his place in the Church as a whole. Observe the reaction of the people in Almonacid de Zorita (Guadalajara) when the door fell off the church as they were leaving on Saint Blaise's Day, 1566:

> The feast of lord Saint Blaise is kept because a few years ago, when most of the village out of devotion was ob-

serving his day anyway, when all the village was coming
out of high mass that day by the main door of the church,
very crowded together, one of the two main doors of the
church fell in their midst because a hinge broke, and God
saw fit that no one was injured. And when the people
contemplated the mystery that God had worked in harm-
ing no one, given the devotion that they had, they all
ordered those who govern this republic and with them its
clergy to promise and endow it to be kept from then on.[48]

While a dispassionate observer might wonder whether an
impartial reading of this sign might not counsel staying as
far as possible from the church on Saint Blaise's Day, the
local interpretation was that the people had been spared injury because of their devotion to Saint Blaise, and that therefore they should formalize that devotion in a vow.

The sign—a bloodless ram, a pillar of flame in a river, the
breaking of a bowstring, or the falling of a church door—
did not have to be a disaster, although disasters seem to have
been the commonest signs and cried out for action. No, the
sign was an anomalous event, invested with meaning by its
occurrence in relation to the annual calendar and the way
it "fit" with the village's devotional history. For the signs
that were seen as punishments directed at the village for not
observing popular (but technically optional) feast days
shaded off into signs that were punishments for violations
of vows previously made. In all the miracle books of shrines,
which began to be published in the mid-sixteenth century,
were examples of divine punishment of individuals who did
not fulfill their promises to the shrine saint; generally whatever affliction they had had returned to them until they paid
up. In terms of village vows, the villages themselves imposed formal mechanisms like fines on recalcitrant citizens.
But when an entire village lapsed in its observance of a vow,
the punishment was sometimes seen to come from a saint
or from God. That these lapses continually occurred cannot
be doubted, especially since some vows were very old, and
their occasions—perhaps two hundred years earlier—long

forgotten. The incentive to fulfill a traditional obligation had to be weighed against the need to work, given an overwhelming number of obligatory feast days even without additional vowed observances.

Dramatic cases of the return of the community disaster following a lapse in observance are evidence that throughout this region fear must have accompanied tradition as an incentive to maintain vows. The invasion of locusts in the fields of Yebra in 1545, described above, takes on a deeper meaning when seen as retribution for not observing a vow made in the previous century to Saint Maurus as protection against locusts:[49]

> Afterwards, either because of our sins or our weakness in being remiss in observing this holy day and vow, or because God saw fit, His Divine Majesty about thirty years ago allowed many grasshoppers to return to the lands of this town.

In Cabezarados (Ciudad Real) the lapse was of a vow to Saint Quiteria for relief from rabies. The chastisement was the loosing of a rabid wolf on a group of holidaymakers:

> This vow is very old, and when there was some laxness in observing it, it came to pass that about forty years ago on a fiesta day Isabel Martín, citizen of this town, and her brother and other people were in the common pasture land of the town when suddenly a rabid wolf sprang out and bit the young man and inflicted many wounds upon him, and he became rabid and died of them eight or nine days after he was bitten. The last days he was so rabid that they bound him with chains until he died. The wolf also bit many oxen and cows in the pasture, and when trying to bite a mother cow that was defending her calf, the cow killed it. Since these events the townspeople have observed and do now observe the old vow with much devotion and hold a solemn procession and feed all the poor in the town; and everyone from the town eats in the house of the mayordomo that day, each paying his share.[50]

Divine punishment also fell on individuals who violated communal vows. In the Madrid town of San Sebastián de los Reyes, the vow to Saint Sebastian on account of pestilence was to fast the eve and eat neither animal products nor fish on the feast day. According to canon law, one is responsible for keeping the vows of the village where one is staying, not of one's home village.[51] So a villager went to a neighboring village to eat well and escape the dietary restriction. When he came back his wife and children were eating beans, and he died suddenly after telling them that they need not observe the vow.

> For Saint Sebastian's Day, which is always January 20, it has been vowed in this town that on the eve there will be fasting and no meat eaten, and on the day itself there be no animal products or fish eaten, or anything that ever had or has blood, nor cheese, milk, or eggs. This was vowed because of the pestilence. About sixty years ago on Saint Sebastian's Day, at a time when the people of the town of Alcobendas used to come in procession to the church of this town before high mass, a citizen of this town, named Portazguero, went back with the procession to Alcobendas solely in order to eat meat in that town. He ate lunch and dinner that day in Alcobendas, and at nightfall he returned to his home in this town. He sat down in a chair and found his wife and children and servants keeping the vow by eating broad beans. And he spoke to them in a way that showed his lack of respect and scorn for the vow by saying how good they were eating their broad beans while he had come all full from eating meat. Without saying another word he was suddenly dead in his chair.[52]

Two more of these cautionary tales. In Puertollano (Ciudad Real) a reaper tried to harvest grain on the feast day of the local shrine, Our Lady of Grace:

> In said chapel hangs a sickle for reaping grain, which they say was put there in memory of a man who went

to reap with it on the day of the Visitation of Our Lady, which is the advocation of the chapel and a vow of this town. At the first sweep that he made in the grain the sickle turned against his hand and stuck to it in such a way that he could not reap anything. The old people say that this happened, that they heard it from their parents and many other people.[53]

Even the worms could take their revenge. The one person in Castillo de Garci Muñoz (Cuenca) who did not observe a vow had his house attacked by worms.

The reason why this feast of Saint Ambrose was vowed was because of the worm that was eating the *villas* [towns? vines?]. And when the town vowed it—so they have heard from their ancestors—the worm stopped immediately. But one person from this town did not want to keep the day, and the worms got into his house, so that he vowed once again the day and observed it, and there was no more worm.[54]

SPECIALIST SAINTS

Disasters like earthquakes, fires, floods, and attacks of locusts, which tend to occur suddenly, were more likely to be taken as signs related to a day than, say, a slow epidemic or the more gradual infestation of vines with worms. In the latter cases the choice of a saint was more problematic; most villages turned to saints known for their specialties.

In the case of pestilence, the peasants of New Castile above all turned to Saint Sebastian, especially in the epidemic of 1507. But by the 1570s Saint Roch was being called on for more new vows than Saint Sebastian. The first dated use of Roch in the reports was in Lupiana (Guadalajara) about 1527, and throughout the century Roch was more popular in the Guadalajara area than in other parts of New Castile. For Spain in general, Saint Roch did not come into use until the end of the fifteenth century, when his relics were stolen from Montpellier and taken to Italy. He did not attain great popularity until the seventeenth century.[55] The two other saints used most for diseases were Mary and Anne, but on a very much reduced level.

For insects attacking the vines the saints most preferred were Saint Gregory of Nazianzus, Saint Gregory the Pope, and Saint Pantaleon. One of the reasons that Gregory of Nazianzus was chosen was that his feast day, May 9, occurs about the time the tender vine shoots would be emerging, a moment of critical danger from vine worms. For the same reason in some villages processions around the vines were held on the day of the Finding of the True Cross (May 3) and other days at the beginning of May. Saint Pantaleon may have been chosen in part because around his day (July 27) the grapes would be in danger from vine beetles. Often the reports refer only to "San Gregorio," but some reports specifically mention Saint Gregory the Pope or Saint Gregory "of March," so we know that this saint, whose feast date is March 12, was also used.

The matter is complicated even further, and the confusion may in fact have been originally caused by another Gregory, called Ostiense, whose shrine in Sorlada, Navarre, was the major Spanish shrine for the control of locusts and other insect pests. This is supposedly a different Gregory, a bishop sent out by the pope as a missionary to Spain to help eradicate locusts. The shrine, magnificently decorated, still exists, and the fields of the region are still blessed with water poured through the reliquary skull of the saint on May 9. March 12 is also celebrated at the shrine.

Our villagers were aware of this shrine. In fact, during the great locust attack of 1545, one town, Almodóvar del Campo (Ciudad Real) sent a representative to Navarre to bring back holy water from the shrine:

> The day of Saint Gregory of Nazianzus is kept, which is May 9; it was vowed because of the plague of many locusts that Our Lord permitted to come down on all this region and crop and destroy the grain. This town sent a representative to the kingdom of Navarre to a place where

they say the body of the Blessed saint lies, and from there he brought back water that was sprinkled on the fields, and God saw fit to lift the plague of locusts. So that solemnity was vowed, and a wooden image was made that is taken around the entire village on that day in a general procession.[56]

Here the confusion of Gregory of Nazianzus and Gregory Ostiense is clear, and the people of Almodóvar consider them the same. The shrine seems to have adapted to the confusion, for there are statues of several Gregories within it. In its present form the shrine was constructed with funds donated by Charles V. The first dated vow to Saint Gregory of Nazianzus in the reports is about 1540. As late as 1757 the government sponsored a nationwide tour of the famous relic to combat an epidemic of locusts.[57]

Even before the Gregories came into vogue, another theologian, Saint Augustine, was used to combat locusts. Indeed, in New Castile, Saint Augustine was a locust specialist, while the Gregories were used against both locusts and vine worms. An Augustinian chronicle published in 1569 claimed that Saint Augustine appeared in Toledo in 1268 to drive locusts into the Tagus.[58]

The doctors of the church were considered to have special power over insects and other agricultural pests. In Socuéllamos (Ciudad Real) a lottery was held among the doctors of the church to choose the saint for a vow against locusts and vine worms. In other towns Saint Ambrose and Saint Thomas Aquinas were used. Perhaps this use of theologian saints can be explained by the custom of ritual excommunication of grasshoppers and insect pests. (See Figure 1.) In an ecclesiastical trial, what lawyer could present a more convincing case than a doctor of the church?[59]

Disease and insect devastation accounted for about three-quarters of all the vows in New Castile for which a reason was given. Other reasons separately accounted for only a small proportion of the vows. Hailstorms, as we have seen, were more likely to be ascribed to the saint on whose day

Figure 1. Saint Augustine conjuring locusts at Toledo. Painting by Miguel Jacinto Meléndez. Prado Museum, Madrid, Archivo Mas.

they occurred. They were also more likely than any other disaster to have been taken care of by female saints. In Valdeavellano (Guadalajara) the crops were ruined seven years in a row by hailstorms, but apparently not on the same day every year. So a lottery was held by burning candles to eleven different virgin saints.[60] In the Guadalajara region the high number of vows to Saint Agatha in olden times probably resulted from her specialty in hail.

Compared with other problems, drought occasioned few vows, and those were mainly to Mary and the Cross of May. Mary, the childbearing saint, was a logical choice in matters of fertility, particularly since the Marian shrines were located in the countryside. The Cross of May (May 3) was probably used because the feast occurred at the time when water was essential for the wheat. The rogation processions doubtless served the same function. Vows to Mary, however, would have been redundant, since most Marian feast days were obligatory; for this reason Mary was addressed more with petitionary processions and novenas at her shrines than with vows.

Both the records of the Barcelona city council and those of the cathedral chapter of Seville confirm that drought, although a chronic problem, was addressed above all with processions and provoked relatively few vows. From 1515 to 1631, sixty-four dry spells occasioned over six hundred petitionary processions in the streets of Barcelona. This was five times more petitionary processions than for all other reasons combined. (There were about eighty in the course of seven outbreaks of the plague, forty-five for royal military campaigns, and others for royal health, Catholic military endeavors, etc.) But in an even longer period (1474–1687) there were no vows because of drought in Barcelona, although there were three for the plague (1501, 1590, 1651), one for hail and tempests (1474), one for locusts (1687), and others out of devotion.

In virtually all crises in Barcelona in the sixteenth and seventeenth centuries it was customary to hold a series of processions to the "Seven Chambers of Mary," convents with Marian images, in honor of the seven joys of Mary. But the saint used especially for drought was Saint Madrona. In five out of six droughts her bones were brought down to the cathedral from a hermitage on nearby Montjuich. When enough rain had fallen, they were returned.[61] In Seville, as in New Castile, Mary was the saint most prayed to for rain in the early modern period.[62]

LOTTERIES

When the choice of a saint was not obvious because of signs or reputation, some communities let Providence take a hand by organizing a lottery among saints. Such a procedure was entirely orthodox. Lots were used for devout purposes in the apocryphal Gospels, and for Augustine and Aquinas it was lawful to seek reverently to know God's will by casting lots if there was urgent necessity. Throughout medieval Europe the *sortes sanctorum* was used to find helper saints in times of need.[63]

Some of the lotteries of New Castile may have been held in the same way that some towns chose their *alcaldes*. In La Solana (Ciudad Real) names of members of the cabildo were written on slips of paper, which were then rolled into balls and dipped in wax. The wax balls were then shaken up in a box so that the choice would be random.[64] In some places the method used to select saints was the burning of twelve candles of equal size and weight, each assigned to a different saint. The saint whose candle was the last left burning was chosen. This procedure was used throughout Europe.[65]

The criteria for selecting those saints to be included in the lottery were usually not reported. In the case of the naming of Saint Bartholomew of La Rana (Toledo) in 1529, the saint was chosen by lot from among "certain saints that they were devoted to."[66] However, the lottery generally took place within a certain class of saints who were considered specialists. We have already seen that in one town the class of saints used against locusts was the doctors of the Church, and in another, the class of saints from which a protector against hail was chosen was that of female virgin saints. In Pareja (Guadalajara) Saints Simon and Judas (Jude) were chosen as protectors against the plague from among the twelve apostles by a system of candles.

> This town is devoted to the blessed saints Simon and Jude, apostles, and hold them its patrons and advocates. The old people were heard to say that this devotion was taken miraculously, because when there was a general plague in the town, they devoutly decided to celebrate the feast of the saint that our Lord should inspire them to choose, and hence they made twelve wax candles and put on each the name of an apostle, and lit them in front of the Holy Sacrament, proposing that the last candle that was live—for all of them had the same weight and wick— would be considered the devotion that they had to cele- brate and give a *caridad* on that day in perpetuity. The last two candles that remained were those of Simon and Jude, and these saints were celebrated in perpetuity, and nowadays the feast is celebrated by giving and dividing up twelve cattle as a *caridad* to the inhabitants of the town and poor outsiders.[67]

Part of the miraculous nature of the choice would have been the conjunction of the two candles, for both saints are cele- brated on the same day, October 28. Was the distribution of twelve cattle seen as a kind of propitiation or a symbol of the twelve apostles?

The apostles were not generally used as protectors against the plague in sixteenth-century vows. However, the custom may have been more common in Alcarria in the fifteenth century, for candles representing the twelve apostles, with two others added for Mary and the *Mártires* were burned to select an advocate for the town of Atanzón (Guadalajara) during a plague about 1463, when "more than four hundred persons died in a short time . . . four, five, or six every day."[68]

The report of Almonacid de Zorita, in the same district,

indicates that the use of lotteries of one kind or another for the selection of divine patrons may have been extensive and well-organized in an earlier epoch. There the vow was made to the martyr saints Justa and Rufina of Seville.

> Some say that it was for locusts that were on the land and eating all the crops; others say it was for the plague, and that they cast lots among the other saints for the one to be kept, and the lot fell to these two Virgins in this town. In each place in this province lots fell to other saints, because it is said that the entire province gathered for this purpose, and so each village or town of the province observes the day of the male or female saint that fell to them by lot.[69]

There are references to lotteries in sixteen of the village reports. Many give some kind of ratification for the vow, some sign that chance was not involved. In Valdelaguna (Madrid) the choice of Saint Toribio during a drought was immediately ratified by a cloudburst.

> Saint Toribio was vowed for water. And in the deposition that was taken on the day of the vow [it says that] there was a great drought, and lots were thrown among saints, and it fell to this blessed saint, and immediately they vowed to keep his feast and build him a chapel. And in the deposition it says that before the people left the church where they had gathered it rained heavily, and they stayed in the church giving thanks to God.[70]

In other towns a simple lottery was not enough. The name had to be repeated three times, as in the case of the Transfer of the Arm of Saint Eugene, a feast day in the Toledo diocese that turned up three times in a lottery on account of the plague in El Campo Real (Madrid) around 1510. Lots also had to be cast three times in the case of Our Lady of Peace, in Puebla de Montalbán (Toledo).

> Seeking this town to take an advocate because locusts and worms were eating the grain and vines, the lots fell twice

to Our Lady. And although they said they already had
her as an advocate, so the lots should be cast again, they
fell once more to Our Lady. From this it was understood
that she herself wanted to be the advocate of the town,
and so her feast is said and mass on Saturdays, and since
then there have been neither locusts nor worms.[71]

This last example is of special interest because it shows
clearly the two-layered system of advocates in use. Mary
was already an advocate in Puebla de Montalbán. But because of the new problem of insect pests, the townspeople
wanted a new, perhaps specialized helper, for whom they
were willing to make new commitments in devotion. Also,
since Mary was already an acknowledged helper, and the
insects had come to town in spite of her, she presumably
needed reinforcement. But the lots showed that it was her
will to be the advocate against the insects. The people's reluctance to use her (accepting her only on the third try)
may help explain why Mary was not chosen more often in
these communities for specific tasks. Apparently she was
considered a general helper, and had been for a considerable
time. New problems necessitated additional helpers.

BROTHERHOODS, DEVOTION, RELIGIOUS ORDERS, AND VISIONS

In the context of group danger, towns selected saints by
sign, by reputation, and by recourse to Providence in the
form of a lottery—a way of provoking a sign. Nine out of
ten vows for which reasons were given were made in this
context. There were other kinds of collective vows. The
need for a divine intercessor was continual, and the people
of New Castile were always alert to it. One of the ways
they discovered their helpers and thereupon made a long-
term commitment was through the gradual accretion of individual favors and protection. Then as now they distinguished simple devotion from votive devotion.

When the church door fell off on Saint Blaise's Day, most
villagers were already observing the day *de su devoción*—

without a vow. The vow was subsequently made because of the clear evidence that Saint Blaise was favoring the village as a whole; it served to institutionalize the relationship. It is therefore not surprising to find villages making into vows de facto or formal devotions that began with one part of the village, perhaps one of its brotherhoods. About 5 percent of the vows for which a reason was given came about in such a way.

The questionnaire did not specifically inquire about brotherhoods, but some villages, often in response to a question about "pious works," volunteered the information. The village brotherhoods, especially those dedicated to a saint, sometimes had property to administer; but most depended upon the entrance fees of new members and the alms gathered during their fiestas to pay for their ceremonies, for the lamp burning before their patrons, for their annual banquets, and for their charitable works. The older brotherhoods seem to have been dedicated to individual saints, especially Sebastian, but the newer were penitential brotherhoods like that of the True Cross, the Five Wounds, and the Blood of Jesus that held processions during Holy Week and participated in village petitionary processions as flagellants. The most active brotherhoods were those of the True Cross and the Rosary, which were building chapels in the decade 1570–1580.

In the larger towns brotherhoods were more numerous and provided a religious focus for barrios and guilds, often providing mutual aid and charitable services. These brotherhoods based on barrio chapels or convents were part of a two-tiered system of devotion, with a local cell for day-to-day devotions, funerals, and poor relief, and a town-wide unit for joint processions, town-wide vows, and other critical moments. There was a corresponding two-tiered system of saints, mainly the specialist saints for the chapels and Mary for the town-wide devotions.

Just as vows to saints preserved a community against locusts, pestilence, and hail, although neighboring communities suffered, so a similar special protection applied to members of brotherhoods. The devotion of Torrubia del Campo (Cuenca) to Saint Augustine for protection against locusts was so old that no one could remember when it began. It preserved the town as a whole and the members of the Saint Augustine brotherhood in particular.

> This saint has been held in great veneration for the very clear benefits as regards the locusts; for although the locusts were in the district they did no harm to this township; so much so that it happened that a brother of this brotherhood had a grain field between two fields of others who were not brothers, and the two adjacent fields were totally ravaged, but no harm was done to the field between them that belonged to the brother.[72]

The brothers made their own vows to their saints, often a feature of admission to the brotherhood. In some villages, like Cuerva and Casas Buenas (Toledo), most villagers belonged to the brotherhoods, and so the village as a whole observed the brotherhoods' vows.[73] Other villages decided to make the brotherhoods village-wide and obligatory, at least as far as men were concerned, so that the village as a whole assumed the brotherhood's devotional obligations as if they were debts. This was the case of Magán (Toledo) on the feasts of Saint Marina, Saint Barbara, the Immaculate Conception, Saint Sebastian, and the Expectation of Our Lady, on which days no one in the village ate meat:

> The reason for all of these days on which meat is not eaten is that there were in this town private brotherhoods (*cofradias particulares*) that had vowed the observance of the days and abstinence from meat on their eves. When the town made town-wide brotherhoods (*cofradias generales*) for these and other saints it assumed the responsibility and custom of fasting and observing those days.[74]

In other cases the villagers said that they observed the feast of a given saint simply out of devotion, whether or not a brotherhood was at the origin of the vow. The saints most involved in such vows—accounting for 7 percent of the total vows for which a reason was given—were Sebastian, Anne, and Mary of the Immaculate Conception. In Almonacid de Zorita (where the church door fell off), Saint Anne's Day was finally vowed because everyone was observing it anyway. In 1573 the town of Carrión de Calatrava (Ciudad Real) also vowed to observe Saint Anne's Day, from devotion. "On July 26 the Feast of Saint Anne is observed by vow because she is the mother of Our Lady, and they are devoted to her in this town; it was voted in the year of seventy-three."[75] We saw before that people were most likely to perceive signs as relating to this kind of popular saint.

There is remarkably little evidence that preachers from the religious orders influenced these vows. Aside from vows made in connection with new relics only one set of vows directly stimulated by a preacher is reported. In Bolaños (Ciudad Real), the people observed the Feast of Saint Joseph "on the instance of Resgente Virués, who was a learned and holy Dominican friar from Almagro, who with his doctrine and sermons was so persuasive that he moved the towns in these environs to vow it, and he died in this year of 1577."[76] Calzada de Calatrava, twenty kilometers south of Almagro, vowed a feast to Saint Joseph in 1576, probably under the stimulus of Virués. So did Miguelturra (although no date is given), twenty kilometers northwest of Almagro, Valenzuela, six kilometers southwest of Almagro, and Puertollano, forty kilometers southwest.[77] Here is a clear instance of a single preacher who introduced into a group of towns a devotion that had not previously existed in the region as a formal practice.

The novelty of the votive devotion to Saint Joseph can be seen from the many different spellings. Of the ten cases of vows in New Castile as a whole, the name was spelled five different ways: Jose, Joseph, Josefe, Jusepe, and Xosepe. There were no chapels at all to Saint Joseph and only one

monastery—a newly founded one in Toledo (of Discalced
Carmelite nuns). Here then is the entry of a "new" saint into the local system—a saint thus far without specialty. The
vows to him were variously for locusts, vine worms, hail,
storms, and simple devotion. Four of the towns around Almagro that seem to have been influenced by Virués listed no
reason or simply gave "devotion" as the basis for their vow.
But Valenzuela had already put the new devotion to a specific use against storms. Thus a devotion passed from the
theology of a Dominican into the practical pantheon of the
countryside.

Dominicans may also have propagated devotion to the
Holy Name in western Cuenca, possibly from their convents of Huete and Villaescusa de Haro. Towns forming two
clusters—Tarancón, Tribaldos, Fuente de Pedro Naharro,
El Acebrón, and Saelices; and El Cañavete, La Alberca, and
Las Pedroñeras—had all made vows or set up brotherhoods
to the Holy Name. A Franciscan monastery to the east in
Villanueva de la Jara was founded with this dedication in
1564. One wonders whether the presence in Castillo de
Garci Muñoz of relics of Saint Bernardino stimulated or
helped the devotion along.

There must have been other cases, but the questionnaire
was not phrased in a way that would show how new saints
were introduced. A saint who became popular was likely to
be picked up by a number of different orders. Saint Roch
was recommended by a Capuchin in Valencia and by an
Augustinian in Toledo. Augustinians would logically encourage devotion to Augustine (at least one Castilian town
enrolled en masse in the brotherhood of the first Augustinian convent in Spain, San Ginés de la Jara, near Cartagena);
but most saints were not members of a particular order and
were thus available to all preachers.[78]

A word of caution is in order here. I think there has been
a clerical bias in ascribing the spread of lay devotion to
clergy and religious. Surely lay reputation and the strategic
success of certain well-publicized vows had much to do with

the popularity of saints. The people and the propagators probably influenced each other.

The most direct sign that a certain saint sought worship and would act as an intercessor for a village or town was the apparition of that saint to a member of the community with instructions for worship. The reports tell of seventeen apparitions of images or saints, of which twelve were of Mary. Most of these stories were probably ex post facto justifications for the importance of shrines, serving to explain and confirm a shrine's location as a sacred place.

MUTUAL OBLIGATIONS OF SAINTS AND COMMUNITIES

All the vowed saints were chosen—whether by reputation, divine sign, lot, or devotion—to represent the community to God ("so that he plead to God for this place"). In the reports, the term commonly applied to the intercessor is advocate (*abogado* or *abogada*). It is still used in some parts of Spain today for this purpose, primarily in Galicia. The trial of locusts at Párraces shows how refined the judicial metaphor was for human-divine relations. As in that trial, the saint was the town's lawyer or advocate. The ultimate judge, however, was not Mary (although the judge in that trial, she was explicitly described also as an advocate) but God, who sent the storms, locusts, and epidemics, or who allowed the devil to send them. In a 1466 vow to the Immaculate Conception because of plague and civil strife, the town of Villalpando (Zamora) asked Mary "to undertake to plead with her glorious Son Our Lord Jesus Christ; and that he by mercy and pity, and by his holy passion, which he suffered for all sins, should see fit to listen . . . and grant her request and order his Angel to desist from wounding and killing us." Similarly, from a vow of the lay and clerical authorities of Madrid during a plague in 1597, "We humbly beseech [Saint Anne and Saint Roch] to be our patrons and advocates in the presence of God, placating the wrath of God we have so justly merited."[79] If these disasters happened on a certain day, it might be because a certain saint was not intervening to stop them. In any case, if the community could find the right intercessor, one who would accept the obligation to help, then all would be well.

The village or town was subject to a number of hierarchies in addition to the saintly pantheon. Castilians' application of the term *advocate* to helper saints fit their earthly circumstances. Communities were constantly litigating: over who was their lord, exemptions from taxes, and common lands.[80] Many lawsuits had to be argued by lawyers paid by the community as a whole in the distant courts of Granada and Valladolid. Just as they paid their lawyers, sometimes going into debt to do so, so villages and towns entailed their resources in the form of future masses, penance, and work time to pay saints to be their lawyers before God.

In the sixteenth century the bureaucracy of Hapsburg Spain became more dense and complex, calling for new legal strategies and expertise from communities. An ominous example of judicial expansion and complication was the superimposition of the Inquisition on previous judicial systems. It may be that the people of New Castile applied lessons learned in the secular courts to the heavenly court by invoking a greater variety of saints and intercessors, and making more and different kinds of prayers, processions, and promises.

The saints did not merely seek to placate an angry God upset by sin. At times there appeared to be other unnamed antagonists trying to get the judge's ear. Here the analogy of a monarch who rewards and punishes after multiple intrigues and influences of favorites would serve just as well as that of a judge. "We well know the importance of the help of the intercession of the saints to defend us from our adversaries," announced the villagers of Quer.[81] Were these adversaries spirits like the devil, animals like locusts, or humans like nobles or other villagers? In any case the villagers' own sinfulness or devotional sloth was not their only adversary in the economy of divine retribution.

From the reports it is unclear whether any of these vows were made conditional on the acceptance by the saint of the duty offered, as in the case of most present-day personal vows. Many of them were unconditional promises, to be fulfilled whether or not they resulted in averting the disaster that occasioned them.

All vows contained some kind of commitment from the citizens—all of them—in exchange for the saint's protection. Such a commitment was sometimes made by acclamation in a mass ceremony, but in most cases it was sworn by the community authorities after a consensus had been reached. The vows might include any of the following: not working on the saint's day; fasting on the day before; holding a procession to the saint's chapel, to the saint's image in the parish church, or to a distant shrine; the carving of an image to the saint; the construction of a chapel; holding a bullfight in honor of the saint; or, quite commonly, holding a food-sharing with participation of the entire village and the poor of the district.

The towns of New Castile reported a wide variety of these public charity feasts. From the earliest times Christians celebrated the anniversary of the death of saints by feasts—the original meaning of "feast day." Such feasts were also common features of Spanish funerals in Old Castile through the nineteenth century, and provisions for them were often included in wills. As part of vows, they were a kind of communal homage to a helping saint. They were held after mass on the vowed day, and usually consisted of certain symbolic items as specified in the vow—wine, bread, and cheese, or a certain number of cows—to be given out to all present, to the poor, or to children. In some places they must have been expensive. The town of Talavera reportedly fed two thousand poor at one *caridad* each year. The charity feasts could be paid for by the town council, by whoever made the vow, or by direct contribution from the citizens.[82]

Observe that both abstention from the eating of meat products (fasts, generally on the eve of given saints' days) as well as the eating of meat products (charity feasts on the day itself) were vowed. Besides being a prerequisite for receiving communion on the saint's day, fasting honored the saint's death. Communal feasts, like the brotherhood banquets regularly deplored by bishops and ecclesiastical visitors, were ways to celebrate the saint's glorification in heaven and were a commemoration of the saint's pact with the village. These compacts of abstention and consumption were village or town adaptations for local religious use of Church law and custom regarding Lent and Easter, Fridays and Sundays. The rules for abstinence on Fridays and during many days in Lent are well known. Less well known is the *prohibition* of fasting on Sundays, Easter, and Pentecost—virtual injunctions to eat in celebration. The *Siete partidas*, composed for Alfonso X in the mid-thirteenth century, explain: "Moreover, where the festival day of some saint to whom vigils belong happens to come on a Monday, persons should fast on Saturday, and not on Sunday, because this is a day on which man should not fast, in honor of the resurrection of Our Lord Jesus Christ." Another law made the same injunction in regard to Easter and Pentecost. Similarly, the report of Perales del Río (Madrid) mentioned that the town had to postpone a vowed fast day if it fell on Easter, "in honor of the Resurrection." Fasting and feasting were thus in theory always coupled: both were in honor of God. The people of New Castile applied this procedure to honor their chosen saints.[83]

Participation in processions and observance of vowed days was enforced in many places by specific laws, rules, and fines. On the days of Saint Sebastian and on Michaelmas the villagers of Argamasilla de Alba (Ciudad Real) went in procession to the chapel of Saint Sebastian:

> One of the adults from each house is obligated to go in the procession, and mass is said in the chapel, and they return in procession and a *caridad* of bread, cheese, and wine is given both days.[84]

The fines for nonparticipation in processions ranged from five to forty maravedis.[85] Another punishment was public shaming—the priest requiring nonobservants to stand and ask forgiveness in mass.[86] In one town, Pezuela (Madrid), if villagers did not belong to the village-wide brotherhood of Saint Benedict vowed in the fifteenth century because of plague and locusts and did not observe its days, they lost their rights as village members ("all citizens of the town are obligated to be members of that brotherhood or not be citizens").[87]

The desire to maintain a united front manifest in these regulations stemmed from the contract with the helper saint —not with the individual inhabitants, but rather with the community as a juridical entity. In the diocese of Sigüenza in the seventeenth century priests had the power to enforce the celebration of these votive masses by holding the town officials responsible and denying them the sacraments until they gave in.[88] The vows were definitely governmental acts. Although the villagers usually paid for the feasts that they ate on these occasions, and so were simply feeding themselves, legally the money or the produce went from them to the town as a corporation, whence it returned as food in a ceremony of commensality not only with neighbors or the poor of the region, but also with the saintly protector. Such ceremonies served as a solemn renewal of the annual contract with the protector. By eating, as it were, with the saint, they confirmed their trust in the protector's benevolence. By going in processions and eating with each other, they actualized, put into physical form, the juridical entity of the community that met in the first place to make the vow.

Effectiveness of Vows

How successful were the vows? For perhaps a third to a half of the vows, the people of New Castile were no more able to answer that question in 1575 than we can now, for they had forgotten the reason for the vow. The vows had to be observed, however, because even if the original cause was unknown, it was most likely a disaster, and a lapse in observance could cause whatever that had been to recur. Most evidence points to the fact that these vows were observed, indeed tenaciously so, even in the face of diocesan opposition.

That many saints were not completely effective as long-term protectors is evident, for communities made vows on different occasions to different saints for the same reason. Such vows were cumulative. Though a vow ceased to have a desired effect and another vow to another saint had been made, the first vow was nonetheless observed. In Getafe (Madrid) Saint Quiteria was first used against insects in the vines. But then the pests came back, and Saint Gregory was called in:

> Lady Saint Quiteria is kept for the same reason [vine pests], which they say was vowed in olden times, and when it was vowed they erected a chapel and brotherhood, and had a bullfight every year on the eve of her day. And this was done for a long time, and the old folk say it got rid of the pests. But eventually they returned, and a new vow was made, this time to Saint Gregory, and both feast days are kept for the same reason.

I found only one instance of villagers remarking on the ineffectiveness of a vow, one made in 1570 to Saint Gregory of Nazianzus, "for love of the worm that was eating the vines, and still is eating them." But this is an exception.[89]

By contrast, there are numerous instances of claims that since making a given vow that particular problem did not return. Some of the cases of immediate dramatic success must have been well known in the districts where they occurred. In Esquivias (Toledo) about 1476, the villagers threatened by grasshoppers

> promised and vowed a chapel to Saint Barnabas . . . and the entire town went out and began to dig the trenches

to make the chapel. And the next day when the people went to do their ploughing they found that the trenches they had dug were full of locusts, and since then they have never suffered from them. So they took the devotion, and built a chapel, where they go in procession on that day and give a *caridad*.[90]

As in the case of the vow to Saint Toribio in Valdelaguna (Madrid), cited above, a number of towns tell of rain falling on the day of a drought vow. And for the plague, there is the moving case of the vow of Móstoles (Madrid) to build a chapel:

Another [chapel] is the old one to Saint Sebastian to the north, which this town built when there was a great pestilence so severe that men fell dead as they were putting up the walls of the chapel. But the construction did not stop, and since then God has seen fit that no like pestilence has been seen. On the contrary, the town has been and remains very healthful. The town keeps it well repaired, and all the people go to it in a general procession, where a public *caridad* of bread and wine and cheese is given that day, and a solemn mass is said.[91]

Similarly, if more succinctly, from the report of Buendía (Cuenca) about the chapel of Our Lady of the Rosel: "They say that they built this chapel because of a plague, and that it stopped when they laid the first stone."[92]

Some vows were dramatically effective in the short run (which was, after all, the primary goal). Others, we are assured, had been completely effective over the long run. A few examples will have to stand for many. In Alcolea de Almodóvar (Ciudad Real) they had made a vow long before to Saint Scholastica because of locusts; they gave a *caridad* to all those present on the eve of the feast day and the day itself.

The inhabitants of this town are very devoted to this holy day because they have seen that in the area there have been great numbers of locusts that have done much damage; in this township the locusts have done no harm, although they have been present in great numbers.[93]

In Ballesteros (Ciudad Real) the Visitation of Mary to Saint Elizabeth (July 2) was vowed because of the great locust attack of 1547:

> It was an enormous plague that consumed the crops, and since it was vowed there has not been any, although there has been much in the area, and nothing has done any harm here. On the eve no meat is eaten, and on the day there is a general procession and other solemn offices.[94]

The town of El Peral, in eastern Cuenca, was threatened by the plague brought by two Valencians:

> It is said that one or two men from Valencia slept in the house of a citizen of this town, for at that time people were dying of the plague in the city of Valencia, and that on the very next day the daughter of one of the guests was wounded with the pestilence. At once [the town] swore a holy day to the martyrs Saint Cosmas and Saint Damian, and built them a chapel that is held in much veneration and devotion in this town at present. As a result, never again has anyone died of the pestilence, except for the daughter of the guest in that house, although people have died in the neighboring towns, one or two leagues away, and this is certain and true.[95]

A fine reading of the report of a vow to the Immaculate Conception in the town of Almonacid de Zorita shows that to some extent, as one might expect, continued devotion from the village did depend on the divine's fulfillment of its side of the bargain:

> The feast of Our Lady of the Conception is kept in this town, and no meat is eaten on its eve, and a *caridad* of bread, cheese, and wine is distributed on the day to citizens and any outsiders in town. Our old people say that

it was vowed because in the past there was a plague here; and because they promised it, Our Lord continues giving us health *and so the devotion has been maintained* and handed down to the present [y como lo prometieron nuestro Señor va dando salud, *por donde se va continuando la dicha devocion* y a venido de mano en mano hasta aora]. [My italics.][96]

These instances of immediately successful vows and the way they are recounted show that even after a vow was made, people were by no means sure it would work. They were in suspense. They had just given away one more of their work days; would it be in vain? Was anyone listening? Hence the success of a vow was also a sign as well as a practical help: a sign of divine attention to their place, to their devotional community. The extent to which the saint responded (or to which God responded to the saint) would govern the enthusiasm and perseverance with which the villagers maintained the vow.

Graduated Responses to Crises

The vow was only one of a number of graduated responses available to a community in time of trouble, and certainly not the first it would try. For the visible approach of a hailstorm or a cloud of locusts, the first response would be the conjuring of the danger by the priest with a cross, on the supposition that storms and locusts were works of the devil and could be reversed by divine power. If the conjuring failed, one conclusion might be that the trouble was a punishment sent by God, and religious remedies would be of the petitionary or placatory variety.

As we saw in the case of droughts, the most common attempt to alleviate a disaster would be a petitionary procession, sometimes called a *rogativa*, to a local chapel or district shrine. These processions sought help from saints who had shown their intercessory powers in the past. In the reports they were mentioned only in passing. A set of processions,

for instance, was fresh in the minds of the people of Chillón (Ciudad Real):

> In April 1576 we witnessed a great drought in this town,
> and after many processions were made to the chapels on
> the outskirts—Saint Sebastian, Saint Catherine, and Saint
> Bridget, which are near the town—and considering the
> dryness of the township, and that everything was being
> ruined as it was already April, almost all the people of the
> town decided to go [to the shrine of Our Lady of the
> Castle] in procession one morning, including a great num-
> ber of men, women, and children and some brothers of
> the Holy True Cross who went flagellating themselves.
> All of these people, together with the clergy, left the town
> under calm skies [con gran serenidad]. And [at the
> shrine] they celebrated mass and preached and then left
> to return to the town. And it pleased Our Lord through
> the intercession of this Holy Lady Saint His Mother to
> send so much rain that everyone got wet and had to re-
> turn very quickly because the roads turned to rivers. As
> a result all of the townspeople held it certain that this
> grace and many others in remedy of the needs of this town
> had been done through the intercession of this Holy
> Lady.[97]

Note the typical pattern of seeking help first from the more
specialized lesser saints, whose chapels were located close to
the town, and only afterward from Our Lady of the Castle,
the major shrine image, still venerated by the people of
Almadén and Chillón today. The people of fifteenth-century
Florence similarly saved their most venerated image for true
crises, even formulating an ordinance in 1435 against its excessive use.[98]

This strategy seems to have been predicated on a desire
not to burden the major intercessor with minor problems.
At the time of the report, in 1579, Chillón, an agricultural,
mercury mining, and textile town, had a population of eight
hundred households, about three or four thousand persons.

In addition to its two parish churches, to Saint John the Baptist and Saint Dominic of Silos, and its shrine to Mary, it had six chapels dedicated to saints, four brotherhoods (the Holy Sacrament, the True Cross, the Rosary, and a general brotherhood for the burial of the dead), and four vows, to Saints Ildefonso, Catherine, Bridget, and Lucy. Some of the saints for whom there were chapels, and some of the saints to whom they maintained vows were doubtless what could be called dormant devotions. Saint Sebastian, Saint Catherine, and Saint Bridget were either considered to be more powerful or more concerned with the town; hence out of the ten saints for whom there were either vows, chapels, or churches, they tried those three first, finally turning to Our Lady of the Castle as the ultimate recourse.

It will be noted that the people of Chillón did not turn to the titular saints of the parish churches for help. With very few exceptions—which fall into two categories, parish churches with important images of Mary and parish churches dedicated to saints for whom there is a major relic —titular saints of parish churches in sixteenth-century New Castile were no more actively used for practical devotion than they are today. If they ever were used as divine patrons it was long before 1575. At most they provided (as today) the occasion for an annual fiesta on their days.

Faith per se was not a factor in these consultations with saints. Moving from saint to saint in time of need, people did not view the desired outcome when it finally occurred as a confirmation of fundamental beliefs so much as proof of the intercession of a particular saint. The occurrence of a cloudburst during a petitionary ceremony was not interpreted—as it would be today—as confirmation of the existence of divine power. That was taken for granted; the drought, too, was evidence of divine power. Rather, it showed just whom to turn to in the future in such matters, who was helping out the town in the heavenly court. It was this information that was important for the people of Chillón: "As a result, all of the townspeople held it certain that this grace and many others in remedy of the needs of this town had been done through the intercession of this Holy Lady."

The vows of annual observance were made either when all previous devotions had been exhausted as a kind of invitation to a new saint to take an interest in the town, or else after a saint, through a patent demonstration of interest in the town (by signs or responses to processions) showed that he or she would like to set up this kind of long-term relationship. A vow entailed a perpetual commitment of time and resources, and it was not entered into lightly. When the people of Castillo de Garci Muñoz (Cuenca) held a petitionary mass to Saint Sebastian in his chapel during a plague, a clear sign from heaven let them know that he was listening; only then did they make the commitment of a vow.

> The reason the feast of Saint Sebastian was sworn was a great pestilence in this town. It is known, for they heard it from their ancestors, that the people went to the chapel of Saint Sebastian and held a sung mass with great devotion. And while the office of the mass was being said, a dove entered and perched in the transept of the chapel and stayed quietly [*quedica*] all during the mass; when the mass was over, it flew out, and the plague soon stopped.[99]

"ACTIVITY" OF SAINTS

Vows and chapel dedications help tell which saints were most popular in sixteenth-century New Castile. For about half of the vows the people did not report when or why they were made, in spite of the request for this information in the questionnaire. Instead they gave answers like "It is not known why it was made," or "It is very old." I have assumed that in a good number of those cases for which no reason for a vow was given the vow was made before living memory. Only five out of a hundred vows for which the people gave dates occurred before 1500. The year 1500 corresponds roughly with the earliest memories of the oldest living persons in the villages, and it was upon their memories that the reports largely depended. In Table 2.2, I have shown the number of vows made to various saints or advocations (to whom more than ten vows were made), the number of vows for which reasons were given, and the vows with reasons as a percentage of the total vows for each saint

Table 2.2. Vows of Towns and Villages of New Castile
in Effect, 1575–1580
(Saints or Advocations with More Than Ten Vows)

Saint or advocation	Total vows	Number of vows with reason given	Vows with reason as percentage of total vows
Gregory of Nazianzus	90	65	72%
Barbara	16	11	69
Roch	55	36	65
Augustine	37	24	65
Pantaleon	38	24	63
Sebastian	216	133	62
Quiteria	33	20	61
Gregory	63	35	56
Anne	67	37	55
Blaise	36	19	53
Our Lady of Peace	22	11	50
Benedict	28	13	46
Abdon and Senen	13	6	46
George	13	6	46
Conception of Our Lady	42	18	43
Name of Jesus	12	5	42
Finding of the True Cross	58	23	40
John at the Latin Gate	24	9	35
Catherine	31	11	35
Michael	26	9	35
Anthony (the Abbot)	42	12	29
Bridget	18	5	28
Agatha	40	10	25
Mary Magdalen	12	3	25
Eve of the Ascension	12	2	16
TOTAL	1,042	545	52%

or advocation. The resulting tabulation may be regarded as an indication of the relative activity of the devotion.

Some words of caution are in order. Some saints, like Gregory of Nazianzus and Roch, were relatively new to the system. Others, like Mary Magdalen, Agatha, and Anthony the Abbot, were clearly old and survived mainly in vows whose reasons everyone had long forgotten. The saints in between are less easy to categorize. Anne and Blaise, for instance, had been popular for a long time and still were popular. The causes of the more ancient vows to Anne and Blaise had been forgotten, but these saints were still quite "active" in 1575. We are helped by a limited amount of direct evidence—exact or approximate dating of vows. Table 2.3 shows the most popular vows within the past twenty-five or thirty years before the questionnaire.

Table 2.3. Vows Made after 1550*

Saint or advocation	Number of vows
Gregory of Nazianzus	7
Anne	6
Roch	3
Sebastian	3
Conception of Our Lady	3
Finding of the True Cross	2
Catherine	2
Blaise	2
Ursula	2
Other saints (one each)	8

* Since dates of vows were given infrequently, these should be seen as a sample, not a population.

An additional complicating factor in Table 2.2 is that some saints, like Sebastian, Augustine, and Quiteria, had very specialized functions (plague, locusts, and rabies, respectively). It would be easier to hypothesize the original reason for vows to those saints. Conversely, the remembrance rate would be lower for Saint Anne, the Immaculate Conception, or the Invention of the True Cross, whose powers were more generalized and could be invoked for various problems. Nevertheless, if these factors are taken into account, Table 2.2 gives a rough picture of a devotional chronology of the peoples of New Castile in the fifteenth and sixteenth centuries.

THREE

Chapels and Shrines

The well-known chapels and oratories in its territory and
the miracles that have taken place there.

I USE the word *chapel* to designate any public devotional
center outside of the parish church and monasteries. In the
reports they are called *ermitas*, and there were an average of
two per community (three for the towns of Ciudad Real).
Many towns of five or ten hundred households had five or
six chapels to different saints. The city of Toledo had twenty. Generally speaking, the bigger the town, the more chapels. But the larger towns had fewer chapels in proportion to
the number of inhabitants, probably because side chapels in
monasteries served many of the same functions. (See Table
3.1.)

These chapels served as headquarters for brotherhoods

Table 3.1. Chapels in New Castile
(By Size of Town)

Households	Number of towns	Number of chapels reported	Chapels per town	Average number of households per chapel
0–49	85	57	0.7	36
50–99	103	76	0.7	107
100–149	75	102	1.4	89
150–199	40	76	1.9	92
200–299	68	122	1.8	139
300–499	64	164	2.6	154
500–999	55	234	4.3	174
1,000–3,000	14	65	4.6	435
11,000	Toledo	20	20.0	550
TOTAL	505	916	1.8	

and as locations of endowed chaplaincies. Some of them were built as votive offerings of towns, others by brotherhoods, and still others by individuals. Because of costs in material and labor, the vow to build a chapel was probably one of the most important commitments a town could make to a saint. After its completion the chapel would be the site of the annual votive mass to the saint on her or his day. Some chapels were simply converted houses, willed by devotees of a certain saint. Others would be small oratories on the outskirts of the villages, typically used as stopping points for the rogation processions of springtime.

CHAPEL DEDICATIONS

When chapel dedications are compared with vows, there are a number of major differences. (See Table 3.2.) The saints or advocations with many chapels but few vows largely fall into two categories: those devotions most favored for brotherhoods—the brotherhoods of the Passion and the Rosary; and chapels dedicated to apostles or other saints whose days the villagers kept by diocesan edict (Mary Magdalen, Bartholomew, James, Peter, and Mary). Some of these latter chapels were the abandoned parish churches of deserted villages. The explanation for their having few vows, I think, is that since their days were observed anyway, it would have been redundant to vow them; instead, the vow was to build them a chapel.

Conversely there were a number of saints to whom there were many vows but few chapels, particularly the saints used to combat locusts and other insects: the Gregories, Pantaleon, and Augustine. To these saints there were 228 vows but only 9 chapels. There were also few chapels dedicated to saints who were protectors from hail: Saints Agatha, Bridget, and George accounted for 71 vows and only 4 chapels. Insects and hail, however harmful, were not matters of immediate life or death. When chapels were put up in the course of vows, it was primarily in cases of epidemics.

Table 3.2. Chapel Dedications Compared with Vows (Saints or Advocations with at Least Three Chapels or Ten Vows)

Vows	Saints or advocations		Chapels (ermitas)
120	Mary*	277	
216	Sebastian	156	
0	Rosary	33	(23 in Guadalajara)
12	Mary Magdalen	31	
67	Anne	28	
42	Conception of Our Lady	28	(12 in Madrid)
6	Bartholomew	27	
24	John the Evangelist	26	
55	Roch	25	(17 in Guadalajara)
1	Christopher	22	(8 in Ciudad Real, 6 in Cuenca)
5	James (Santiago)	21	
14	Peter	19	
42	Anthony the Abbot	18	
28	Benedict	15	
33	Quiteria	14	(6 in Ciudad Real)
58	True Cross	14	
10	John the Baptist	12	
0	Blood of Jesus	10	
8	Lucy	10	
16	Barbara	10	
5	Andrew	9	
26	Michael	9	
36	Blaise	9	
17	Mark	8	(6 in Ciudad Real)
0	Our Lady of Remedies	8	
6	Ildefonso	6	
22	Our Lady of Peace	6	
31	Catherine	6	
90	Gregory Nazianzus	3	
8	Barnabas	3	
37	Augustine	3	
63	Gregory	2	
40	Agatha	1	
38	Pantaleon	1	
18	Bridget	2	
13	Abdon and Senen	0	
13	George	1	

* Including Conception, Rosary, Remedies, and Peace

Why, given the large number of Marian chapels, were there relatively few vows to Mary? Eliminating for the moment general advocations of Mary, like the Immaculate Conception, Our Lady of Peace, and Our Lady of the Rosary, which were treated much like other saints with vows and brotherhoods, there remains a large number of Marian chapels dedicated to very specific, local, Marys. The devotion to this kind of saint (generally called Our Lady of such-and-such a place) was qualitatively different from that accorded other saints. These chapels were used for general relief from many problems, especially for curing the lame, the halt, and the blind; they were used not only by the community, but also by groups of communities and by individuals. The buildings were more likely to be at a greater distance from the town center than the other chapels, in some cases on the site of a castle or a previous settlement. As in the case of Our Lady of the Castle of Chillón, they represented a higher, more permanent level of advocacy than the saints of the local chapels. It was at these special chapels that miracles took place and votive offerings were left. Chapels that attracted the devotion of more than one town, or that were used for curing, or to which the villagers were especially devoted, I will call shrines. Shrines were overwhelmingly dedicated to Mary. (See Table 3.3.)

Relatively few vows were made to Marian shrines by these towns and villages because the people were so devoted to Mary that vows would have been superfluous. Most Marian feast days were already obligatory. On these days, particularly August 15 and September 8, communities made processions to their Marian shrines even without a vow. Indeed, as in Chillón, in some places masses to Mary were held in the shrine every Saturday.

The qualitative difference of Marian devotion is shown by the legends of the shrines. The Marian legends recounted in the reports were like the signs for vows in that they provided information from the divine about an intercessor. But in other ways they were different. In the first place, they

Table 3.3. Devotion to Mary, the Saints, and Christ in New Castile, 1575-1580
(For 530 Villages)

	Number of vows (and % of all vows)	Number of chapels (and % of all chapels)	Number of shrines (and % of shrines in each category)			Number of images or chapels with origin legends (and % of all)
			District attraction[1]	Curing sites[2]	Regional attraction[3]	
Mary	120 (9%)	277 (32%)	41 (62%)	36 (68%)	12 (86%)	17 (59%)
Saints	1,155 (83%)	544 (62%)	23 (35%)	14 (26%)	1 (7%)	8 (28%)
Christ	115 (8%)	50 (6%)	2 (3%)	3 (6%)	1 (7%)	4 (14%)
TOTAL	1,390	871	66	53	14	29

[1] Shrines to which people of more than one village go (exclusive of regional shrines); see Appendix B.
[2] Shrines where there is habitual curing, or more than one cure cited.
[3] Shrines to which towns beyond neighboring towns go; see Appendix B.

were not remembered as having occurred in the context of a natural disaster, when the people had already initiated the search for a helper. In the legends of the shrines it was the saint (who was generally Mary) who initiated the encounter, who chose the community. The choice occurred through apparitions or through the providential placement of statues, like the Greek palladia that were said to have fallen from the sky. Such statues exhibited a stubborn will to be venerated in a specific place. The apparations and the statues told the people not only who would help them, but also where to go for grace. This then was another characteristic that distinguished shrines from ordinary chapels— their location had sacred significance.

These legends were encapsulated devotional charters. The ones in the reports are particularly significant, for they represent one of the oldest sources of oral origin legends of shrines anywhere in Spain.

ORIGIN LEGENDS

In all but three of the stories mentioned in Table 3.4, the image made its desire to be worshipped in a particular place known by some kind of sign.[1] Some signs involved the way the image was located; there was some kind of tip-off of an extraordinary nature. Typically this sign came through animals, usually domestic ones: a hunting dog stubbornly digging in one spot, or an eagle that kept returning to one place; or a horse that shied. In Catalan legends oxen usually pointed the way to images. Sometimes strange lights (as at Cazalegas) or celestial music played this role. But the most common sign was that the statues persisted in returning, usually at night, from the parish church to which they had been taken to the sacred location where they were found. Such was the case for Saint Bridget, Saint Mary the Egyptian, Our Lady of the Eagle, Our Lady of Valverde, and Our Lady of Madroñal. A shrine historian acknowledged the ultimate mystery of why images return to the site of their

Table 3.4. Images That Were Found

Image	Town	Date	Sign
Crucifix	Albalate/Zorita (G)	1514	Hunting dog
Cross	Chiloeches (G)	1571	Ploughed up; old church site
Crucifix	Griñón (M)	1569	Cured
Saint Mary of los Llanos	Santa María de los Llanos (Cu)		Found during ploughing
Our Lady of the Cross	Cazalegas (T)	ca. 1549	Light during storms; cured
Our Lady of the Eagle	Ventas/Peña Aguilera (T)		Eagle's roost; image returned
Our Lady of Virtudes	Santa Cruz de Mudela (CR)		Found in foundations
Our Lady of Valverde	Fuencarral (M)		Found(?); returned to site
Saint Anne	Puertollano (CR)		Found in cave; juniper tree gave oil
Saint Bridget	Brugel (T)		Returned to site; found with bell
Saint Mary the Egyptian	Luciana (CR)		Returned to site; found with bell

finding. "By these situations we are taught that our Lord wishes these most holy images to be adored and venerated on the very spot where they appeared and nowhere else: he knows why (*él sabe por qué*)."[2]

There is a gray area between images that were found and images that "appeared" (see Table 3.5), which in some cases ought to read as "turned up."[3] The legend of Our Lady of the Madroñal shares the characteristics of the legends above. There are two versions of the legend of Our Lady of Salceda (the patronal image of a Franciscan monastery), one in the report of Peñalver and another in that of Tendilla; the shrine is on the boundary between the two townships. Both say that the image was discovered by Knights of Saint John. The Tendilla people say it happened when the knights were lost in a nighttime storm, and Mary appeared with a light in a willow; that they built a chapel in thanks, and that later

Table 3.5. Images That Appeared

Image	Town	Date	Sign
Crucifix	Montiel (CR)	1520	On altar of Santiago chapel, December 25
Our Lady of the Madroñal	Auñón (G)		To shepherd on tree stump; returned to site later
Our Lady of Salceda	Tendilla (G)	ca. 1236	To knights on willow
Our Lady of the Baths	Fuencaliente (CR)		At hot spring
Our Lady of Holy Spring	San Pablo (T)		"Appeared"
Our Lady of Consolation	Iniesta (CU)		"Appeared there"
Saint Vincent	Puerto San Vicente (T)		"Appeared there"

the Franciscans built the monastery there. The story told by the people of Peñalver is that the knights found the image in the willow when one of their horses shied; and that upon the discovery the horse knelt down, and the knight had a revelation that he should found a monastery there.[4]

Most stories about saints appearing in the flesh (see Table 3.6) were given very briefly, either because the informants did not take the trouble to go into detail (the questionnaire did not ask for details) or because the traditions themselves were fragmentary.[5] The Virgin usually appeared to only one person. At Daimiel and Belmonte, she appeared to persons in trouble, a characteristic of early medieval apparitions of the "Mother of Mercy."[6]

One of the oldest apparition legends of Spain, known from the eighth century, is that of the "Descención" of Mary to Saint Ildefonso, in which she rewarded him with a chasuble in the cathedral of Toledo for his devotion. According to the Toledo report, this event took place on December 18. In 1575 people venerated the stone on which Mary had stood—as they do today. The story was one of the most popular legends in all of Europe in the late Middle

Table 3.6. Apparitions of Saints in the Flesh

Image	Town	Date	Sign
Descent of Mary	Toledo		Gave cape to Saint Ildefonso; stone marks spot
Our Lady of the Crosses	Daimiel (CR)	1465	To boy in trouble; proof with candles
Our Lady of Peace	Daimiel (CR)	before 1507	To girl in time of pestilence; proof a tile
Our Lady of Grace	Belmonte (Cu)		To woman in well
Our Lady of the Cross	Cubas (M)	1449	To girl over nine days; her fingers fixed in shape of cross
Our Lady of los Llanos	Hontova (G)		Ordered shrine built, named it
Our Lady of the Olive Tree	Almonacid de Toledo (T)		To shepherd
Saint Blaise	Cubas (M)		To ploughman; ordered chapel built
Saint Lucy	Ventas/Peña Aguilera (T)		To woman; proof a spring
Saint Gregory	Fuenlabrada (M)		To a good woman
Saints Stephen, Augustine	Toledo	1312	At funeral of Count of Orgaz

Ages, and it inspired imitative visions in Jaén in 1430 and Quintanar de la Orden in 1523. As a shrine the cathedral appears to have been ranked with Guadalupe. A laborer from Budia (Guadalajara) tried as a false prophet by the Inquisition of Toledo in 1541 had boasted he could make Our Lady of Guadalupe and Our Lady of the Descent come to wherever he was.[7] (See Figure 2.)

The villagers appear to have believed, at least in retrospect, that Mary's ultimate purpose in appearing was to have a shrine built to her and to serve as their advocate. A key message was thus the location of the shrine. In the Cu-

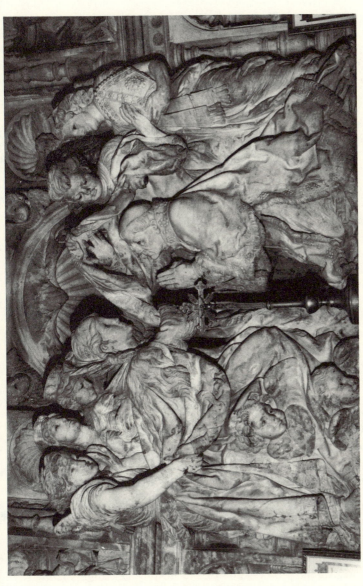

Figure 2. The Virgin Mary bestowing a chasuble on Saint Ildefonso. Sculpture by Felipe de Borgoña (1527) on the altar of the Descención, Cathedral of Toledo, next to the sacred stone on which Mary stood during her appearance. Photograph by Cristina García Rodero.

bas story Mary made it clear. When a procession came out of the town toward the apparition site, with the seer Inés and other village children in the lead, Mary called Inés away, took the cross made of pieces of a loom from Inés's hands, and herself planted it in the ground.

> . . . In the territory and jurisdiction of this town, at a distance of two crossbow shots, is a very important convent of nuns of Saint Francis, very cloistered. It is called Our Lady Saint Mary of the Cross, because 120 or 130 years ago, more or less, according to documents and notarized reports, the Virgin Our Lady appeared in the township nine times from March 1 until March 9, to a young herding girl of this town, said to be nine or ten years old. The herding girl by order of Our Lady came to this town to tell us how Our Lady ordered her to go to the priest and the authorities [*justicia*] so that they would at once go in procession to said site. And so that she would be believed she made her a cross out of the fingers of her hand, with the thumb on top of the forefinger. . . . And so she came, and when they saw her thus they tried to unstick the said cross with much force, and they could not do it. And so they believed what Inés had told them and organized a procession and went with much devotion, and in the lead went many children with said Inés, who carried in her hand a cross of wood made from boards of a loom. And when they were a little ways from the place where Inés said Our Lady would be found, the Mother of God called to her, according to what she said, and together with her went to the place which was planted with vines and known as the Valley of Acirulero. And when they got there the Virgin Our Lady took the said cross in her hands and stuck it in the place where the church is now and said: "Here it is my will that a church should be built called Our Lady Saint Mary of the Cross." And afterwards the girl was not able to unstick her fingers from the form of the cross, until finally Our Lady told her to go

to her house of Our Lady of Guadalupe, where she would see her, and unstick her fingers. Which she did, for she went to Guadalupe, where when they showed her certain images she found one of which she said, "This is the Lady that was there and ordered me to come here." And at once the cross came apart; and concerning all this there is a notarized report held by the nuns of said convent in which what has been said can be seen in more detail.[8]

When images were found, the image was there to show. With apparitions nothing was left to show, so that some proof was needed. How were the people and the authorities to believe the seers, particularly when they were so often marginal figures like shepherds and children.[9] In the case of the "inventions" of statues, the question was where to place the shrine. That was not a problem with apparitions, since the Virgin or the saint made clear where the shrine should be. With apparitions the problem was convincing the authorities. The legend thereby became a dramatic tale in which the poor and the young, with the help of the Virgin, were vindicated in the face of the skepticism of the powerful.

The unnamed boy of Moral de Calatrava to whom Our Lady of the Crosses appeared (after the mule carrying his wheat fell over, and the sacks were too heavy to lift) had to deal with the ridicule of his mother (until she discovered that the wheat had been ground miraculously) and was flogged and strung up on a tree by the authorities of Ciudad Real (because they did not at first find the candles Mary assured him would be burning on the site of her apparition as a proof) before he was finally vindicated. In Cubas Mary forestalled such ridicule by providing the seer Inés with proof—crossing her thumb and forefinger so that no one could separate them.

The proof of the apparitions of Our Lady of Peace in Daimiel and Saint Lucy in Ventas con Peña Aguilera was something the authorities would find when they dug at the

shrine site: a piece of tile at the former, a spring at the latter.
And in Belmonte, when a woman fell in a well, her very
survival gave credence to her account of seeing and speaking with Mary. This last type of vision was a regular item
in shrine miracle books of the seventeenth and eighteenth
centuries. In Talavera a man was known as Miguel del Pozo
because in 1555 he miraculously survived the collapse of a
well after invoking God and Our Lady of Prado, the major
devotion of the town.[10]

In all of these cases, whether in the form of a location
choice by an image that was discovered or a proof of an
apparition, it was the extraordinary that certified the legiti-
macy of the divine desire to be worshipped in a given place.
The stories involve a dialogue between the image (or the
image and the poor seer) on the one hand, and the village or
town with its lay and clerical authorities, on the other. In
the process of working out a site for the image, or a proof
of an apparition, a relationship between the saint and the
community is in formation, a bond that will be all the more
secure for the doubts and the mistakes of the people. In these
situations the saint, usually Mary, has to make an effort so
that she may eventually be of service to the community. The
moral is that the saint, Mary, has chosen them; her patronage
and advocacy was something that was meant to be. How
different from the saint who is beseeched for help, and who
may or may not listen, who may or may not vouchsafe a
sign. The poor or the powerless have the visions, and the
eventual imposition of their truth upon the town authorities
is a sure way of showing that Mary or the saint has come to
serve everybody; that the bond set up between the saint and
the town is also a direct bond between the saint and each
person of the town, beginning with the powerless.

Most of these stories of apparitions are vague about dates,
placing them in the remote past. Of the findings of images,
only a few are contemporaneous, mainly crosses and crucifixes found with little supernatural intervention in circumstances by and large believable. Some of the most elaborate

legends correspond suspiciously to those shrines in the hands
of monasteries (those of Tendilla, Hontova, and Cubas).
None of these considerations inspires trust in the historicity
of the stories of apparitions or miraculous findings.

How, then, did the shrines actually start? Did the actual
event have any relation to the story? The reports for Our
Lady of the Remedy (at Fuensanta, Albacete) and for Our
Lady of Charity (in Illescas, Toledo) give clues to how other shrines started. Of the Albacete shrine, still important today, the informants tell that it began when a spring was
noticed in a place where the water table was supposedly
low. Since the water in the spring maintained a constant
level, the people thought it was of supernatural origin (*negocio de milagro*) and came to bathe there and cure their
ailments, especially those of eyes, and hernias of children.
Because of the cures they built a chapel and called it the
Holy Spring ("y con esta devocion y efecto del agua se
fundo la dicha ermita y se le puso el dicho nombre de Fuensanta"). Their story is an easily believable series of events.
At the time of the reports the shrine was under the aegis of
the Trinitarian Fathers. Apparently the Trinitarians heard
of the popularity of the new shrine, and came over from
their monastery-shrine at Garaballa (Cuenca) to colonize
Fuensanta.

A league toward where the sun rises is a monastery of
friars of the Most Holy Trinity, called Our Lady of the
Remedy of the Holy Spring [Nuestra Señora del Remedio
de la Fuensancta], where in olden times, the earth being
dry and the water deep, there appeared a spring which,
although when discovered they began to take water from
it, neither decreased nor increased. And thinking that this
was a miraculous situation, many people came to bathe,
and the water cured all infirmities and had manifest power
for the eyesight and hernias of children, and because of
this devotion and the effect of the water the aforementioned chapel was founded and called Fuensanta. It has

been and is a house of much devotion, and Our Lady of
the Remedy has worked many miracles in it, giving sight
to the blind, curing the lame, and freeing captives from
the power of the Moors who asked for her help. And it
is very popular and visited from towns within a fifteen or
twenty league radius, and there is a great fiesta and fair
every year on the day of Our Lady of September, when
nine hundred carts and ten thousand persons gather there
out of devotion and because of the miracles that are daily
worked in this house of Our Lady of the Remedy. And in
said monastery there are normally twelve Trinitarian
friars.[11]

The story related by the townspeople was transformed
over time so that it resembled many of the legends cited
previously. In 1648, the Trinitarian Cristobal de Granados
wrote that the shrine originated with the apparition of a
statue that stated its wish to be venerated on the site and
that the new spring should be used for curing. According to
Granados, the statue was taken twice to La Roda, a nearby
town, and twice it returned at night. The first miracle of
the shrine was the resurrection during her funeral of the
daughter of the man who found the statue. A seer was cre-
ated and named, and a specific date was assigned to the
event: March 24, 1482.

This same process of sacralization undoubtedly took place
with a number of shrines associated with curing through
the application of water, oil, or ointments, such as those of
Our Lady of the Baths (Fuencaliente, Ciudad Real), and
Our Lady of the Holy Spring (San Pablo, Toledo), both
of which have very weak, brief statements to the effect
that the Virgin or her image appeared there. Such may also
be the case for the apparition of Saint Lucy in Ventas con
Peña Aguilera (Toledo), where a spring cured eye problems.

The origin given for the shrine of Nuestra Señora de la
Caridad at Illescas is also plausible. The first miracle at the

shrine, which is a chapel in a hospital by the same name, reportedly occurred on March 11, 1562, when a young woman who had been totally crippled for more than six months was cured after an hour of prayer.

In Illescas there is a most famous hospital, called Our Lady of Charity, where each day very great miracles have been and are worked, which would take too long to describe. It is the most visited and popular shrine in all of Spain. His Majesty the King, our lord, Her Majesty the Queen, our lady, the most serene Princess of Portugal, Doña Juana, have come to visit and hold novenas here, as well as many prelates, dukes, counts, and other great princes, *oidores* of His Majesty's councils, and an infinity of persons, who never cease to come and visit this most blessed image. . . .

This town keeps as a vow March 11, which they call the day of Our Lady of Charity, because on that day in 1562 the first miracle took place. A woman arrived at the hospital who was so crippled and helpless that they had tied her to an animal between two large sacks of straw, because for more than six months her calves had been stuck to her thighs, and as they were letting her down she asked them to put her in the chapel where this most holy image of Our Lady is, and after being there for something over an hour asking the Virgin Our Lady for help, she thought she felt much better, and calling the nurse she said, "O sister, since it seems to me that I am well, if I am not dreaming, bring me a staff and I will try to get up and see what it is I am feeling." When she had been given the staff she tried to get up, and she got up as well as if she had never been crippled, and leaving the staff she walked and was as healthy as all of us.[12]

There is a contemporary painting of this first miracle in the shrine today. (See Figure 3.)

We know of the popularity of the shrine (which was subsequently decorated by El Greco) not only from the re-

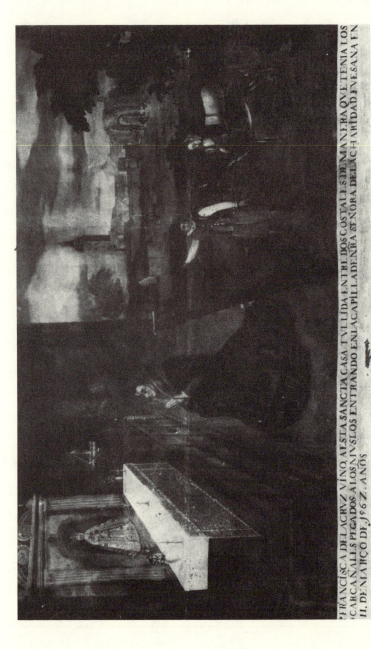

Figure 3. The miracle of Our Lady of the Caridad, Illescas. To the right, Francisca de la Cruz approaches Illescas on a mule; to the left, she prays in front of the altar. Anonymous painting (late sixteenth century?) in the shrine. Photograph by Cristina García Rodero.

port, but also from Lope de Vega, who in *La entretenida* ranked it with Guadalupe, Atocha, and Rome as a pilgrimage site. La Caridad did not retain its popularity for long, and its rapid rise in importance doubtless had much to do with its location near the court and royal favor. But its origin in a dramatic miracle (that is, its origin as a shrine) must have been common to many shrines before it, and certainly applies to many shrines throughout Spain that became popular later. It is a logical beginning for a curing shrine. How many of the major curing shrines in the area began as simple votive chapels or images in churches, and once they began to cure acquired the legends to explain the special interest the saint was taking in a given community?

For all its hyperbole, the seventeenth-century miracle book of Salceda confirms the same process. Still remembered at the shrine was the cure of a blind child from Fuentelaencina:

. . . Because of it her fame was extended throughout the land, and thousands of sick persons came each day.

. . . Each of these cripples who returned to his home cured was a trumpet who wherever he went called out to many others to come to this Holy House for medicines and cures . . .

. . . By now there was hardly a maimed or crippled person in the entire area nor in many neighboring areas whom the most holy virgin had not restored to health . . .[13]

Similarly in Auñón, at the shrine of Madroñal:

In 1524 a man mute from birth, according to him and everyone else, was going through the villages and towns of the district begging; he lost his way and ended up at the mountain of the said chapel of Our Lady, and he said that the Virgin Mary appeared to him there and that as soon as he saw her, he was able to speak Castilian like any other man. *When this miracle was known the devotion of all the people of this district increased, to the great benefit of the shrine* [my italics].[14]

These spates of miracles, which can convert chapels into shrines or revitalize dormant devotions, seem to play out over time for all but the most important shrines. Some village shrines "used to" be miraculous—as if it were a condition that came and went. To the shrine of Saint Anne in Alvares (Guadalajara) people reportedly had come from as far away as Seville. Miracles also used to occur in the Marian shrines of Peñalver (Guadalajara), Our Lady of la Zarza, Cogolludo (Guadalajara), Our Lady of Remedio, San Silvestre (Toledo), Our Lady of la Fuensanta, and Talamanca (Madrid), Our Lady of la Fuensanta.

Some legends arise from a misinterpretation of iconography. According to the first history of Our Lady of Salceda (1616), in 1566 a medallion was found in the foundations which supposedly depicted the discovery of the image by Knights of Saint John.[15] The finding legend may have been reconstructed from that medallion, which could explain the differing stories of different villages, for the medallion, reproduced in the 1616 volume, is quite ambiguous. The time of the finding of the medallion, 1566, coincides with an assertion in the Peñalver report that there had been many miracles in the past ten years. A spate of miracles may have followed the discovery of the medallion.

The specific form the legends take is surely a result of contagion and imitation of one shrine by another. For these local and district devotions exist within a matrix of regional, national, and international shrines. The extensive legend in verse of Our Lady of the Crosses, written by a devotee of the shrine in 1560 and included in the Daimiel report, laments the relative lack of devotion to the shrine in the district, and mentions the most famous Marian shrines of the country:

> I will say but one thing more
> if that is permitted—
> that the exceptional establishment
> that they call Guadalupe

and another that I visited
in Montserrat
and another that is on the border
of Castile and Portugal [Our Lady of Peña de Francia]
all three alike
and of a tone
along with that of Aragon [Our Lady of Pilar]
are much revered
because they are completely one
with that of heaven,
then with how much more zeal
should she be honored here
because she presented herself here in person.[16]

The poet makes a distinction between his shrine, based upon an apparition, and the "national" shrines of the time. In fact, by the sixteenth century the legend of the apparition of Our Lady of Pilar to Saint James was quite well established. The legend of Guadalupe was a combination of an apparition with the discovery of the image with a bell and the resurrection of the finder's child. It was widely imitated in Castile and may have influenced the legends of Saint Bridget (Brugel), Saint Mary the Egyptian (Luciana), and the Cristobal de Granados version of Our Lady of Fuensanta (La Roda). Montserrat and Peña de Francia both had legends of the discovery of an image. That of Peña de Francia was well known in New Castile; among the relics of the Order of Santiago at Uclés was a piece of the stone on which the image was found.[17]

Finally, a caveat against excessive skepticism in regard to the legends. That most of them were stereotyped or derivative by no means rules out the discovery of images or the historical phenomenon of apparitions. Real discoveries and visions were stereotyped: people organized these experiences into known patterns. The findings of crucifixes were recent enough to preclude major falsification. Indeed, in the parish archive of Griñón (Madrid) is an eighteenth-century copy of the original investigation of the finding of the crucifix there in 1569. Comparing the original investigation and the account in the 1579 village report, we note a reversal of sorts: In the original depositions, villagers testified to heavenly odors, changes in color of the crucifix, the appearance of a cross in the sky over the site of the discovery, and miraculous cures performed not only by the crucifix itself, but also by the earth around it, a plant near it, and the cloth in which it was wrapped. The village report, made by some of the same men who took down the testimony ten years before, is quite restrained and omits most of the sensational aspects.[18]

Findings of images did occur; so did apparitions. By the early sixteenth century, however, an apparition was a rather dangerous enterprise. By then a number of nuns, friars, beatas, and an occasional peasant had been taken before the Inquisition for false or diabolical visions. In his *Aviso de Gente recogida y especialmente dedicada al servicio de Dios* (1585), Diego Pérez de Valdivia, who himself had been tried by the Inquisition of Córdoba as a confessor of beatas, warned beatas and nuns to pray that they *not* have visions or apparitions.[19] The bishop of Cuenca's instructions to his parish visitors in 1602 well represent the spirit of the times in a region where the alumbrados were by no means forgotten. The inspectors were to inquire not only for bewitchers, cloudchasers, faith healers, people who believe in books of chance, palm readers, physiognomists, usurers, curers of the evil eye, homosexuals, and pimps, but also for "those . . . who say that they see visions of saints: or that they have revelations from God in what they do or say."[20] The one person mentioned in the reports as having "raptos y extasis" is a case in point. Francisca de la Concepción, a nun in Cifuentes who was twenty-eight years old at the time, was subsequently investigated twice by the Inquisition of Cuenca.[21]

It is not surprising that all the apparitions described took place in the period before the Inquisition started paying attention to Catholics. The apparitions to Inés at Cubas did, in fact, occur (by which I mean that there was a girl named Inés who said she saw the Virgin Mary). A copy of the original investigation is held by the nuns at the convent on the site.[22] In the fifteenth century similar visions occurred at Santa María del Miracle (Lérida, 1458) and Nuestra Señora de la Cruz (Escalona, Segovia, ca. 1490).[23]

In a wider perspective, all of these legends served to locate sacred images in places of universal significance for agricultural and herding communities: near water, near important trees, on cliffs or peaks.[24] Mary offered alternative sacred places to the village center, taking the villagers out from the society to nature. The medieval parish church of Our Lady of the Baths at Fuencaliente (Ciudad Real) was a telling exception. The shrine, at the center of the town, was built over a holy hot spring. As with Guadalupe and Compostela, the shrine apparently came first, and was the origin of the town.

Elsewhere I have suggested that the renewed use of images in the eleventh and twelfth centuries led to a kind of Christianization of the landscape in the form of shrines and chapels. Devotions that had previously centered on relics in parish churches could move out to strategic locations, which were sacralized by the images. This kind of referral to nature for sacred places is a slow, constant process, which continues today. Essentially, in Spain, it has been a Marian movement. The legend motif of the return of the image to the country site, rejecting the parish church, may be an echo or a metaphor for what was in some sense a liberation of devotion from parish control—or, put another way, the resistance of local religion to the growing claims of the Church.[25] It may also have been an expression of the implicit tension between the intensely social life-style of these urban-type villagers and their agricultural and pastoral vocation. In this sense it was a statement of peasant or rural "otherness."

THE USE OF SHRINES IN CRISES

How did shrines fit into the system of vows, chapels, and protectors? As discussed above, there was a hierarchy of protectors and a progression of responses (see Table 3.7), depending upon the gravity of the danger and its persistence. Minor problems were taken to the chapels. Major problems were taken first to the chapels, then to the shrine. People referred to the sacred figure in their shrine as their general advocate, as distinguished from their advocate for the plague, or other specialties. As seen above, the choice of this advocate was explained by elaborate legend and reinforced by regular ceremony. By the seventeenth century the advocates were commonly referred to as patrons (patrón, patrona), and their status was formalized through canonical procedures by an edict of Urban VIII in 1630.

Table 3.7. Response to Community Disaster in New Castile
(Expressed as Hypothetical Gradient)

A. Conjuring (of storms, clouds of locusts)

B. Petitionary processions and novenas
   to chapels
   to local shrine(s)
   to district shrines

C. Vows
   to fast on saint's day or its eve
   to observe saint's day or its eve
   to give a *caridad* on saint's day
   to build chapel to saint

D. Acts
   the building of a chapel

If on the most critical occasions, over a certain period, the general advocate consistently failed, then a community might associate with it a co-patron (often of the opposite sex) or might begin to treat another saint as the patron. Typically the replacement of these advocates when they were statues of Mary involved the substitution of one Marian advocation for another. Vows were emergency measures that supplemented the community pantheon when its standard helpers did not respond. Because vows were usually not made to Mary, but rather to the specialized saints, their success or failure did not lead to the replacement of the overall patron.

IMAGES USED FOR CURING

The reports told of "hospitales," but these were generally places for paupers to die or hospices for wayfarers. A number of curing hospitals were located in Toledo and Madrid and a major one in Illescas, which, as we have seen, doubled as a shrine from 1562 on. What help people could get from doctors or folk healers was supplemented by prayers and promises to images and relics known for their healing powers. About thirty villages reported curative powers of images or relics, or ex-votos, normally associated with curing. In addition, twenty-one other villages mentioned that a given image or relic performed many miracles. I assumed that these also were curing shrines. These wonder-working images or relics were not the only curing sites in the area, and possibly not even the only sites among the villages in the area who answered questionnaires. But they probably include most of the major curing shrines and are representative of the minor ones. More than two-thirds of these shrines were dedicated to Mary. (See Table 3.8.)

The curing images were overwhelmingly located in the chapels, generally apart from the village center in the countryside. Relics that cured were more likely to be in the town, whether in a monastery or a parish church.

The cures varied according to the saint. Considering the generic specialties (as opposed to specific miracles) noted by the villagers in the reports, the saints were seen as specialized, while the Marian shrines were more generalized in

Table 3.8. Curing Images and Relics
(By Province and Type of Location)

Province	Mary	Saint's statue	Saint's relic	Crucifix or cross	Total
Toledo	11	3	2		16
Madrid	5		2		7
Guadalajara	6	1	4	2	13
Cuenca	6	1			7
Ciudad Real	8	1		1	10
Location					
Chapel	31	3	2	2	38
Monastery	3		2		5
Parish Church	1	3	4	1	9
Hospital	1				1
TOTAL	36	6	8	3	53

their powers. The specialties mentioned for saints, some of which, like those of Saint Lucy and Saint Christopher, corresponded to events in the saints' lives, are the following:

Saint	Specialty
Saint Lucy	Eyes (cured with water from a spring)
Saint Christopher	Eyes (with water poured over bones)
Saint Matthew	Throat (stone in image's hand brings disease to climax in three days)
Saint Babiles	Hernias
Saint Martin	Quarternary fevers

Saint Anne seems to have been the only saint other than Mary frequently consulted for more general curing.[26]

Riansares of Tarancón (Cuenca) and Monsalud of Córcoles (Guadalajara) were two Marian shrines with a single specialty: hernias and rabies, respectively. But by and large the Marian shrines were advertised as curing a variety of conditions, listed below in the frequency with which they were mentioned:

Condition	*Frequency*
Cripples	16 (*cojos, tullidos*)
Hernias	6
Mutes	2
Wounds (*lisiados*), deaf, eyes, nipples, rabies	1

In addition, some Marian shrines were used to provide rain and to free captives.

The questionnaire requested information on specific miracles as well. Most of those reported were of dramatic recoveries from accidents and personal impediments. (See Table 3.9.) Generally the miracles included names and dates; many were quite recent.

One wonders at the general absence of illness from these lists. The absence may in part be explained by a bias in votive offerings, which were prime sources of evidence for shrine specialties. Votive offerings, or ex-votos, were gifts

Table 3.9. Miracles Mentioned in the Reports

Agent	*Miracle*
Mary	Cured cripples (11 cases)
	Saved people who fell in wells (5 cases)
	Cured mutes (3 cases)
	Cured hernias (3 cases)
	Revived person from death (2 cases)
	Cured cancer of nose
	Saved fallen child
	Saved man from fallen rock
	Saved persons in collapsed building
	Saved person from drowning
Saint Blaise	Revived dead child
	Saved gentleman choking on fish bone
Saint Benedict	Cured paralyzed man
Saint Cecilia	Saved knight who fell off cliff
Saint Mary the Egyptian	Revived dead girl
Various saints' relics	Cured woman of deafness; cured insomniac

to a shrine, often promised should a prayer be granted. The most commonly mentioned votive offerings were wax members of parts of the body, crutches, trusses from hernias, and an occasional coffin—representing a revival from the dead. (See Figure 4.) Votive paintings, which could better express the idea of sickness (the standard picture is one of a person in a bed, and another person praying to the saint nearby) seem to have been only in limited use in these shrines. While votive paintings at Madrid's Atocha shrine were numerous from at least 1564 on, and even earlier, in 1528, Alfonso de Valdés listed among common ex-votos "babies painted on boards," only two shrines in the reports mentioned paintings as votive offerings. Of one, Our Lady of la Granja, in Yunquera (Guadalajara), "hay cuadro de un milagro." The painting was of a man drowning, something, like most accidents, difficult to express with a wax

Figure 4. Votive offerings in the regional shrine of Our Lady of Cortes (Alcaraz, Albacete), 1976: wax parts of the body, locks of hair, depictions of persons cured, and descriptions of miracles. Photograph by Cristina García Rodero.

offering. The other was a painting of the founding miracle of the shrine of Our Lady of Grace in Belmonte (Cuenca) —the apparition of Mary to a woman in a well—which was incorporated in the reredos of the church.[27] The exhibition of votive paintings may have been inhibited by the edicts of Trent, both against crude or indecent paintings, and against the publication of unverified miracles. The Minims who kept the shrine in Madrid of Our Lady of the Soledad, for instance, did not allow paintings of miracles to be hung there between the founding in 1565 and 1605–1610, when there was a more relaxed attitude toward these matters.[28]

It may also be (although for this we have only circumstantial evidence) that illness in this period was considered more a collective affliction, to be dealt with collectively, as opposed to the more individualized afflictions catalogued above. For these curing shrines, the pride of their communities, were not in fact used in epidemics as much as the specialized epidemic saints. In the mentions of the plague or other epidemics the miracles performed by the epidemic saints were not in curing individual people so much as stopping the spread of the disease. Villages and towns routinely mentioned the hundreds of persons who died in epidemics, but did not cite as a miracle a single cure from an epidemic disease, much less list epidemics as specialties of curing shrines. Perhaps epidemics, like locusts and hailstorms, were seen only as collective afflictions with a collective etiology.

Why was Mary not the primary agent to be dealt with in these epidemics?[29] With quarantining as one of the main curative techniques, one could not expect the sick to go to the shrines; but why was Mary not used in vows? The explanation (in addition to the redundancy of vows to a saint whose days were obligatory) may lie in the sense of collective afflictions as chastisements, for which one must do penance. These chastisements were administered by God or his angels, with the participation of, or at least the nonintercession of, the specialist saints. People's behavior caused divine anger, and possibly the anger of saints. God then chastised

them, and the saints did not intercede. Mary's role was also
one of intercession, but she was never seen as angry. Therefore she was not directly involved in the chain of cause and
effect that led from sin to anger to punishment. It was not
her anger that had to be placated. Mary's only actions were
benevolent. She acted or did not act, in response to petition;
but when she acted it was to grant people what they wanted
but did not have. There are no cases in the reports of communities concluding that because some disaster occurred on
a Marian day, Mary wanted to be worshipped in some additional way. They applied that reasoning to other saints, but
not to Mary. Mary could warn people of impending punishment, but she did not punish.

One clue to the different attitude toward Mary, and by
extension, to her mother, Anne, is their motherhood. As
mother (and grandmother) saints they were particularly appropriate helpers for mothers with sick and injured children. Childern and babies were not considered to be sinful
until they distinguished right from wrong, as with Adam
and Eve in the Garden of Eden. So their sickness or injury
could not be in retribution for their sins. For such cases
(for example, birth defects, hernias of newborn children)
the placation of an angry God by means of specialized saints
would have been inappropriate. Rather, one turned to the
benevolent mother saint, who took care of injuries directly.
At least for children, the idea of accidental, or at least non-
responsible injury must have entered the common theology.
This nonretributory mode, I believe, applied to adults as
well as children, for people of all ages were, figuratively,
the children of Mary, and shared in her mercy.

Curing at shrines worked through the establishment of a
theater in which grace could plausibly be delivered. The
cures at the shrine were more likely of long-term afflictions,
problems which, however serious, left their victims capable
of making their way to the shrine. Other cures took place at
home or in the course of an accident. Cures away from the
shrine usually occurred after a simple invocation or a prom-

ise to the shrine image. When people had ailments that ordinarily would be taken to the shrine for curing, but were unable to go (because they lived too far away, or were cloistered nuns, for example), it was customary to send an offering to the shrine by a proxy pilgrim. This procedure might also be used for incapacitating ailments that did not require immediate attention. Catalan and Aragonese cities and villages sent proxy pilgrims, called romeros, to shrines during epidemics, but this does not appear to have been a Castilian custom in the sixteenth century.

From the miracles in the reports and contemporary miracle books a kind of gradient can be constructed of the different points at which people were healed, away from the shrine or in the process of a pilgrimage. (See Table 3.10.)

Table 3.10. Sites and Occasions of Cures

Site of cure	Occasion of cure
Away from shrine	On invocation of saint
	On promise to saint
	After sending gift to shrine
	On application of shrine water, oil, ointment, or insignia
On visit to shrine	While on trip
	On first coming in sight of shrine
	On entering shrine grounds
	On touching shrine building
	On entering building
	On catching sight of image or when veil around image is opened
	At first prayer to image in its presence
	On spending night at shrine, often while asleep there
	During novena at shrine, especially at its conclusion
	During mass at the shrine, especially on holy day
	On application of shrine water, oil, or ointment
	When touching or kissing the image or relic
	During procession of image on holy day or rogative
	During moving (traslación) of relic

By the sixteenth century the major shrines of Spain had various kinds of insignia or tokens, sacred souvenirs for pilgrims capable of effecting cures and other miracles away from the shrine. For Montserrat in the sixteenth century special candles stimulated cures in distant villages and cities.[30] For the Christ of Burgos they were *cruzetas*, small crucifixes given to members of the shrine brotherhood.[31] Among other items distributed at Guadalupe were *estampas*, prints of the image, which sometimes cured people when placed on the injured part of the body.[32] Other, similar items included *mides* or *medias*—ribbons the exact measurement of an image, which had been touched to the image before their sale (in use at the shrine of Fuente de la Salud, Castellón, among other places); medals, and small replica images.[33]

There is only one mention in the reports of the use of such insignia in New Castile: that of the use of a scapulary of Santa María de la Varga in Uceda (Guadalajara) to cure a cancer of the nose. From other sources it is known that *estampas* were also in use at about this time at the shrine of Our Lady of Prado, Ciudad Real. In 1582 one of these prints miraculously did not burn, and another, which a Ciudad Real soldier was carrying with him as protection, was successfully used to calm a lion at a Valencia zoo! By the seventeenth century prints of images were in use at shrines throughout Spain, as they are today.[34]

Many of the idiosyncratic religious lore, practices, and ceremonies of Spanish communities center on their shrines. Until recently, much curing at or away from shrines was done with natural substances at the shrine site. In the sixteenth century, two such curative agents were in use at the shrine of Fuencaliente (Ciudad Real): the water and an unguent (sulphur?) in the hot springs below the church. Holy water from wells or springs cured eyes at the shrine of Lucy at Ventas con Peña Aguilera (Toledo), eyes and children's hernias at Fuensanta of La Roda, and cripples at Fuensanta of San Pablo (Toledo). At the Christ of Burgos water that had been used to wash the feet of the crucifix performed cures; similarly at Almoguera (Guadalajara) water in which the bones of Saint Christopher had been dipped cured eyes and other injuries. At the shrine of Saint Anne in Puerto-llano they used the oil, leaves, and wooden chips from a holy juniper; and at Our Lady of the Dados (Dice), small cubes from a mosaic cured people with fever.[35] Oil from the lamps of the shrine of Monsalud was used for healing from the fourteenth century on. Also at Monsalud a kind of holy bread was baked and used for curing, sometimes when dipped in the oil.[36]

The *velada* (vigil, or wake) at the shrine, often the night before the shrine feast, but in theory any night, was considered to be a time at which a cure was especially likely. About a third of the miracle cures reported in the 1554 miracle book of the Christ of Burgos took place during *veladas*, typically after the supplicant fell asleep after long hours of prayer. When she or he awoke in the morning the cure was accomplished. This kind of cure is similar to the incubatory cures of the Church of late antiquity, associated with dreams at the shrine. The men of Cabezarados tell of a cure during a vigil in the shrine of Our Lady of Finibus Terrae and its verification and documentation:

It is a shrine of much devotion and has worked many miracles, especially one on March 26, 1554, when Isabel Martín, wife of Pero Martín de Lorencio, resident of the town of Corral, came to the shrine to spend the night in prayer (*velar*). She had been crippled for more than a year in her hands and feet, and when she was praying at night in the shrine to Our Lady suddenly she felt herself better and could walk and use her hands very well. A report and a very thorough investigation with a number of trustworthy witnesses was made by Mateo Muñoz, the alcalde ordinario of this town at the time on the request of bachiller Martín Alonso, parish priest of this town. Because the miracle was so spectacular, a procession was held from this town to the shrine, and the woman was healthy and remained so until she died several years later. The report and the testimony of the miracle is held by the mayordomo of the shrine in a chest, and I, Christobal Sánchez, notary, certify that I have seen and read the aforementioned dossier and testimony.[37]

Miracles were critical, dramatic evidence of the power of the shrine image. Without such evidence a shrine could not attract the votive devotion necessary for its maintenance, and it would revert to a simple chapel, without keeper or chaplain. Without miracles, monasteries that maintained shrines would lose considerable income.

Once it was clear that an image performed miracles, it could become a long-term shrine. For orthodox theology and modern psychology would agree that on some level people must believe in a saint for the saint to cure them. Once they believe in a saint's power they will invoke it in time of need. And since in a certain percentage of cases they would be cured, freed, or spared (whether by divine intervention, luck, or the psychological boost of faith) these new graces or miracles were in a sense self-generating. An image built up a momentum of miraculousness. This momentum is understood by the faithful, who collaborate in it, as it were, with their votive offerings, which are patent proofs and demonstrations of the effectiveness of the image, advertisements for their countrymen. The ex-votos on the walls of these chapels set up the atmosphere of power in which new miracles can take place.

As at Our Lady of Finibus Terrae, at other shrines testimony of witnesses and participants in miracles was taken down by notaries and made available to the skeptical. Such depositions could be read at Our Lady of Salceda (Peñalver, Guadalajara); Our Lady of Socorro (Loranca, Cuenca); Our Lady of Madroñal (Aunón, Guadalajara); La Concepción of Trascastillo (El Cañavete, Cuenca)—"many miracles have been done there, as will be seen from the testimony

of the authorities of this town in front of notaries that will
be shown to anyone who wants to see them . . ."; and Our
Lady of Oliva (Almonacid de Toledo)—". . . many miracles, which are written down and put up for posterity on
a signboard, and taken in evidence. . . ."[38] Miracle records
were also being kept at this time at the Marian shrines of
Los Llanos (Hontova, Guadalajara), Monsalud (Córcoles,
Guadalajara), Prado (Ciudad Real), and Atocha (Madrid),
and at the shrine of the Crucifix of Griñón (Madrid).

The very existence of this kind of formal proof is evidence for a spirit of doubt in the land. The publication of
shrine histories-cum-miracle books, including those of Saint
Isidore of León (1525), Montserrat (1536), Our Lady of
Peña de Francia (1544), the Christ of Burgos (1554), Guadalupe and Santiago (1575), the Niño de la Guardia (1583),
and Our Lady of Puig (1591), spread models of miracles,
some of them highly unlikely, throughout the peninsula.[39]

Not only Protestant reformers, but also Spanish Erasmians had occasion to question some of these miracles in print.
The Council of Trent, in reaction to this kind of criticism,
set up norms for the declaration of miracles and apparitions,
which henceforth needed the approval of the bishop. These
norms, calling for the testimony of witnesses as well as
signed, notarized statements, were reaffirmed and strength-
ened by Urban VIII in 1625, but in fact were merely the
continuation of the practice of many of the shrines in Spain
as early as the mid-fifteenth century. Documents certifying
miracles of the Christ of Burgos were collected beginning
in 1454 because even at that time there was skepticism of
miracles. By the end of the sixteenth century, most printed
books containing miracles also carried careful explanations
of how the miracles were verified, openly admitting that
many people in Spain did not believe in miracles at all. The
history of Our Lady of Salceda published in 1616 describes
how the prior in 1565 requested that a commission from
the archbishopric of Toledo examine the shrine's miracle
registers and certify their authenticity. To eliminate any

question of influence the prior absented himself from the
monastery while the examination was under way.[40]

That this kind of proof was necessary can be seen from
Martín de Azpilcueta's *Manual for Confessors*, from which
it seems that in order to open up for "business," pious or
otherwise, at a new shrine, the keepers would hang up fic-
titious votive offerings. His condemnation came in the form
of a consultation as to whether a given act was a sin:

> [From Chapter II, de bien honrar a Dios:] If one put
> forth false relics of saints to be adored; or offered votive
> images of false miracles to the image of the crucifix, or to
> that of Our Lady, or to other saints, so that others, in-
> spired by them would offer, or in order to offer purchase,
> other similar (votive images), and hence profit from it.
> *Mortal Sin.* Because one does a notable irreverence to
> the divine cult by making the people believe in lies.[41]

The votive offerings in shrines were purchased at the
shrine itself. In fact, such is often the case today in Spain.
The sale of these offerings can be of considerable significance to shrine keepers. They would be the prime—but not
the only—beneficiaries of false miracles. Sixteenth-century
Spain was plagued by con artists who made their livings off
the shrines and the pilgrim routes, and who won alms and
celebrity status by faking miracles at shrines. A chapter in
the Synodal Constitutions of Toledo of 1536, repeated in
those of 1566 and in those of Uclés in 1578, warned against
"some tricksters disguised as pilgrims who say they have
been sent for the health of souls, going under aliases and
false pretenses, using many other frauds and deceptions to
fool ignorant folk and make off with their money and other
possessions that they can get a hold of."[42] Some pretended
to be captives miraculously released from North African or
Turkish captivity and delivered at night to the shrine. A
pragmatic of Philip II was directed against them in 1590.
Shrine histories reveal other highly suspect miracles, like

one in Burgos in which a man seemed to vomit up a huge lizard at the climax of the crowded Friday mass.[43]

Careful documentation sought to avoid some of these false miracles and restore public confidence in the shrine's power. In addition to ultimately providing a source of income from new offerings, the documentation and proclamation of miracles at a shrine was a source of local pride. An element of competition with other shrines and images was clearly involved. In some villages even today the shrine is the only attraction the village has to outsiders, the shrine feast day the only time when strangers come. A shrine can put a town on the map, and miracles make a shrine.

Shrines, Shrine Keepers, and Fiestas

The reports give few physical descriptions of shrines. An exception is Our Lady of Madroñal outside of Auñón (Guadalajara).

> The chapel is a large church that could serve more than four hundred households; it has large guest rooms because it is much frequented by people from this district and from many other parts due to the great devotion that they profess to this shrine and the many miracles that have taken place there. It has a *huerta* and gardens, for which men had to bring soil because it was located on top of bare rock, and wonderful trees have been grown in them, including mulberry, apple, plum, pomegranate, and much ivy, jasmine, violets, lilies, daisies, figs and grapevines. All of the trees bear wonderful fruit each year. At times chaplains [*Capellanes de Misa*] have led a holy life in this house, and a *santero* and *santera* keep the place clean and cultivate the *huertas* and gardens; and when there is no chaplain, the patrons provide a chaplain of good character to come on all Sundays, days of the Apostles, and feasts of Our Lady to lead mass, sung or

prayed, with organ music, for the people who go to the shrine.[44]

The shrines operated at certain monasteries were on a larger scale. Pedro González de Mendoza, archbishop of Granada in the early seventeenth century, published in 1616 a history of Our Lady of Salceda, where he had been a monk, and which he had had renovated at his expense. As he describes it, the shrine was a kind of Renaissance palazzo set among lush gardens and orchards. In the library were portraits of noted scholars; outside the monastery was an elaborate set of devotional chapels, satellite shrines; with easy access to the shrine chapel there was a clinic for pilgrims; and in all the chapels and halls there were plaques with edifying verses for the visitors. The pilgrim was encouraged to approach the shrine image and relics gradually, moving from one wondrous place to another in a kind of ritualized sacred tourism. The shrine seems modeled after the national monastic shrines of Montserrat and Guadalupe.

By and large, however, shrines were relatively small. They were used by large numbers of people only intermittently, and most of the fiestas occurred in warmer weather, when people could spill over outside for the services. Many of the shrines of the sixteenth century still exist, and few of them approach the size of parish churches. (See Figures 5 and 6.)

The relative well-being of New Castile in the early sixteenth century led to the establishment of substantial numbers of *obras pías*, pious foundations in the form of chapels, hospices (generally private houses willed with or without endowments for use as almshouses, old age homes, or shelters for transients), hospitals (usually supported by endowments, brotherhoods, or both), funds for the annual awarding of dowries for orphans or reformed prostitutes, or monasteries (of which a surprising number was being built at the time of the reports).

The erection of a monastery was a kind of spiritual investment, for one of the duties of the monastics was to pray for their benefactors. The endowment of chaplaincies served the same purpose: it provided income for a cleric to say a given number of masses per week for the souls of the founders. It was also a way of assuring family property, for succession to the chaplaincy was often limited to the deceased's family. Some of these chaplaincies were set up at shrines, but generally they were established in parish churches and cathedrals. The chaplaincies were private foundations for private prayers, and the priests at the shrines, by definition, had a public to serve.

The majority of the shrines were probably served by the parish priest. Others did, however, have full-time *capellanes*, who were paid by the patrons or owners of the shrines, whether the village council, a brotherhood, a lord, a monastery, or a cathedral chapter.

Depending on these different arrangements, the number of masses said in a shrine varied greatly. Shrines in monasteries would have a daily mass, as would any shrine with a resident chaplain. Saturday masses seem to have been an honor sometimes accorded a saint whom the village or town considered its chief advocate.

The day-to-day administration of a shrine (except in the case of monasteries) was in the hands of a layman, the mayordomo, appointed by the owners to keep accounts, supervise the rents and loans from the shrine patrimony, and pay the priest for his services. Beneath the mayordomo was the *santero*. In some of the poorer shrines there might be no chaplain or mayordomo, simply a *santero*, a man or a couple who live at the shrine and maintain it, and farm the *huerta*. There is no mention in New Castile of single women shrine keepers, who operated many of the shrines of the Basque country (under the title of *serora*) and the Montaña (under the title of beata) at this time. In other parts of Spain the shrine keepers were expected to be celibate and wear a costume, but in New Castile they seem merely to have been caretakers, as today.

The people distinguished mere shrine caretakers from

ermitaños (hermits). Hermits lived at the shrine for devotional reasons. One near the Escorial in 1575 was "old and thin, but healthy."[45] The *capellanes de misa* referred to in the Auñón report quoted above ("who have led a holy life in this house") were probably what are called in other reports *ermitaños de misa*, clergymen hermits. There were also lay hermits. Cervantes, in *Persiles and Segismunda*, distinguished between wealthy or noble hermits, for whom self-interest was out of the question, and poor people, who might in fact have bettered their standard of living by taking over a shrine and fomenting contributions. The *santero* or *ermitaño* inevitably profited from the offerings brought to the shrine saint.

We should not marvel that a rustic shepherd should retire to the solitude of the countryside, nor wonder that a

Figure 5. The chapel of Saint Quiteria, Huete (Cuenca), May 1977. Photograph by Cristina García Rodero.

pauper who is dying of hunger in the city should retreat to the solitude of a place where he will not lack for food. There are ways to live sustained by idleness and laziness, and it is no small laziness for men to live off the work of other hands, however generous. If I saw a Hannibal of Carthage shut up in a chapel, as I saw Charles V closed in a monastery, I would be amazed and astonished; but that a common person retires, or a pauper goes into retreat, neither astonishes nor amazes me.[46]

Persiles and Segismunda was written about twenty-five years after the reports were made. Relatively few hermits were mentioned in the reports, and it was only as economic conditions in New Castile worsened, toward the end of the century, that hermitism became a social problem. Restrictions on hermits in the Synodal Constitutions of Toledo appeared in 1566, repeated in 1583 and elaborated in 1601. In Cuenca they were restricted as early as 1531, the restrictions repeated in 1602 and 1626.[47] (See Chapter 5.)

Figure 6. Ritual dance before the image of Saint Quiteria, May 22, 1977. Photograph by Cristina García Rodero.

In spite of Cervantes, or perhaps implicit in Cervantes'
position, the hermits of this period had a kind of aura, as
the physical, if not spiritual successors of the saintly hermits of the Middle Ages. The villagers of Illán de Vacas
(Toledo) believed their town to have been named after a
hermit, San Illán: "And it is not known why it is called
Illán de Vacas, except that we have heard from our ancestors
that it was called Vacas, and that in this town there lived a
holy man, called Saint Illán; his hermitage, where he is
buried, is a league from the town, and that is why we say and
we heard it said that the town is called Illán de Vacas."[48]
   The medieval tradition of eremitism was alive also in the
Madrid town of Los Santos de la Humosa, where the bones
of the founding hermit, Pedro, were treated with veneration
greater than that accorded the relics of other saints and
apostles in the same church.

> In addition to the holy relics listed, for more than five
> hundred years the residents and their ancestors have held
> in devotion and respectful memory the bones of a good
> and holy man that are in a pinewood chest in the parish
> church, which are said to be of a hermit named Pedro,
> who led a solitary and eremitical life where the town is
> now located, which, as was said before, was a mountain
> thickly forested with oak and holm oak. He lived in a
> small chapel and hermitage on the summit of that moun-
> tain, which is the old chapel section of what is now the
> parish church. And there are still today old, honorable,
> and trustworthy persons in this town who remember
> having seen the bones of this holy man taken out and
> placed on the heads of women who were giving birth and
> seemed to be in danger, and that once they had been
> placed there the patient soon felt the favor and aid of
> God and gave birth. And that when a church Visitor
> came to inspect the church they showed him the bones
> with the skull and told them what happened with them,
> and he ordered them that they take much care with them

and keep them in a decent and enclosed place until God was pleased to make known his saint, if he was one, and so the bones were placed in the chest in a niche in the main chapel of the church where they have been and remain today.[49]

Medieval hermits throughout northern Spain became local saints. Their bodies and their dwelling places became devotional centers and are still used that way in many places today. There are few cases of this kind south of the Tagus because the reconquest of the South came after the golden age of eremitism. In contrast, with a few striking exceptions —Saint Pascual Bailón, Ven. Pedro Muñoz, Ven. Pedro Pecador—very few of the hermits of the sixteenth and seventeenth centuries became saints in the eyes of the local people. For many of them the perfect life was not so much one of isolation and direct service to the people as it was the stimulation of devotion. Their vocation was to make shrines; the image or the saint, not the hermit himself, was the central figure. The kind of person who was a hermit saint in the early Middle Ages was a monastic in the sixteenth century—Teresa of Avila, Peter of Alcántara, and John of the Cross.

The hermit entrepreneur of the sixteenth and seventeenth centuries, who retired to a chapel and drummed up devotion in the countryside to his chosen image is also found in the reports. There was one in Fregacedos (Madrid) who brought relics approved by the bishop. And the hermit Pedro de Castillo of the chapel of Our Lady of Altomira (Mazarulleque, Cuenca) went so far as to go to Rome for relics and a bull from the pope. He was successful enough to attract the Discalced Carmelites to found a monastery there, and by 1616 it was considered one of the major shrines of the Alcarria.[50]

The bishop of Cuenca complained in 1601 about the maintenance of hermitages as a source of income for their proprietors. He wrote that chapels were being built "by private persons and by village councils, who set people up in the chapels to ask for and obtain alms for them, and what they get they convert to their own uses, without having to account to anyone, which is against all law and causes scandal and is a bad example." Unlike other bishops he did not forbid the establishment of the chapels without his license, but he did rule that they be brought under ecclesiastical jurisdiction, with account books checked by diocesan inspectors, and all alms spent on the chapel.[51]

Eremitism was one way laymen could consecrate themselves to the religious life without the taking of orders. The reports mention only one woman hermit. Catalina de Cardona (1519–1577) had been nurse to the children of Philip II. In 1562, taking the name of Catalina de la Cruz, she retired in solitude to a cave in Alcarria. Ten years later she founded a Discalced Carmelite monastery near the Jucar River, where at the time of the reports she lived in semi-isolation. For most women the equivalent of eremitism was a vow of voluntary chastity and, at times, retirement from the world as a beata.[52]

There is little information in the reports about the income of shrines. For most shrines, income in the form of votive offerings and alms was probably little more than sufficient to maintain the building, pay for the oil needed for the altar light, help feed the *santeros*, and pay for the masses. The largest ones were worth more. The alms of Saint Mary of the Baths of Fuencaliente (Ciudad Real) amounted to 300 ducats and 100,000 marvedis for the feast day, September 8, alone.[53] The alms must also have been substantial at the monastic shrines (Monsalud, Salceda, Sopetrán, Fuensanta of La Roda), where they were needed to feed, clothe, and cure needy pilgrims, and at the major shrines of Illescas, Talavera, Ciudad Real, Madrid, and Toledo.

The typical shrine feast in La Mancha today is in two parts: the image is taken to the town from the shrine and then triumphantly returned after a period of weeks or months. Such processions may have been customary in the sixteenth century, but we know of only one image—Our Lady of Castillo of La Membrilla (Ciudad Real)—that was regularly moved.[54] The processions on feast days in the sixteenth century seem rather to have been of the townspeople to the shrine, where the image was waiting. Such a procession included musicians and dancers, in contrast to penitential processions to the same shrines in times of need. Witness the description of the fiesta of the regional shrine of Saint Anne, in Carrascosa del Campo (Cuenca):

> There is a chapel they call Lady Saint Anne's, which this town considers its señora, advocate, and patron. Sixty-five years ago the chapel was founded and built from devotion by a private brotherhood. In other parts of this district they also hold it in great reverence. This town and republic comes many times to it in procession with its crosses and celebrates its day with great ceremony. A very solemn procession departs from the parish church of the town, accompanied by many clergy, crosses, pennants, and musicians—all that can be gathered together, and sometimes flageolets and sackbuts, cornets, and flutes; many dancers come and different kinds of instruments. There are many skits performed [*hay muchos entremeses*]. On arrival at the shrine mass is said with the maximum dignity. There is a sermon, and the most learned preacher that can be found is chosen to speak. Bulls are run, the best ones available. So many people come from far away, that although this town is as large as we said [670 households], for each person one meets from this town, one meets many from other towns; all in all it is one of the most notable and principal fiestas in the bishopric of Cuenca.[55]

As at Carrascosa, in many other shrines bulls were fought, killed, and divided up in the afternoon of the fiesta. One of Spain's oldest bullrings is part of the shrine of Our Lady of Virtudes, near Santa Cruz de Mudela (Ciudad Real), and despite repeated ecclesiastical censure, bullfights still character-ize the fiestas of La Mancha. In at least three of the more important shrines, La Fuensanta of Albacete, Santa María Egipciaca at Luciana (Ciudad Real), and Fuencaliente (Ciudad Real), a fair was held on September 8. Shrine feast days were occasions for the massing of the poor as well as the faithful. Then as well as now the way to the shrines was lined with beggars, and all gathered for a free meal after the shrine ceremony.

Both the people of Carrascosa (Cuenca) and Terrinches (Ciudad Real) boasted of wise and learned preachers at their fiestas. A "notable event" (Question 56) reported by the men of Alcorcón (Madrid) demonstrates the frequency of preaching in the region. (It also points up the significance of Good Friday as a very important holy day in this time of devotion to the Passion.)

> In this town there was a man named Juan González, who died five years ago; he was a poor man who did not know how to read or write, very rustic in his comportment [*muy rustico en su trato*]. God saw fit to give him an illness such that he was in bed crippled and without speech for a year. One day on Good Friday, as ill as he was, he made them take him to church, and to please him two men carried him seated in their arms. He went to the middle of the church and with a loud voice began to speak and said a sermon so coherently and with such good style and citations from the Holy Scriptures and with such good doctrine as if he were a man of letters and experienced in preaching.[56]

What better evidence for the spread of the idea and ideal of learning than that in a miracle an unlettered peasant becomes a learned man. What better evidence of religious saturation that when the mute speak, they preach!

In addition to the major feast day, many villages celebrated other feasts of Mary. Five of them, the Purification (February 2), the Annunciation (March 25), the Assumption (August 15), the Nativity (September 8), and the Immaculate Conception (December 8) were obligatory in the region. Others, optional in some of the dioceses of New Castile, were commonly celebrated anyway: the Visitation (July 2, obligatory in Cuenca and Sigüenza), Our Lady of the Snows (August 5, obligatory in Cuenca), the Presentation (November 21), and the Expectation (December 18, obligatory in Toledo). Some villages, through custom or vow, also observed the eves of these nine Marian days. The obvious place to celebrate them was the village's major Marian chapel. Bishops encouraged fasting on the eves of these days with indulgences.

Throughout New Castile it was customary to make regular visits to shrines in springtime processions. These visits were generally made between April 25 and May 9, to implore protection for the crops.

April 25	Saint Mark; obligatory (= Greater Litanies)
May 1	Saint Philip and Saint James; obligatory
May 3	Finding of the Holy Cross; obligatory
May 6	Saint John at the Latin Gate
May 8	Appearance of Saint Michael Archangel
May 9	Saint Gregory of Nazianzus

Saint Mark's Day, on which the Greater Litanies were observed, by Church custom entailed a procession to ask for a successful harvest, and apparently succeeded the Roman feast of Robigalia. There were processions to a number of Marian chapels on this day, particularly in the western parts of New Castile. In addition, the towns in the archpriestric of Madrid had jointly vowed not to eat meat on Saint Mark's Day, although none of the communities could explain why.

May 1 had been another Roman feast day, and as late as the seventeenth century the diocesan constitutions of Sigüenza forbade the choosing of May queens or kings and the decoration of doorways with branches (*lamparas*).[57]

The day, however, was an obligatory holy day, and was the occasion for processions to a number of chapels in the region, notably that of Saint Anne in Maqueda (Toledo).

The Cross of May, May 3, was also obligatory, and was a day on which processions were made as protection against vine worms and hailstorms, particularly in the provinces of Madrid and Toledo. These processions were directed especially to shrines of saints—Mary Magdalen, Peter, Babiles, and Bartholomew. In some towns the processions were simply around the fields and back, as in La Despernada (Madrid) and Fuenlabrada (Madrid).

May 6, the Feast of Saint John the Evangelist, was similarly observed with processions to shrines, particularly in the Toledo region, where processions converged on the abandoned churches of San Juan de Hurtado, San Esteban de Rodillas, and the Marian shrine of Our Lady of Gracia, at Velada.

On May 8, the feast commemorating the appearance of Saint Michael at Monte Gargano, in Italy, processions were held from a number of villages to Marian shrines, predominantly in the Toledo and Cuenca regions. And May 9, the day of Saint Gregory of Nazianzus, was the date of many vows to that saint for protection against vine pests. In some towns, processions were made to the vines, or around the boundaries on this day. Whereas the vows the villagers had made were a part of their collective obligations—something like a corporate debt or like the kind of interest on loans that had to be paid in perpetuity—once the initial crisis that provoked the vow was over, the annual observance of the vowed day also took the form of a petition that the plague, the pests, or the hail not recur. In this way critical ceremonies became calendrical ceremonies not unlike the obligatory petitions of the rogations.

The concentration of processions and vows into this two-week period indicates its critical importance in the agricultural cycle. It was a time of great danger to the vines from worms, which attacked the first buds, as well as from late frosts, hailstorms, and drought. Its equivalent was a period of danger from hail in the late summer when the wheat was ready for harvest. Spring rains are crucial for the ripening of the wheat. It was not only a time for supplication, but also of celebration. Is there any fertility ceremony of a sexual nature involved? It is impossible to say. The report of Huecas, in respect to the annual visit of the town to the shrine of Mary Magdalen (whom Alfonso de Valdés termed the Christian successor of Venus) comments sourly that the people when at the shrine on Saint Mark's Day "dance with too much enthusiasm" (*bailan con demasiado negocio*). In earlier times people had spent the night at the shrine.[58]

In addition to the fixed days, there were three more days of processions on the movable feast days of the Lesser Litanies, the Monday, Tuesday, and Wednesday of the seventh week after Easter—some time between May 10 and June 17. These processions took the form of the rogations of April 25, and were usually each to a different chapel, generally ones within the village boundaries, theoretically at the four cardinal points. In some villages oratories were placed at four entrances to the village for this purpose.

In keeping with the villagers' own desire for unity and completeness in the observance of its divine obligations, diocesan constitutions encouraged participation in these processions. Those of Sigüenza (1532) fined families not sending a member one *real*. Those of Cuenca (1531, repeated 1566, 1592, 1602) offered positive reinforcement—forty days of pardon for those participating in the rogation, Corpus Christi, or votive processions. "And we exhort one member of each household to attend the rogation processions."[59]

The result of the concentration of processions on these days was that at times processions from several settlements would be converging on the same chapel on the same day. In a history of the Benedictine shrine of Our Lady of Sopetrán (Guadalajara) published in 1615, the author describes the assembly of many surrounding towns for a day of the Lesser Litanies.

All of these villages come in procession the Wednesday of Litanies, the day before Ascension, and a great fair is held in this place attended by merchants of silk and woolen cloth, goldsmiths and silversmiths, vendors of dry goods, and numerous artisans of all kinds because of the multitude of people who come from so many places. It is very pleasing to see them eating in family groups. Each village separately spreads out very large tablecloths in the meadow. The parish priest, clergy, mayors, and corregidor sit at the head, and then the mass of the people. The *concejo* generally gives each community bread and wine, and each person brings his own food. To see in one meadow thirty or forty entire towns, some with two hundred, others three hundred men all together around their food is very pleasing to the eye.[60]

Such gatherings were not always so bucolic. Often there was friction over precedence, and it was a natural time for intervillage disputes over boundaries, stray animals, and common lands to come to a head, sometimes in pitched battles between village youths. For this reason the bishop of Burgos in 1575 and the bishop of Toledo in 1583 decreed that villages should go in procession to shrines on separate days. At the ruined shrine of Saint Mary of Batres on the Guadarrama River many village processions once coincided on May 1. By 1576 only a few went—"more processions used to meet there, but because of some diputes [*pasiones*] that took place there they have stopped coming." Apparently this problem also arose between the towns of Daimiel and Torralba (Ciudad Real), for the shrine of Our Lady of the Crosses was located on the boundary between them. "The people of Torralba go there in procession, and sometimes have their differences with those of Daimiel." Within the city of Toledo the same kind of problem arose when brotherhoods had to make joint processions. The priest who wrote the extensive Toledo report argued that the brotherhoods ought to be consolidated, "so that when we receive the Bull of the Holy Crusade or we go on roga-

tions, or processions or funerals, there not be arguments or
irreverences over who should carry their sceptres and
crosses ahead or behind."[61]

In some shrines ceremonies with clear and fixed rules of
precedence served to defuse those conflicts that were pro-
tocolary in nature. The ceremony described for the shrine
of Our Lady of Arroyo de Viñas in Móstoles (Madrid) is
still practiced in many places throughout Spain.

In the territory of this town is a chapel of Our Lady of
Arroyo de Viñas, which is so called because it is on the
bank of the stream by that name. It is of much devotion,
and every year on Saint Mark's Day the processions of
this town [Móstoles], Arroyo de Molinos, Sacedón, Zar-
zuela, Odón, and Navalcarnero meet there. The procession from this town must receive all the rest, and no other
may enter before her, and when they leave [this town's
procession] must dispatch all the rest, and leave last of all,
because the chapel is in its jurisdiction. It has some income
in rents, which might total a *cahiz* of grain, and the rest
is provided by the council, which out of devotion keeps
it well repaired.[62]

The reception of the visiting procession by the home procession at such ceremonies generally entails the "embrace"
of the parish crosses.[63]

Villages also went to shrines in petitionary processions
(known as *rogativas*), especially for water. Certain shrines
were used on a district basis only in times of drought, and
do not seem to have been used for curing.[64]

Valtablado del Río (Guadalajara)	Relics of Saint Vincent	Up to 29 villages
Villarrubio (Cuenca)	Relics of Saint Silvestre	Repels storms
Villarejo de Salvanés (Madrid)	Saint Peter Salvanés	For water
Cardiel (Toledo)	Saint Benedict	For water

The gathering of large numbers of villages at a shrine to
pray for water (as at Valtablado del Río) is still customary
in the northeastern half of the province of Guadalajara, and
in adjacent Soria. It used to be a common feature of certain
shrines in Huesca and Lérida also, but there it has died out
in this century, partly because of irrigation in the lower
villages and depopulation in the higher villages. These gatherings have a fixed etiquette of ritual and precedence. At
Valtablado del Río the skull of Saint Vincent was taken out
and dipped in a well during the ceremony. This was also
customary at the shrines of Saint Urbez (Nocito, Huesca)
and Saint Magín (Pontils, Tarragona).[65] Most of the shrines
now used for group rainfall requests are Marian.

In addition to the fixed days and to petitionary or votive
processions, individuals and families would normally be
coming to the more popular shrines throughout the year.
While trips of gratitude might be saved for the annual fiesta,
individual pilgrimages of petition would be made as the need
arose, and might take the form of a nine-day stay at the
shrine. Many shrines had lodgings for these guests, and presumably then as now *santeros* derived some of their income
by supplying food to the petitioners.

Among these corporate villages with their separate contracts with the divine, their individual arrangements with
secular lords, their own special rights and exemptions, their
own long-standing traditions, the shrines and their festivals
provided occasions for transcending boundaries and celebrating those things the people from the different communities had in common. The shrines, generally in the inter-
stices of social geography—at times, as in the cases of Our
Lady of Salceda, the Rey de Magestad in northern Guadalajara, and Our Lady of the Crosses in Ciudad Real, exactly
on the boundary between villages—were a kind of neutral
ground where especially powerful divine helpers could be
shared by neighboring villagers, entire districts, or regions.
The *caridades*, rituals of commensality, particularly symbol-
ize the communion of devotion and obligation to the divine

of groups of villages in New Castile. Carmelo Lisón has emphasized the number of festivals of sharing in present-day Spain, and certainly what he says holds true for the sixteenth century.[66]

One in six villages had a shrine to which other villages came. About one in forty had a shrine to which more than the surrounding settlements came. (See lists in the Appendix.) Most of the shrines with the wide zones of attraction were Marian, and all were used for curing. With the possible exception of the Cathedral of Toledo and Our Lady of Charity at Illescas, in the sixteenth century there does not appear to have been a shrine in New Castile with an extraregional appeal.

On the other hand, the reports mention a number of shrines outside the area under study. First and foremost, Guadalupe. To this shrine in Extremadura (but still in the diocese of Toledo), a Hieronymite monastery, were headed many pilgrims passing through La Mancha. It was to Guadalupe that the child Inés of Cubas had to go to get her fingers unstuck after the apparition. The historian of Salceda compared his shrine to Guadalupe more than any other. In the sixteenth century Guadalupe was the most important shrine in the kingdom.

Montserrat was to Catalonia what Guadalupe was to Castile. It too was cited in the Salceda monograph and the Daimiel romance. Peña de Francia was to the Dominicans what Guadalupe was to the Hieronymites and Montserrat was to the Benedictines—the most important shrine operated in Spain by the order. There had been a chapel to Our Lady of Pilar, the major shrine of Aragon, in Villarrubia de los Ajos (Ciudad Real).[67]

Other extraregional shrines mentioned included that of Saint Gregory of Sorlada (Navarre) used by the town of Almodóvar del Campo (Ciudad Real); the Seville shrine of Our Lady of Antigua, to which a nobleman in Barajas (Madrid) built a chapel that became quite popular; Our Lady of Tentudia (Badajoz) of which there was a relic of the stone on which Mary appeared in Uclés (the shrine being in the territory of Santiago); and in Santorcaz (Madrid) a chapel to Our Lady of Valvanera, the major shrine of the Rioja region. The most important shrine in northern Andalusia, Our Lady of the Cabeza, was mentioned in the report of Almodóvar del Campo (Ciudad Real) as receiving "great and constant devotion in this kingdom." La Cabeza is described at some length in Cervantes's *Persiles and Segismunda*, and there was a chapel and a brotherhood dedicated to it in Toledo.[68] There is no mention in the reports of other important sixteenth-century shrines: the Veronica in Jaén; Our Lady of Puig north of Valencia; the Christ of Burgos; or even of Saint James of Compostela (although there were a number of chapels and a small number of vows to Saint James).

People from New Castile certainly visited the shrine of Guadalupe in cases of great necessity. And one of the miracles in the history of the Christ of Burgos, published in 1554, was the resurrection from the dead of a woman from Cogolludo (Guadalajara) in 1525.[69] The woman and her husband visited the shrine in thanks three years afterward. But, considering the home villages of persons cured in the miracles given in their respective miracle books, I doubt that many people from New Castile made special trips to visit the other shrines mentioned. The very existence of devotional chapels to Antigua, Pilar, Valvanera, and Cabeza are evidence that the shrines themselves were too far away. Questors, gathering alms and votive offerings, had permission to beg in this region from Guadalupe, Peña de Francia, and Montserrat. The questors from Guadalupe, at least, were active there shortly before the reports.[70]

The existence of this kind of national network, the chains of hospices for pilgrims, and the hospitality for pilgrims at larger shrines, encouraged the flowering of a kind of pilgrim vagabond. We have already mentioned the con artists. From the miracle books we know that people with serious ailments, deformities, or mental problems sometimes tried a number of shrines until they found relief; typically they tried smaller, closer shrines first, then the major national shrines. The miracle book of Our Lady of Prado in Ciudad Real gives a case of this kind—a man possessed by the devil from Daimiel, who tried a number of shrines before he was cured in Ciudad Real in 1580, when the veil around the image was opened. In addition there were other pilgrims, like a woman in *Persiles and Segismunda* who had worked out an annual itinerary, who were essentially vagrant tourists for whom the various shrines were a means of livelihood and spiritual entertainment.[71]

The active, important shrines within New Castile, when mapped out, fall into a pattern that may give a clue to their historical evolution.[72] Above the Tagus there was a 26:20 mix of shrines to Mary and her mother, Saint Anne, on the one hand, and shrines to other saints, on the other. Below the Tagus the ratio was 27:3 in favor of Mary and Saint Anne. I believe this difference stems from the time of the Reconquest. (See Table 3.11.)

Table 3.11. District Shrines North and South of the Tagus
(Exclusive of City of Toledo)

Shrine figure	North of Tagus	South of Tagus
Mary or Saint Anne	26	27
Other saints	20	3
Crucifix or cross	2	1

The shrines present in the sixteenth century would be an accumulation of the chapels that had become miraculous or effective over a long period of time. Prior to the eleventh century, shrines in Spain were almost uniquely based upon important relics. Beginning at that time, the use of images made possible shrines to saints whose relics were not available. The conquest of the region south of the Tagus did not come until the thirteenth century, and at that time the cult of Mary was in full tide across Christian Europe. It is natural that the castles and chapels that the conquerors founded at that time should be devoted to Mary. The reports mention a number of shrines in castles, or on sites where castles are believed to have existed.[73] (See Table 3.12.) All were Marian shrines, and almost all were south of the Tagus.

Table 3.12. Shrines Associated with Castles

Province	Town	Name of Shrine
Madrid	Alcolea de Torote	Na. Sra. del Castillo
	Arganda	Na. Sra. del Castillo (in town)
Toledo	La Cabeza	Na. Sra. de Batres (ex-fort?)
	Castillo de Bayuela	Na. Sra. del Castillo
	Villarrubia de Santiago	Na. Sra. de Castellar
Cuenca	El Cañavete	Na. Sra. de la Concepción de Trascastillo
	Carrascosa del Campo	Na. Sra. del Castillo (legend of siege by Moors)
	Uclés	Na. Sra. de la Dehesa (formerly Defensa)
Ciudad Real	Carrión de Calatrava	Na. Sra. de los Mártires (site of battle)
	Chillón	Na. Sra. del Castillo
	La Membrilla	Na. Sra. del Castillo de Tocón
Guadalajara	Jadraque	Na. Sra. de Castejón

Through shrines the sacred was permanently present in the landscape of New Castile. Just as vows established special times and procedures for a local religious order, shrines were that order's most sacred places. There, because of the cumulative experience of cures, or because of supernatural signs and visions, people knew that a powerful saint, usually Mary, was particularly receptive to their prayers. The importance communities placed on shrines can be seen in the annual feasts and processions, the employment of lay and clerical guardians, the careful registration of the shrine history and miracles, and even the way shrines were included on maps (see Figure 7). The saints of these shrines were considered the resident patrons of their communities. Our Lady of This-Place, located by this particular spring, tree, or castle, with that particular view, was different from any other Mary. Just as today, in the sixteenth century shrines were the quintessential institutions of local religion.

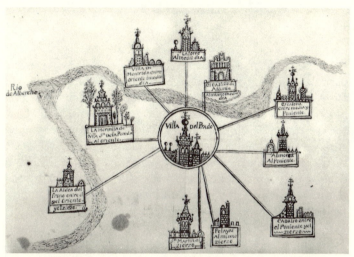

Figure 7. Map sent by parish priest to Cardinal Lorenzana (1782). In this town-centered view of the world, the shrine of Our Lady of the Póveda (left of center) is second only to the town of Villa del Prado (Madrid). Archivo Diocesano de Toledo.

FOUR

Relics and Indulgences

The notable relics that said churches and towns possess . . .

RELICS

As in the rest of Catholic Europe, the cult of relics was a part of Christian religion in Spain long before images of saints were objects of devotion. Bodies of Spanish martyrs like Vincent, Eulalia, and Leocadia probably were the basis for the first Spanish Christian shrines. In the tenth and eleventh centuries the shrine of Saint James and the reliquary shrine of the Camara Santa of Oviedo were two of the major devotional centers. The introduction of a vital Marian cult into this system, a cult based on images, reduced the importance of relics. By the sixteenth century most active shrines in Spain were Marian.[1]

Many of the relics that had been so highly valued in Spain before the Moslem invasion were taken back into the northern mountains or into France. And as the Reconquest moved back across the peninsula, many of the relics stayed in the north. As a result, by the sixteenth century there were fewer relics the farther south one went.

Nevertheless, the old devotion to the bones of saints was very much alive in sixteenth-century New Castile. From the reports it is clear that there were two different types of relics; one, an older kind, of highly prized, miracle-working bodies or bones of saints in parish churches, used for curing and other needs; the other, large collections of relics, many of them quite recently arrived from Rome or the Protestant countries. The latter were treated with veneration, but were not the basis for deep and persisting devotion.

Again, as with shrines, the Tagus appears to have been a historical divide, and new relics were evenly divided north and south of the Tagus. (See Table 4.1.) But most of the older ones, like the shrines to non-Marian saints, were in the north. My hypothesis is that many of the relics and many of the shrines to non-Marian saints north of the Tagus originated in the period when that land was Christian, the land south of the Tagus was under control of the Moors, and the cult of Mary was not fully developed. The saint with the largest number of relics, Blaise, fits this pattern persuasively.

Table 4.1. Distribution of Relics

	Villages Reporting Relics	
When relics obtained	North of Tagus	South of Tagus
Before 1500 or unknown	28	6
Definitely after 1500	10	9
Total villages	349	181

In all, about 13 percent of the settlements questioned had relics, mainly in their parish churches. In about a dozen cases, the relics are said to have worked miracles. In only one of these cases had the miraculous relics arrived recently. The other eleven were of a type: all but two were in parish churches, and all but one were relics of a single, male saint: Blaise (2), Babiles, Christopher, Germain, Macarius, Matthew, Silvestre, Vincent. (The exception was not a female saint, but rather a fragment of the True Cross.) Five more relics (three to Blaise, the others of the Eleven Thousand Virgins and Saint Bernardino) were said to be accorded special devotion, but without mention of miracles.

The relic shrines had a common ceremonial: on the saint's day people from the town and the surrounding towns came to the parish church and were allowed to touch the relics. At Fuencaliente (Ciudad Real) on certain holy days the head of one of the Eleven Thousand Virgins was shown to the people, and everyone touched it "with their heads, eyes, mouths, bowls, and other objects out of devotion." Similarly, many people went to Atanzón (Guadalajara) on the feast of Saint Blaise to touch the relic in its monstrance during the offertory of the mass.[2]

Two of these relics warded off storms. That of Saint Silvestre in Villarrubio (Cuenca) was brought outside when storm clouds bearing hail approached. "It has been seen many times that when bad storm clouds are coming and the holy relic is taken outside, the hail has stopped and changed into clear water." In Campo de Criptana (Ciudad Real) was a fragment of the True Cross, mounted in a golden cross. "It is considered very certain that when hailstorms come and the Cross is taken outside, hail never falls on this township."[3]

Other relics, as noted, were used to obtain rain. That of Saint Vincent was kept in a chest in a recess of the wall of the church of Valtablado (Guadalajara). Nine villages observed a day of litanies with a *romería* in its honor, and when there was a drought, many more came to bathe it, a ritual common in sixteenth-century Iberia, though frowned on by some bishops.

> In times of a need for water many other villages come to the relic; and sometimes as many as twenty-nine crosses from as many villages have gathered; and together they take the relic out and carry it with great veneration and reverence, and carry it to a spring and bathe it, and it has been the will of Our Lord that many times it has given them much water.

The villagers of nearby Ocentejo confirmed the effectiveness of the ritual: "Very many times on the third day or on the very day they gather, our lord has given them much water." The villagers were unsure of the origin of the relic, except that it might have been left by monks of the Order of Santiago. Only a handful of houses still stand in Valtablado. The people told me in 1975 that their precious relic was destroyed in the Civil War. It had been bathed for rain until the first years of this century.[4]

In Almoguera (Guadalajara) a number of relics found by a priest by revelation under the church altar "more than 110 years ago" (i.e., about 1460) were also deployed to obtain rain. Again it was a question of petitionary processions from district towns, and the rain is said to have come at once. "Seldom or never has it been taken outside for water that it did not rain immediately or within a few days." From this shrine people carried home water "touched by the bone of Saint Christopher, which they drink and keep, and wash their faces and eyes, and other honest parts of the body where they have felt some sore or pain and they find great health and relief. . . ."[5]

Strangers who died in these villages were also a source of relics. The Cuenca town of Castillo de Garci Muñoz, according to its report, was the place to which Francisco de Milan, one of the three companions with Saint Bernardino of Siena when he died, brought one third of the saint's staff, a third of the chain he wore as mortification under his habit, and two small containers of oil that came out of the saint's feet upon his death. De Milan died in the town, so the story goes, and that is why the relics are there.[6]

The same scenario is reported in Escalonilla (Toledo). There relics, particularly those of Saint Germain, cured small boys and men, both from the village and from other villages. (Of what we are not told; was it hernias, as with so many of the shrines of the region?) The cures apparently occurred especially on the saint's day or the night before, when the supplicants were keeping vigil, and were commemorated by wax votive offerings. The passerby that died in the village did so before living memory. The relics of Fuentenovilla (Guadalajara) had the same origin, in that case a clergyman coming from Rome. The relics were of unidentified saints, in a reliquary, and had not worked miracles.[7]

The other miraculous relics were given no legends at all. In two cases, Saint Macarius and Saint Matthew, parish churches were dedicated to the saint; it is possible that the relics dated from the earliest times of the Reconquest.[8]

Other localized saints were honored by the villagers. The people of Almodóvar del Campo stated somewhat diffidently that Saint Roch grew up in the area ("y que en esta tierra dicen que crecio"). Uceda, in Guadalajara, claimed the head of a hermit named Ysidro—apparently Isidro Labrador, canonized in 1622.[9] Mesones (Guadalajara) also claimed him, and his body was supposedly in Madrid. Other local saints whose bodies were in cities included: Saint Eugene in the cathedral of Toledo, whose arm was brought from France in the thirteenth century and body in 1565; Saint Leocadia, some of whose relics were in Toledo, and whose body was brought there in 1587; Saint Ildefonso, whose body was returned in 1584; and Saints Justo and Pastor of Alcalá.[10] We see little evidence of these devotions in the country.

Rural New Castile had its own holy people. All through the early modern period and up to the present in western Europe there have been people revered while alive and venerated after death, whose bodies are seen as working miracles. The reports mention a number of these local, uncanonized saints, really as much relics, in the true sense, as the fraudulent bones sent out from Rome and Cologne.

Of two of these, Saint Babiles and Saint Macarius, we are told only that their bodies were venerated in the villages of Boadilla del Monte (Madrid) and Valdesaz (Guadalajara), and that they worked miracles for people in the district. Babiles was a specialist in hernias.[11]

The memory of the holy founder of the monastery of Fitero and of the Order of Calatrava, "Fray Reimundo," (Saint Raymond of Fitero, d. 1163) was alive in Ciruelos (Toledo), where his body had been kept (and where it had performed *miraglos et vertudes,* according to Alfonso el Sabio) until its removal to the Cistercian abbey in Toledo. Similarly, the memory of a saintly prior of the order of Santiago lived on in Uclés. "In addition there are three chains, which with a hair shirt were found on the body of a prior who died here, named Pero Alonso de Valdaracete. They are held in great veneration and give off a celestial odor. He is thought to have died a saint."[12]

Saints Vincent, Gabina, and Cristeta were thought to have been martyred in Avila. Devotion to them appears to have been strong in the region north of Talavera, much of it in the diocese of Avila. Talavera claimed them as natives. Puerto San Vicente (Toledo) claimed that Saint Vincent appeared there, and the Cazalegas parish church was dedicated to him.[13]

In Valenzuela (Ciudad Real) was a relic of the habit of "Fray Diego." Diego of Alcalá was canonized in 1588 at the petition of Philip II, who credited Diego's body with the cure of his son Carlos. Diego (ca. 1400–1463) had lived in a number of monasteries in the region, including Our Lady of Salceda. His body was preserved in Alcalá.[14]

Saint Blaise is generally thought to be from the East, perhaps Armenia. His cult was very strong in the northern part of New Castile. Fully eighteen towns reported having his bones, typically a finger. In the seventeenth century unscrupulous forgers that provided saints and legends for towns concocted a Spanish Saint Blaise who lived in Cifuentes (Guadalajara).[15] But it seems that some kind of legend already existed in the sixteenth century, for the Uceda (Guadalajara) report specifies that their relic is of "San Blas el menor." The Blas relics in a Dominican convent in Cifuentes were the most complete and had performed the miracle of resuscitating a child. Seven of the twenty relics that performed miracles or received special devotion in the entire region were of Saint Blaise. One of the few apparitions of saints other than Mary was of Saint Blaise in Cubas (Madrid); and one of the few miraculous statues other than Mary was of Blaise in Camarena (Toledo).[16]

The area of concentrated devotion to Blaise was southwest Guadalajara, Madrid, and northeast Toledo. Only two relics are reported in the area south of the Tagus. There were thirty-two vows to Blaise in Toledo, Madrid, and

Guadalajara; in Cuenca and Ciudad Real there were only four. This long-standing devotion to Blaise is something of an enigma. Traditionally his specialty has been the curing of throat ailments. But this power was mentioned only in reference to a couple of the vows. None of the relics was described as having a particular property; while they performed occasional miracles, it was not for curing, it would seem, that they were generally revered. They were simply revered in general. Nor are the vows to the saint consistently for a special purpose. All of this generalized devotion is consistent with the tradition of a local saint.

We have transcribed the traditions of the holy hermits of Illán de Vacas and Los Santos de la Humosa. The latter, Pedro, left bones that were used in difficult childbirths. Juana de la Cruz was a holy woman who revived the convent of Our Lady Saint Mary de la Cruz of Cubas founded by Inés on the site of her apparitions. Juana died in 1534, and the Cubas villagers remember her, though confusedly: ". . . which monastery was built by a woman named María de la Cruz [sic], who today lies in flesh and bones in said monastery. She died more than forty years ago, and they say that she was a saint and performed many miracles in her life."[17] In addition to the body of Fray Reimundo, Toledo had two other holy but uncanonized bodies—that of a certain María of Ajofrín, in the Hieronymite convent of La Sisla; and that of the Count of Orgaz, in the parish church of Saint Thomas, buried (as in the El Greco painting) by Saint Augustine and Saint Stephen: "In Saint Thomas the body of the blessed Don Gonçalo Rruiz de Toledo, Count of Orgaz, whom Saint Augustine and Saint Stephen came visibly and in the flesh to bury with their own hands in the year 1312."[18]

The example of Francisca de la Concepción of Cifuentes, "through whom God has worked and works miracles," demonstrated that the region continued to produce human sources of divine power, sources powerful while alive and after death.[19] A cursory glance at the bibliography of any

major Spanish city in the seventeenth century shows numbers of sermons and biographies of monastics considered to
have died in odor of sainthood, to have worked miracles
during their lifetimes, and whose bodies for a time after
their deaths must have been the object of cults. This kind
of popular canonization, of a comparatively short-term nature, continues even today to provide local sources of holy
power. It is a kind of sub-rosa, precanonical sainthood rem-
iniscent of the early Middle Ages.

Relics from outside the area formed part of its devotional system from the time of the Reconquest. In the sixteenth century some of the earlier relics from outside the
area were working miracles and were treated with special
veneration; but the more recent the arrival of the relic, the
less likely it was to be considered to have miraculous power.

Until the sixteenth century collections of relics, as opposed to an individual relic or two, seem to have been located by and large in monasteries, cathedrals, and collegiate
churches, institutions with more resources and more means
of contact with Rome and the Holy Land than the average
parish church. In the sixteenth century, Spain's new role as
a European imperial power, the use of the Jesuits by the
papacy as a Europe-wide spiritual militia, the increased frequency with which Spanish priests visited Rome, and the
Protestant Reformation itself meant that it was very much
easier for Spaniards to obtain relics. The towns of New
Castile, because of their proximity to the court, were especially privileged in this respect.

Cardinal Gil de Albornoz sent back a shipment of relics
to Alcocer (Guadalajara) from Rome some time between
1353 and his death in 1367.[20] And in the fifteenth century,
if not earlier, a passing pilgrim left his reliquary in Escalonilla (Toledo). These are the only collections of relics
that one can tell from the village reports came into the region before 1500. However, from other sources it is known
that a group of relics dating from 1469 was in the parish
church of Ciudad Real,[21] and the massive collections in the

cathedral of Toledo, the collegiate churches of Talavera and Pastrana (the latter containing over three thousand relics), and the convent of Santiago in Uclés, dated at least in part from earlier times.

Philip II's questionnaire did not ask about the origin of relics or their date of arrival in the village; some places, however, volunteered the information. (See Table 4.2.) Of the nineteen cases of relics arriving in the region in the sixteenth century, fourteen were lots of relics, as opposed to individual relics. In the five remaining cases, three were heads of the Eleven Thousand Virgins, and the other two were relics of Saint Sebastian and Saint Benedicta. (Here then, is additional circumstantial evidence that most of the single relics of Saint Blaise, all of which were undated, predate this period.) The relics arriving in the villages in the sixteenth century came in collections from Rome, often mounted in reliquaries. The exceptions were relics of the Eleven Thousand Virgins, some of which, at least, came directly to Spain from Flanders and Germany.

Table 4.2. Bearers of Relics to the Villages of New Castile

Clergymen or religious born in or attached to village	12
Inhabitants of village, not necessarily clergy	4
Clergy, not necessarily attached to village	3
Hermits in village	2
Passing people who died (all before sixteenth century)	3
Royal secretary (Alemán) or wife (of Eraso)	2
Princess Isabel	1

Typically the local priest, or a priest from a town who had moved into a privileged position in the church or imperial hierarchy, such as royal chaplain, obtained the relics in Rome. He then announced in advance their arrival in the town, and the town authorities arranged a procession and ceremony for their reception.[22] In some villages formal agreements were signed in which the town undertook to observe certain feast days in honor of the relics. The relics would normally be installed in the parish church.

A number of the relics were obtained through the royal family. In one case the gift was direct, relics of Saint Sebastian from Isabel, princess of Portugal, to the town of San Sebastián de los Reyes. In other instances it was indirect: from Queen Isabel (Philip's second wife) to a Franciscan, who in turn gave them to his home town of Tendilla, in 1575; from Queen Mary (Philip's fourth wife), who brought them with her from Flanders in 1570, to a Jesuit, who in turn gave them to his home town of Fuentelaencina (adjacent to Tendilla), also in 1575; and from Doña Juana (Philip's sister) to the prior of a convent she founded in Madrid in 1559, a friar from Yebra (Guadalajara), who passed them on to the town. Other donors connected to the monarchy were the royal secretaries Juan Alemán, who gave a set of relics to Mocejón (Toledo) and the wife of Francisco de Eraso, who gave a relic of Saint Benedicta to the town of Humanes (Guadalajara).[23]

That the court should be a source of relics is not surprising. Charles V brought to Spain new devotions and relics from Germany; but the cult of relics was especially pronounced in the court of Philip II. Another study has shown the zeal with which Philip gathered relics in the Escorial from all over Europe, using his ambassadors and his royal relatives.[24] The first delivery of relics for the Escorial arrived in 1564. Formal, ceremonial deliveries continued to arrive until Philip's death. The story of how his ambassadors, through discreet but persistent pressure, were able to obtain the relics is told by documents in the Escorial and by W. Telfer (in relation to the collection of one ambassador, Juan de Borja). The over seven thousand relics in the Escorial were mostly presents to the representatives of a powerful nation from churches or convents in central European nations weakened by religious struggle. Large numbers were obtained in Flanders, Germany, Hungary, and Bohemia; but substantial presents also came from countries not rent by Protestant discord, as in the case of Venice. For Mediterranean nations, as well as for the more northern countries, Spain, the most powerful Catholic nation, whose fleet played a prime role in defeating the Turks at Lepanto, was a nation to be pampered. Philip's desire for relics was known, and it was a relatively painless way to please him. Relics were perquisites of power.

To a certain extent, also, it was a way to put relics threatened by heretics into safekeeping, a kind of reversal of the flow of sacred treasure from Spain to Europe that had taken place during the invasion of the Moors. Archbishop Quiroga of Toledo made this point when celebrating the return of the body of Saint Leocadia to Toledo from Flanders in 1587.[25] Philip and his daughter Isabel were there for the festivities, just as he had arranged the arrival of the body of Saint Eugene in Toledo in 1565 so that he could be there —indeed, so that he could carry it.

The report of Uceda (Guadalajara) gives a good description of the origin of a set of relics brought back in 1574 from Flanders by an army officer from that town, a certain Juan de Bolea. Bolea ("capitan de campaña y gran prevoste de Justicia") was the assistant of the duke of Alba in the Netherlands, and it was in Uceda that Alba was quartered after his disgrace.

> On this last trip Captain Bolea brought back two heads of the Eleven Thousand Virgins who received martyrdom with blessed Saint Ursula in Colonia Aggripina. He was given them to bring back by the abbess and nuns of the Carmelite monastery of Saint Thomas, near Groeninga in the diocese of Belduc, in the provinces of Flanders, who had them, with many other relics, in their convent. The reason for this gift was that as a good captain and defender of the Christian faith, he had saved the convent and its relics from fire and theft by heretics. The story can be read in the letters of donation, not only from the abbess and the nuns, but also from his Holiness, our very holy father Pius the Fifth, who, informed by a pious father of the deed, gave permission to bring the relics to Spain be-

cause of [Bolea's] valiant defense of the Faith, the Catholic Church, and the Holy Relics in those provinces against the heretics.

The relics were brought back with much solemnity and a great procession including many crosses from the district and a great mass of people. He placed them with permission of His Holiness and the Ordinary on the day of Saint Mary of August in the year of Seventy-four in the church of Santa María de la Varga in this town, in a chapel and a niche that he had made for them at his own expense next to the main altar on the side of the Gospels, with a vault underneath for his burial, and a strong, handsome, and well-crafted grille of iron as protection for the Holy Virgins. This town holds as its patrons the two Holy Virgins and for their intercession voted the feast of Saint Ursula and the other saints at the instance of the captain.[26]

The papacy cooperated in this massive reallocation of relics, especially in the 1570s and the 1580s, by providing authenticating documents. We know so much about the relics precisely because the Council of Trent had required stricter procedures (if not standards) for the certification of relics; certificates accompanied all of the relics brought for Philip and many of those going to the villages after 1550.

The Jesuit order collaborated with the Spanish throne and the papacy in the redistribution of relics. Jesuits in countries affected by religious wars sent lots of relics out to Spain, Portugal, and to missions in newly discovered lands. Their privileged access to some relics (especially the Eleven Thousand Virgins in Cologne) gave the Jesuits the possibility of using relics as a tool of religious renewal. Jesuit colleges springing up in Spain were richly endowed with relics from Rome and Germany, as can be seen in the report of Belmonte (Cuenca).[27] Juan de Borja's father, Francisco Borja, had been the superior of the order, and it was to the Jesuit chapel of São Roque in Lisbon, rather than to the Escorial, that Juan de Borja gave the relic collection that he had amassed as a royal servant. The Jesuit Valentín Josep was favored by Queen Maria with relics from Flanders in 1575, which he passed on to his home town of Fuentelaencina (Guadalajara); and there is evidence that in the years immediately succeeding those in which the reports were written, Jesuits were in New Castile distributing relics to villages.[28] As a very active international order, often connected by birth to the administrators of the empire, the Jesuits were ideally suited to facilitate the movement of relics across Europe and obtain the certificates necessary for their worship. It was a Jesuit who brought back to Toledo after much travail the body of Saint Leocadia from Flanders.[29]

In addition to the inexhaustible supply of the Eleven Thousand Virgins in Cologne, the major source of relics was Rome. On the one hand there were the catacombs, explicitly mentioned as the origin of relics in Talavera. On the other, it appears that many of the relics from northern Europe were "processed" through Rome as Protestantism advanced. Hence we find specifically German relics, like those of the Eleven Thousand Virgins, in lots of relics coming to Spain from Rome. In Rome the relics would be provided with documents by certain delegated cardinals and with these "passports" would travel on to Spain.

Some finds in the Low Countries were potentially embarrassing. An officer who was a native son wrote to the Barcelona council in 1610 from Cambrai that he had access to a head, originally from Germany, which bore the inscription "Saint Eulalia, virgin and martyr in Spain." He wondered if the head might be missing from the body of Saint Eulalia, patron saint of Barcelona. The council forwarded his letter to the bishop, who checked his records and confirmed that the body in the cathedral included the head. The bishop advised the councillors not to obtain the relic from Flanders, "because it would give rise to the suspicion that the holy body is not, as it is, in the cathedral of Barcelona. . . ."[30]

But this was an exception. The influx of relics in the six-

teenth century was welcomed, indeed provoked by the people, or at least the clergy of these villages. For some of the
donors, the relics sanctified the church that would be their
burial place. For others, especially the hermits, the relics
like bulls of pardon, were a source of income. But the ceremonies welcoming relics, indeed the petitions of villages like
Pareja (in 1599) for relics indicate that there was a genuine
veneration of them among the common people of the villages. Communities were proud of their relics, felt enriched
by them. Was it a coincidence that the adjacent towns of
Tendilla and Fuentelaencina (Guadalajara) both obtained
relics in the same year from different sources, or is there an
aspect of competition among these chauvinistic communities? Many of them, like Uceda, celebrated the feast days of
the relics.

Yet by and large this new group of relics did not provoke
the kind of devotion accorded shrine images, or the older
relics of more local saints. Perhaps the very magnitude of
the influx served to debase the value of the relics. Perhaps
also the ridicule and the criticisms of the Erasmists and the
Protestants had some effect. In any case in all of the reports
there is only one set of these newer relics that worked miracles—those brought by a religious from Pius V to Villanueva de Alcardete (Toledo) around 1570. By 1578, installed in the hermitage of the Concepción, where they were
maintained by an *ermitaño de misa*, they had worked two
miracles. On the night of their arrival a woman was cured
of deafness; and on one of the feast days a man who had
been struck by lightning was cured of a nervous disorder.[31]
But this shrine was an exception. Many of the relics of this
epoch are still in the reliquaries in parish churches where
they were deposited in the years 1560–1620, but they were
not then, nor are they now, objects of the kind of practical
devotion that results in promises, pilgrimages, or gifts. (See
Figure 8.)

This influx of relics may have been important, however,
in reviving an interest in the older, local relics. Southern

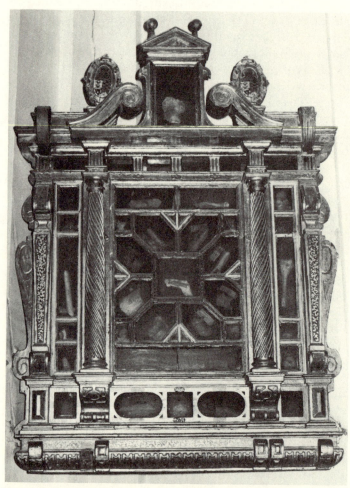

Figure 8. Reliquary at the shrine of Our Lady of the
Caridad, Illescas. Photograph by Cristina García Rodero.

Spain was left relatively bare of relics of early martyrs by the Moslem invasion. This scarcity was somewhat compensated for after the Reconquest by the establishment of Marian shrines whose images were sanctified by a history of miraculous apparitions or discoveries. But at the time the reports were being made and in the fifty or so years afterward, the southern cities (and some of the northern ones, too) began to feel the need to recover their own local saints. The return of Saints Justo and Pastor to Alcalá in 1568, and of Saint Ildefonso in 1584 and Saint Leocadia in 1587 to Toledo are cases in point. Alcalá gained a new saint, Diego, in 1588, as did Madrid—Saint Isidore the Farm Servant—in 1622. Towns that could not find their saints elsewhere or canonize new ones invented them. Three saints, Fausto, Januario, and Marcial, were "discovered" in Córdoba in 1575, and their veneration approved by the Toledo Council in 1583.[32] The remarkable fraud of the martyrs of Sacromonte in Granada was perpetrated in the year 1588, and false chronicles, distributing saints and miraculous origins to images in hitherto uncharismatic cities, were written and circulated throughout this period (in large part by Jesuits).[33] The new influx of relics from central Europe and Rome contributed to the intervillage and intercity competition for sacred history.

Relics may have been, as Peter Brown puts it, the common coinage of Christianity, linking Christians across the Western world more surely than pilgrimages. But from the tenor of the reports, relics in the sixteenth century seem to have also had an opposite effect; they reinforced community pride and chauvinism.

INDULGENCES

The reports tell little about the sacramental aspects of the religion of the people of New Castile: church attendance, communion, and confession are rarely mentioned in these accounts. From other studies it appears that most New Castilians knew the Pater Noster, the Ave Maria, and, less well, the Credo; and that they confessed annually during Lent, although not necessarily with the parish priest. In some places, at least, certificates of lenten confession were given out.[34]

Juan de Avila described the typical rural confession as very perfunctory, not unlike most rural confessions today.[35] Francisco Farfán, a native of Toledo writing about 1585 about rural religion, criticized the common practice of confessing and communing but once a year, "y essa por fuerça."[36] If manuals for clergy and parish visitors were being followed; one can understand why peasants were reluctant to make their annual confession. A manual of 1530 instructed the parish visitors to "[teach the priests] how they should treat more gently the *letrados* and nobles and virtuous people who bring with them great shame and confusion than the rustics and the ignorant who if they are not rudely rebuked neither have shame for nor realize the gravity of their sin."[37]

Because there is little information in the reports to indicate the involvement of the people of New Castile in the salvationary side of religion, one might draw the conclusion that they were largely involved in religious concerns that dealt with the problems and dangers in their present lives, rather than the life beyond the grave. Such an assumption would be mistaken. For one thing, the corporate persona of a village that makes a vow to a saint has no afterlife. It exists only in the real world. Individual villagers might do deeds or make bargains relating to their salvation; they certainly banded together in brotherhoods that sometimes operated as salvation cooperatives; but it is not surprising that vows by villages as a whole do not deal with these matters, and it is the corporate religion of the villages that the questionnaires bring out most.

One index of an interest in the afterlife is the pious works set up in wills: chaplaincies, monasteries, and hospitals include in their foundation prayers for the intentions of the founders. These founders would be the wealthier people, but a similar preoccupation with salvation will be found in the masses and offerings to different shrines willed in the testaments of the less wealthy as well.

The brotherhoods served in part as a kind of group insurance for the world to come. Particularly those that dwelt on Christ's Passion, very active at this time, bespeak an identification with the sufferings of Christ and a thirst for redemption. And virtually every parish in the city of Toledo had a brotherhood devoted to the Souls in Purgatory.

Some of the brotherhoods at this time (particularly those of the Passion and the True Cross), shrines, hospitals, and relics were "enriched" by papal indulgences. Is the success of these indulgences in stimulating participation, devotion, and contributions evidence for a preoccupation with sin, forgiveness, and life after death? Here the evidence is equivocal. While some indulgences are explained by the villagers as involved with the remission of sins, others, as in the case of Fuencaliente (Ciudad Real) and the Bulls of the Crusade, permit the relaxation of fasts, the commutation of vows, or the working on holy days. From the reports we are not told enough to know the theological implications of the success of indulgences in this area.

For successful they were, or had been. By the end of the sixteenth century so many indulgences, real or counterfeit, were in circulation that the currency had been debased. The reports mention a number of indulgences operative in the villages of New Castile. The earliest given is that of Fuencaliente (Ciudad Real), dated era of 1353. This indulgence, apparently of Clement VI, refers to six others granted by other popes, mainly in the thirteenth century. According to the text, it was granted in Rome upon the request of the agent of the master of Calatrava. The bull was applicable to those present at the shrine on September 8 and to members of the shrine confraternity.[38]

The first bulls in their respective zones apparently had a

very great effect. In 1463 the town of Cobeña (Madrid) obtained a bull from Pius II granting thirteen hundred years of indulgence for the parish church on three feast days of every year: those of the titular patron, Saint Cebrian; Saint Sebastian; and Saint Agatha. "And according to what some of the old men said, since in this district that was the only bull, many people came from other towns, so many that the town was not big enough for all the people who came from afar in order to win the indulgences and pardons."[39]

A jubilee was a remission of temporal punishment (or time in Purgatory) for all sins committed up to that point. According to the report of Tendilla (Guadalajara), theirs was the first plenary indulgence in Castile. It was obtained by the count of Tendilla, ambassador to Rome for Ferdinand the Catholic, for the benefit of a hospital he intended to found. The jubilee was apparently granted to all who contributed to the project, and the resulting income was very great. "This jubilee was the first to come to Spain, and that is why many people in this kingdom and outside it were very glad to obtain it; and the offering was so great that it was enough not only for the construction of the Hospital of Saint John, but also for the reconstruction of the monastery of Saint Anne."[40]

Other indulgences mentioned in the reports apply to visits to the parish church on certain days (Bernuy [Toledo], before 1478; Auñón [Guadalajara], ca. 1488; Magán [Toledo], ca. 1560; and Sta. María del Campo [Cuenca]); visits to chapels (Ribas [Madrid], Saint Cecilia; El Peral [Cuenca], Saint Christopher, 1498; La Membrilla [Ciudad Real], Concepción); for brotherhoods (of the True Cross: Cobeña [Madrid], 1579; Daimiel [Ciudad Real], recent; La Despernada [Madrid]; Bull of Minerva for Holy Sacrament: Cobeña [Madrid]; Toledo, parish of Saint James Extramuros, also chapel of Saint Peter); and to visits to relics (Mazarulleque [Cuenca], ca. 1567; Villanueva de Alcardete [Toledo], ca. 1569; Fuentelaencina [Guadalajara], 1575; Lillo [Toledo]; Valdesaz [Guadalajara]).[41] Since the questionnaire did not specifically ask about indulgences, these should be seen as a sample; certainly many of the other towns also had them.

How did these villages and towns obtain them? Virtually the only major indulgences reported were those granted by the pope; they had to come from Rome. It seems there were similarities between the obtaining of indulgences and the obtaining of relics. Prior to the sixteenth century it would seem that indulgences were obtained through the orders (as in the case of Fuencaliente) or the noble lords of a town (as with Tendilla). In the sixteenth century simple priests brought them back from visits to Rome. The reports give three instances of priests who returned from Rome in the years 1569–1575 with both relics and indulgences.

Founders of chapels had an interest in obtaining indulgences. Two lay hermits founded the chapel of Our Lady of Gádor near Berja (Almería) in 1588. One of their first acts was to obtain, on credit, a bull from Rome, through the intermediary of a man in the city of Granada who had a son in Rome. The price was twelve ducats, and when in 1592 the town of Berja purchased from the hermits what was by then a successful shrine (in that it drew devotees in from other villages), it assumed the debt for the bull. The hermits moved on, reputedly to enter a monastery.[42]

Indulgences, then, were available at a price. But a clear implication of the two stories of the impact of early indulgences in the area (Cobeña and Tendilla) was that by 1575 indulgences did not have the same grand effect any longer. On the other hand, the number of indulgences had made them essential for a shrine or brotherhood to be competitive, precisely because there were so many. By the 1570s indulgences were a valued ornament of shrines and brotherhoods, much in the same way that relics themselves, once they were available in numbers, were used to enhance and illustrate preexisting shrines.

New relics from central Europe and indulgences from Rome were two ways that local communities adapted

Churchwide resources for local use. From the way towns-people tell about them in the reports, it appears that their net effect was not so much to universalize devotion in the town or city, not so much to make persons more aware of their brotherhood with all Catholics and the authority of Rome, as to make more attractive and holy their own sacred places and times.

FIVE

Local Religion: Variations, Alternatives, and Reform

THE CAREFUL maintenance of a local religious order interested the people of Toledo as much as those of the smallest village, merchant as well as farmer, the king as much as his subjects. It was "popular" only in the sense that it was predominantly lay. But much of the clergy fully participated in it as well. In Spain it was little affected by the Council of Trent, which merely ensured the precedence of the Church Universal over local churches.

I do not think devotion per se was a matter of wealth or social class. In the early seventeenth century poor and wealthy peasants alike in the villages south of Toledo had a number of religious pictures on their walls.[1] Indeed, joint religious devotions probably helped hold communities together in the face of wracking disparities of wealth and opportunity.

Among country believers there were doubtless differences in style. Noblemen kept private chapels dedicated to the advocations of Seville, Rioja, and Aragon, the saints of distant places and wider societies. The devout wealthy may have been able to pay more attention to salvation than to religious solutions to practical problems. In times of plague they could afford to flee town, and in times of want they could buy food, depending less on divine help. But wealth was only a partial protection against disease and no protection at all against infant mortality, death, or damnation.

By the same token, skepticism and incredulity, if we are to trust literary accounts and Inquisition documents, were to be found as much in a small village as in a large town. In novels like *Lazarillo de Tormes*, *La Vida del Buscón*, and *Persiles and Segismunda* not all hermits are holy, all pilgrims devout, or all villagers credulous. The Inquisition of Cuenca arrested persons in all sizes of towns for propositions like denying the virginity of Mary (nineteen cases between 1515 and 1535), incredulity as to the Eucharist, denial of the efficacy of prayers for the dead, and denial of the divinity of Christ (these last skeptics were priests). Those investigated included the literate and the illiterate, the rich and the poor.

Some of the propositions were more specifically directed against local devotions. A carder in Huete claimed in 1526 that the images of the saints were idols; a man in Belmonte in 1579 charged that a shrine was not a house of God, but rather a den of thieves; and an alcalde in Vara de Rey denied in 1582 that the saints worked miracles.[2] The collective religion of these Catholic communities was not necessarily shared in full by individual members.

LOCAL RELIGION OF CITIES

We can only suggest differences between rural and urban styles of devotion, for we have the report of only one full-fledged city, Toledo. *Urbanidad*, for a Toledo priest, was measured by the absence of ploughs. By this standard even the largest of the other towns surveyed were not very *urbana*. For the fifteen towns with a thousand or more households the proportion of vows for agricultural reasons (insects, rain, hail) was only slightly lower than for the region as a whole (0.38 as compared with 0.44), an indication of their agricultural concerns. In towns known to have had substantial numbers of artisans—Talavera, Puente del Arzobispo, Pastrana, Fuentelaencina, Fuenlabrada, Rejas, and Almadén—the proportion is just as high as for the region as a whole.

Toledo was different. Only one of the thirteen special holidays of Toledo was vowed, as far as I know, for agricultural reasons (locusts). And cities did not depend so much on the saints for their food. Although much city food came from the immediate hinterland, and city dwellers who were landowners had a stake in the crops, urbanites were paradoxically more cushioned from the effects of famine than country dwellers. When prices were high, villages could not compete with cities for imported grain. Cities had more and better grain warehouses as well as the right to purchase grain at advantageous prices in their *aldeas*.

By the same token, it is not surprising that for Toledans sacred places were mostly within the city walls. For urban dwellers, just as sustenance and prosperity were matters of provident institutions and judicious political economy, so their significant saints were located in society, and alertness to the sacred was directed inward, not outward. While there were chapels on the outskirts of the city, these were not the critical places of devotion. For Toledo, sacred places were inside the city—the miraculous images, powerful relics, and sites of apparitions were in parish churches, convents, and the cathedral. In agricultural towns, the most sacred places, the Marian shrines, were mainly outside in the country. The relation of citizen to shrine reflected the relation of town to the land and the constant traffic between these citadels of sociability and the world of nature. The significant sacred geography for Toledo was not in nature, but in society.

Another difference in urban devotion (and this would apply to the agro-towns as well) is that religious activity was more compartmentalized. Toledo had 28 parishes and 147 brotherhoods in 1575. The ratio of brotherhoods to population was about the same throughout the region, about 1 brotherhood for 100 households, attesting to the need for a more intimate devotional community and solidarity groups not based on kinship. But the bigger and more socially complex the settlement, the more likely it was to have a socially segregated settlement pattern. Toledo had parishes that were almost exclusively peopled with artisans and poor. Thus parish brotherhoods would be more class-based in Toledo than in smaller towns. Furthermore, many Toledo brotherhoods were directly based on occupations. Those in

1575 included barrelmakers, blacksmiths, clothiers, day laborers, harnessmakers, inheritors of vines, market gardeners, money-changers, regidors and *jurados*, silk spinners, silk weavers, silversmiths, and hosiers.[3]

As a result, different kinds and classes of people had helper saints for their group, in contrast to a smaller community, where all people had the same saints for different problems that everyone faced. In cities saints could become symbols for differences. Townwide processions in Toledo were occasions for acrimonious disputes over priorities among the brotherhoods. And anyone who goes to Seville for Holy Week will hear the most outrageous insults hurled at the images of other brotherhoods or barrios.

Mere size also meant that in a larger place there were more devotional resources for any one person. While a villager of Cobeña (Madrid) had a choice of ten chapels to visit, possibly fifty images to see, any resident of Toledo had at least ten times as many options. There was a convent or a monastery in only one of eleven places in New Castile. In Toledo there were thirty-six.

But Toledo was more than large: it was cosmopolitan. "To walk through Toledo is to walk through the world, because there you will find people of all nations, provinces, professions, crafts, estates of life, and languages. It is the center and heart of Spain, and therefore of the world. . . ."[4] The presence of convents, foreigners, and immigrants from other regions meant that a wide variety of saints was available. Toledo had a chapel and a brotherhood to the Andalusian devotion of Our Lady of the Cabeza; a chapel with a "true copy" of Our Lady of Popolo, of Rome; two brotherhoods to the famous Crucifix of Lucca; and an image of Our Lady of Peña de Francia. The Minims had introduced devotion to Our Lady of the Soledad to Toledo in 1567 or 1568; it was very popular in 1575, although as yet virtually unknown in the countryside.[5]

Finally, a large town could afford religious celebrations, processions, and feasts on a more imposing scale. Only ma-

jor cities could match the floats and pomp of Toledo's Corpus processions, or set up month-long celebrations like those
that welcomed the bodies of Leocadia and Eugene to Toledo, Justo and Pastor to Alcalá, or the canonization of Isidro
Labrador in Madrid and Raymundo Penyafort in Barcelona.

Cathedral cities had a special role in the spiritual economy
of the kingdom, and for this reason their devotions were
more keyed to national and international political events.
Philip II and his successors solicited the prayers of cathedral
chapters (of Toledo and elsewhere) at critical moments in
national affairs—when members of the royal family were
sick, traveling by sea, or in childbirth; at the start of military campaigns; or before major battles.[6] At moments of
great danger entire cities would be mobilized in general processions complete with flagellants. In Toledo the Brotherhood of the True Cross held "very devout and well ordered" flagellant processions "whenever appropriate for the
health of royalty and princes, for victories, or for the common good."[7] In the sixteenth century the Brotherhood of
the Blood of Jesus served this same politico-civic function
in Barcelona.

Cities were similarly asked by the pope through the bishop
to pray for the success of international Catholic endeavors.
Both Seville and Barcelona, and doubtless Toledo also, held
processions for the success of the Council of Trent in 1561.
Other processions petitioned for or gave thanks for victories
of Catholic forces over Turks and Protestants. The city of
Toledo, alone among the 530 towns surveyed, observed by
vow October 7 in commemoration of the victory of Lepanto (1571).

Furthermore, the wealth of cities and royal fiscal depend-
ence upon them gave them leverage in obtaining indulgences
and jubilees for their special holy days, the canonization of
saints, and relics. Madrid and Toledo were veritable ossu-
aries. In Toledo each church had a coffer with relics, and
there was a massive collection in the cathedral. In Madrid
in 1629 there were at least 46 complete bodies of saints, 8

thorns from the Crown of Thorns, and 109 heads of the Eleven Thousand Virgins![8]

As a result of these advantages, cities were devotional centers for the surrounding countryside. In Spain today, and probably in the sixteenth century as well, villagers in a city's hinterland know both geographies of grace—that of the chapels and shrines in the immediate landscape of mountains, rivers and caves, and some of the city's sacred geography as well—selected images in churches and convents. The author of the Toledo report described how on two occasions on a trip to Cartagena, persons at inns where he stayed asked for the worn shoes of his servants in exchange for new ones, because they had been worn in the cathedral of Toledo. Visits to the city for other reasons probably included, as they do today, the fulfillment of promises at urban shrines.[9]

While some devotions, especially those brought in by religious orders, doubtless spread out from the cities, there was also a contrary trend; cities appropriated devotions from the countryside. As Madrid expanded in the last years of the sixteenth century, the number of brotherhoods increased. The new brotherhoods needed venerable images, and some simply appropriated them from rural chapels—quite in keeping with the ancient practice of relic theft. The very act conferred on an image an aura it may not have had in the countryside.[10]

Although the city was less vulnerable, less directly dependent on local crops and weather; although its shrines were more in town and less in nature; although some of its devotions were more compartmentalized and class-bound; and although its pantheon was at once more varied and more up-to-date because of its convents, foreign colonies, and artists; the city had the same kind of corporate relations with its most significant saints as the smallest village had. Devotion in Toledo to native saints like Eugene, Leocadia, and Ildefonso, and to prime images of Mary like the Descension and Our Lady of Sagrario transcended barrio and brotherhood rivalries. Such saints were urban versions of the general advocates of the shrines of villages and towns. They served as objects of citywide, corporate religious attention both in times of trouble and in calendrical ceremonies. Individual citizens in large settlements may have been less accountable than in villages for keeping up corporate religious commitments. Nevertheless, cities too, whether Toledo or Madrid, Seville or Barcelona, had special friends of God who helped them; special times of year to celebrate; and particular places consecrated by proven instances of divine presence.

KINGSHIP AND LOCAL RELIGION

All Castilians, those of hamlets as well as those of Toledo and Madrid, had some kind of psychological bond with the king. In the sixteenth century the nature of the bond was deeply influenced by royal religious policy and royal religiosity. Read the lament of the people of Las Mesas (Cuenca), in 1575 a town of 230 households, for the quality of this relation:

[Forty years ago] in this place there were more than sixty flocks of sheep; and there were more than thirty labradores with four, three, and two pairs of mules, and many others had one pair, or one mule. Of the nearly two hundred heads of household, all but the craftsmen were labradores and planted crops. And now we see that there are not more than fifteen flocks of sheep, and no labrador has more than one pair of mules, and those with a pair are less than twenty-five in number. One labrador had three or four pairs of mules and nine flocks of sheep, and since he died forty years ago his house has almost completely collapsed, and in the part still standing New Christians are living, and nothing is left of his estate except a little land. The rest of the farms that were near his were almost as substantial, and now the sons and grandsons are all

working as day laborers for wages. So that this town has
come to such great ruin that were it not for the monte
and the common pastureland described above it would no
longer exist; and this poverty and decline is due to our
being deprived of our great privilege [access to certain
pastureland] in 1535. And this decline is so severe that
[Las Mesas] can, like the woman from Canaan, ask for
privileges once more. For when the woman from Canaan
called Christ "Son of David," at once he granted that
great mercy on her. So this town can ask and say, "Our
Lord and King: since you are of the progeny and lineage
of the Most Serene Catholic Kings and inherited from
them not only us, but also this holy reknown as Catholic,
and having made it yours by your great power and royal
virtue, have mercy on us Las Mesas, if only with the royal
scraps and crumbs left over from your imperial table.
That is, forgive us and exempt us of half of the *alcabalas*
[sales taxes] with which we are burdened, so that we can
set up a grain storehouse to ensure that these your poor
of Las Mesas are not without bread. . . ."[11]

Although the parallel of Philip II with Christ in the para-
ble of the Canaanite was a rhetorical device, the reference
to Ferdinand and Isabella, the Catholic monarchs, was not.
The monarchy in the late fifteenth century had become
identified with Catholicism. In the century before 1575 it
had established the Inquisition, expelled the Jews, forced
Moors to convert, had its political actions ratified by Rome
with the Bulls of the Crusade, sent ships that defeated the
Turks at Lepanto, and attempted to police the heretics of
the Low Countries.

Who in this petition was the interlocutor of the monarchy? Not the respondents (a priest and a regidor) but
Las Mesas itself. Las Mesas was like the Woman from Canaan. "Habed misericordia de nosotras Las Mesas" (note the
femine ending on *nosotras*): Have mercy on us Las Mesas.
This collective identification of *pueblo* (people) with *pue-*

blo (place) bound up in *us Las Mesas* is at the root of the kind of religiosity we have been studying. Just as Las Mesas talked to the king, so Las Mesas talked to its saints, sought their help, and thanked them in a corporate, collective voice.[12]

Collective religiosity, centered on local sources of grace, was supported by the rulers of New Castile. Villagers considered the king would want to know of supernatural events and new sacred objects. In May 1517, when the townspeople of Peñas de San Pedro (south of Albacete) saw flames on a cross and a crucifix in the sky above their town, they sent off a letter describing it to Charles V.[13] In April 1528, Charles, on his way to Valencia, stayed a night in the village of Albalate de Zorita (Guadalajara). There he was told of the ancient crucifix that had been discovered miraculously by a dog fourteen years before. After mass the next morning, he asked to see it, kissed it, and requested two of the little chains hanging from the arms as keepsakes. The villagers remembered well the date and details of his visit thirty-seven years later, when an official ecclesiastical record was made of the discovery. His adoration of the cross was an integral part of the inquiry.[14] Philip III also venerated the cross, and his visit was recalled in another report one hundred and fifty years afterward. Similarly, in 1576 the report of Illescas boasted of the visits and novenas of the king, the queen, and Princess Juana to the newly miraculous shrine of Our Lady of the Caridad.[15]

Villagers were well aware that Philip II and his family were the sources of many of their newly obtained relics. Philip made sure to be present (and help carry the litter) when the most important acquisitions entered Toledo. Toledo was honored, and had Philip depicted in the reredos and paintings of its chapels. (See Figure 9.) The greatest shrine of all, Guadalupe, was maintained under royal patronage and at times had served as a palace and a royal bank. In building the Escorial, Philip made a palace which, like Guadalupe, would also be a shrine, furnished with the

Figure 9. Detail of altar at the chapel of Saint Eugene, Toledo, apparently showing Philip II at the moving of the relics. Anonymous, sixteenth century. Archivo Mas.

choicest relics that religious wars could provide, and staffed by the same order. Whatever their personal inclinations, visiting shrines has virtually been part of the duties of royal families. It was and is one of the simplest, clearest, and least expensive ways to show respect for local societies and regions. Even Manuel Azaña made an official visit to Montserrat as president of the Republic. Francisco Franco went so far as to make certain Marian shrine images captains general of the armed forces.

There is every indication that as far as the Hapsburgs were concerned, they shared the religious outlook of their subjects. In Toledo women who wished to be cured of *çiçiones* (probably malaria) would sweep the church of Santiago on Saturdays. When Charles V had malaria, he too swept the church, according to the Toledo report.[16] Philip II attributed the cure of his son Carlos in 1562 to the intercession of San Diego of Alcalá. The people of Toledo considered that Our Lady of the Sagrario had cured Carlos, for the image had been taken down from the altar for special prayers. Similarly, a thorn from the Crown of Thorns had been taken on Philip's orders to the bedside of his son Philip in 1857.[17] And in 1619 Philip III was certain he had been saved from death by the presence of the bones of Madrid's patron saint, Isidro Labrador. A Madrid historian writing ten years later proudly reported that when Philip's son wanted to remove the relic, the king said: "All I know is that as soon as I put it on the fever went away; and it did not come back until, thinking the relic bothered me, I put it down on my pillow, and at once the fever returned; so I am not going to take it off now."[18]

The pride with which New Castilians described the association of royalty with their devotions indicates the political value of this kind of devotional style for a monarchy in the process of consolidating a nation-state. Paolo Tiepolo, the Venetian ambassador to Spain, wrote in 1563 that Philip II procured "in all regards to appear to act in all of his enterprises truly as a Catholic king out of conscience and zeal for religion; such acts, however, never fail to be to his benefit and utility." Similarly, Ambassador Tommaso Contarini wrote in 1593 that Philip's reputation for devoutness and piety served him in excellent stead with his subjects, "and leads them to judge his deliberations reasonable, his undertakings just, and his laws holy and inviolable."[19]

Perhaps the people's pride in royal devotion to their saints also points to a kind of double consecration that occurred at such moments—the consecration of local religious objects by the attention of the king and the consecration of the king by the local religious powers. At these moments local corporate societies were themselves being honored and valued by the ultimate secular authority.

Local religion was a fusion of sacred with secular, god-in-society or god-in-landscape. And the ultimate head of that society and lord of that landscape was the king. By going to the cathedral of Rheims to be crowned, the French kings both honored Rheims and became kings. Certain ritual acts of modern diplomacy by heads of state echo the symbolic role of shrines. Laying a wreath on the monument to the Unknown Soldier in Paris or Rome is an attempt to address and honor the entire nation, past and present. Shrines, shrine images, relics of local saints, and sacred places, outlasting individuals as they do, come to stand not only for the *pueblo* of the moment, but also for the eternal *pueblo*. It was the eternal Las Mesas that would benefit from a privilege reducing the *alcabalas*, the eternal Las Mesas that made vows to saints and maintained them over generations.

ERASMIANISM AND REFORM

An assertion of royal authority in religious matters accompanied the political consolidation of Spain under Ferdinand and Isabella. Through Jiménez de Cisneros, who had been a monk at Salceda, they introduced a degree of order and centralization in monastics and encouraged humanist scholarship. In Spain, as elsewhere in Europe, scholars began to

question those traditions of the Church that seemed to conflict with the Gospels. The printing press, a veritable explo-
sion of educational opportunity, and the radically enlarged
bureaucracy that supervised the empire in Europe and the
New World provided the basis for a new class of literate
Spaniards, to be found mainly in the larger towns and cities.

The ideas of Erasmus had a substantial impact on this kind
of person, as Marcel Bataillon has shown. For Erasmus, for
Alfonso de Valdés, for José Luis Vives, the audience in
Spain, although fragmented, was large enough to offer a
theoretical alternative to the local religion of New Castile.
For the religion they favored was counterlocal as well as
counterauthoritarian. On the one hand they sought to put
forms of consecration to God hitherto limited to clerics and
religious at the disposition of lay people, threatening the
authority of the priest and the Church in the process. But
on the other, the personal religion they favored was quite
different from that already practiced by the common people, *el vulgo*. They sought a "spiritual life" centered on
Christ and the Holy Sacrament, purified or depaganized of
"Pharasaic" exterior practices, which they considered ridic-
ulous in common people and reprehensible in the clergy.
The spirituality they proposed was divorced from local
context and contingency; it could apply as well in Ghent as
in Las Mesas, in prosperity as well as tribulation. There are
some parallels between their approach and that of the post–
Vatican II clergy in Spain.[20]

Even before the Erasmians, the alumbrados in New Castile had questioned many of the tenets of local devotion.
According to the propositions for which they were indicted, the alumbrados of Toledo in 1525 shared some of the
same attitudes toward the kind of religion in the reports as
the Erasmians:

13. That exterior acts of devotion are beside the point
and unnecessary, and that to do them is imperfect. . . .
. . . .
15. That it was wrong to dress up the image of Our Lady

and take it out in the streets in procession; and that it
was idolatry, and that they should remove that idol,
speaking of the image of Our Lady.

16. That they not take pains to venerate the image of Our
Lord or Our Lady; that they were sticks. And they
laughed when reverence was paid to them, saying to
ignore them, that they were sticks.

17. Explaining to a person why they did not have an
image of Our Lady [the alumbrado] said that looking
at any woman [she or he] would remember Our
Lady.

18. That a certain person preaching said that one did not
have to adore the Cross, saying that it was a piece of
wood; that they should adore Christ crucified.

. . . .

21. That one should not ask God for anything in particular, that it was unnecessary to say, "Pray to God for
me," for God cares for everyone. And when a confessor said to a certain person that it was right to ask
for things in particular, they said that they held it
better not to ask.

. . . .

27. That what use are excommunications, fasts, and absti-
nences of the Church; that the soul should be free.[21]

The direct contact with God of the alumbrados was an
old strand of privileged religious knowledge, one that continued long after the alumbrado movement had been extin-
guished. The alumbrados took to an extreme what had hitherto been an alternative path of dedicated monasticism and
opened it to lay people. Their spiritual successors (like Saint
Teresa) continued in monasteries or *beaterías*. But the ec-
static union with God became once more an implicit possibility instead of an explicit necessity.

By the 1570s, with the elimination of the more radical
aspects of illuminist doctrine, the contrast of the beatas with
other modes of popular devotion was the old one of degree

—the degree to which one was able to consecrate oneself fully to religious devotion. But there remained the essential difference between treating with the divine as a separate entity with whom arrangements and agreements could be made, and an identification and union with the divine, the *imitatio christi.* The vitality of this latter option in late sixteenth-century New Castile seemed to reside predominantly in the women. It was nuns and beatas, rather than monks, who were referred to in the reports with adjectives such as "very devout," or "miraculous."

Erasmus was willing to let the *vulgo* go its way. But some of the concerns that he and his followers raised about lay practices found their way into the decrees of the Council of Trent and the mainstream of accepted theology. By 1575 the reports of the villages of New Castile bore some evidence, although not very substantial and quite uneven, of reforms.

The kind of reforms of religion on the parish level that show up in the reports and the synodal constitutions of New Castile largely fall into two broad categories. One was the separation of the profane from the sacred, correcting the *mezcla de cosas profanas con divinas.*[22] In practice this separation meant making distinctions between differing notions of the sacred—whether imposing a common standard on a variety of local ones, or revising an older common standard. The other was an assertion of clerical authority over local religious activity. Neither of these categories represented a theological innovation. As Juan de Avila stated in his memoranda for reforms, what was needed was the enforcement of old laws, rather than new ones. The change was rather, in the face of the Protestant challenge, a new sense of urgency and determination.

The church in Spain had long waged a frustrating battle against "pagan" customs and institutions, which it often characterized as traffic with the devil. The manuals of superstition and witchcraft of Ciruelo (1530) and Castañega (1528) are examples of this pre-Trent preoccupation. In

Talavera, Cardinal Cisneros had suspended the Mondas celebration as *cosa de gentilidad*. Julio Caro Baroja believes the ceremony (since resumed) was originally Roman. Erasmians sought to widen the notion of what was pagan to include bullfighting on holy days (which Alfonso de Valdés associated with Roman cults), the specialization of saints (associated with Roman and Greek deities), and the notion that God's grace was more common at certain places (the basis for shrines and pilgrimages).[23]

The effort to question the Christian credentials behind the specialization of saints and the particular availability of grace at holy places was unsuccessful in Spain. This would have been a true threat to local religion. But a number of reforms were made to sanitize local religious custom, ensure that it was under diocesan control, and eliminate any conflicts with religion as ordained from Rome. To some extent the Inquisition performed this function, and so did parish visits; but it can also be followed through diocesan legislation.

The reformers' position on bullfighting won temporary acceptance. Bullfighting as part of vows was prohibited by the Council of Toledo in 1565, and all such vows were declared null and void. The 1566 Synodal Constitutions of Toledo complained that people persisted in running bulls on vowed days saying that in doing so they were no longer fulfilling a vow, but merely acting out of free will. Unsatisfied with this semantic evasion, the administrator of the diocese of Toledo ordered that they change the days of the bull-runs to ensure that they were not part of vows. In 1567 Pius V forbade bullfighting altogether. This extreme position had to give way to popular pressure, and in 1575 Gregory XIII permitted bullfighting in Spain, but not on holy days.[24]

In the reports there are indications that bullfighting on vowed days had been suppressed in Mascaraque (Toledo), El Toboso (Toledo), Alhambra (Ciudad Real), Fuentelaencina (Guadalajara), Getafe (Madrid), and Santorcaz (Madrid).[25] On the other hand, they continued as part of fiestas

in Carrascosa del Campo and Tarancón (Cuenca), Auñón
(Guadalajara), Ocaña, and Talavera. Archbishop Quiroga
himself learned the difficulty of suppressing this popular
custom. During the fiesta he organized in Toledo in 1587
for the reception of the body of Saint Leocadia, he was com-
pelled against his own edicts to accede to bullfights.[26]

Images were supposed to be of real saints and to be dressed
in a seemly fashion, neither profanely nor in religious habits. Decrees in the various dioceses indicate that there were
problems in this respect in New Castile. In the reports such
a matter would not ordinarily be mentioned.[27] An exception
is the removal of a remarkable secular image from a chapel
in Atanzón (Guadalajara) around 1560.

> It is public knowledge that in the town of Villar, now
> uninhabited, there lived a girl who had one body and two
> heads with complete faces, and that when one spoke or
> sang the other replied, and as proof of the truth of this
> they saw and it was public knowledge that in the chapel
> of Saint Dominic there was the statue of a body with two
> heads carved from wood, and it was there as a remem-
> brance of that remarkable phenomenon among other holy
> images of wood that about twenty years ago [from 1578]
> more or less, were taken out by permission of the Church,
> because it was indecent for it to be there, and afterwards
> the statue was lost.[28]

Other popular customs, like the choosing of May queens
and kings, were forbidden in the diocesan synods, though
not mentioned in the reports; but two quasi-religious practices associated with vows were reported forbidden in certain circumstances. John Bossey has described the gradual
abolition of the parish wake in Europe.[29] Many *veladas* were
mentioned in the reports, both of groups and of individuals
at shrines. In only one case was there an indication that a
velada had been suppressed. Until 1568 or 1569 the town of
Huecas (Toledo) had spent the night of Saint Mark (the
Greater Litany) at the shrine of Mary Magdalen, two

leagues away; subsequently they went and came back on the same day.[30] This change probably coincided with the strictures of the 1565 Council of Toledo against spending the night in shrines. The objection to wakes seems to have been to the indecorous mingling of men and women overnight.

In fact, vigils had been forbidden except during Holy Week by the end of the fifteenth century in Old Castile and were permitted only with strict supervision in New Castile up to the 1560s. The reasons for the prohibitions (which seem to have had little or no effect) are similar in all the dioceses: the profanation of sacred places by dancing, feasting, and drinking, farces and plays, and secular, dirty, and lewd songs. The constitutions of Burgos (1411), Avila (1481), Jaén (1511), and Cuenca (1531), explicitly mentioned "fornications and adulteries." Most of the constitutions of the sixteenth century were more circumspect, complaining of "unmentionable lewdnesses," "scandals and sins," and "lewd and enormous sins." Those of Badajoz (1501) and Córdoba (1520) requested that people keep their clothes on when they sleep in the shrine. People were clearly enjoying themselves. The archdiocese of Toledo was one of the most lenient, tolerating vigils in town churches as late as 1601, as long as there was adequate supervision. But by 1565, and in most dioceses long before, vigils in chapels and isolated shrines were theoretically forbidden in almost all of central Spain. As in the case of vowed bullfights, such prohibitions contained clauses that automatically commuted and nullified vows to hold vigils.[31]

In a similar attempt to improve public morality and bring local religion under clerical control, a number of bishops in the sixteenth century (including Sigüenza and Toledo) forbade votive and rogation processions beyond a certain distance, usually a league. Vows for such processions were automatically commuted to other chapels within the township limits. The reason given for the restriction was the immorality that occurred when people had to spend a night at a shrine, or when they ate and drank to excess out of town.

Virtually all diocesan laws were intended to give a legal basis for eliminating abuses, rather than hard and fast rules.[32] At the time of the reports the town of Huecas continued to hold its processions to Saint Mary Magdalen over one league away, even if, in a rare example of obedience, it abandoned its vigil at the shrine. The town of Brihuega had vowed in 1403 to go annually with three tapers to Our Lady of Sopetrán. But by 1615, after the diocesan proscription against long-distance processions, it was required each year to ask permission to fulfill its vow. Every year the permission was granted, but the net effect was that Brihuega each year acknowledged diocesan jurisdiction over its contract with Mary.[33]

The *caridad* was another custom the bishops sought to control. In Osma in 1536 and Astorga in 1553 the synods forbade the "general" *caridades* that were customarily distributed at funerals because of the waste of inheritances that the custom supposed.[34] The bishop of Astorga tried to limit the beneficiaries of funeral charities to the poor and needy. This constitution met so much opposition that it had to be backed up by a royal edict. If such general *caridades* at funerals were distributed in New Castile, the reports did not mention them, and the diocesan constitutions did not condemn them.

Following the Council of Trent, an effort was made in New Castile to eliminate those *caridades* vowed for days when fasting was required by the Church. Constitutions to this effect were promulgated in Toledo in 1566, Uclés in 1578, Cuenca in 1602, and Sigüenza in 1608.[35] The reports bear witness to this trend. Visitors of the Order of Santiago suppressed charities in Torrenueva (Ciudad Real) in 1574, and commuted two of them in Villanueva de los Infantes (Ciudad Real) to alms for the poor. Earlier, some time around 1555–1560, two *caridades* had been suppressed by visitors from the diocese of Cuenca in El Acebrón (Cuenca). And, with explicit reference to the Council of Trent, *caridades* on the eves of holy days were abolished in Getafe

(Madrid) and changed to another day in Cobeña (Madrid) in the archdiocese of Toledo.[36] But as of 1580 the majority of vigils and *caridades* remained untouched. Some village *veladas* (for example in the diocese of Badajoz and the shrine of Our Lady of Chilla, Candeleda, Avila) and *caridades* have survived to the present.[37]

Caridades, because they were under lay administration, also exemplified the renewal, with Trent, of the Church's struggle against lay authority in religious matters. Many of the shrines were operated by lay mayordomos for town councils or lay patrons. Brotherhoods were predominantly lay bodies that hired out priests (the parish priest who wrote the report of the city of Toledo bitterly complained that "with so many brotherhoods, the laymen are in such firm control that they order the priests around as if they were day laborers").[38] Quasi-religious hermits set themselves up in isolated chapels and siphoned off alms that might otherwise have gone for masses or other clerical or monastic uses. Lay women banded together in religious communities without formal vows, and they too went out to ask for alms. Lay questors circulated collecting money for shrines and pardons. And town councils organized much of the village religious festivals and held their meetings in churches. Part of the Church's struggle for authority was perennial, but the new urgency was that it was precisely in these areas that some of the greatest abuses complained of by the Protestants were occurring.

In some cases it was a matter of the elementary authority of the priest. In the 1553 constitutions of Astorga, repeated by the 1566 constitutions of Cuenca, it was even necessary for the bishop to specify penalties for lay persons who talked back to priests during the sermon.

> We are informed that when the parish priests and chaplains teach Christian doctrine to their parishioners and reprove them and impose penances because they have not come to mass or because they violated holy days or for

other just causes, the parishioners raise objections and have words with said priests and chaplains. And this is cause for much scandal, as it happens during high mass.

The constitutions of Burgos in 1575 raised the same issue in different words:

Sometimes it has happened that when priests or preachers are rebuking or speaking ill of vices or sins of the people, the persons referred to, or those that claim authority in the town, stand up and reply to him, and at times speak words that are rude, indecent, and unworthy of such a place.

The priest's authority in his church in the sixteenth century was by no means absolute.[39]

This kind of lay spunk in the face of clerical authority carried over to theological matters as well. We saw earlier how peasants were reluctant to go to confession, and how they refused to admit to their sinfulness once in confession.[40] On a number of matters, such as work on holy days and Sundays, peasants had their own theology. One such matter that the church pursued with zeal toward the end of the century was the "heresy" that sexual intercourse among unmarried persons was not a sin; large numbers of people were condemned by the Inquisition in the last quarter of the century for expressing this proposition. Francisco Farfán, in his *Treatise on Simple Fornication*, complained at length about "rustic and ignorant" peasants who presumed to discuss theological matters, at risk of their lives and property.[41] The comparison of practices described in the reports and forbidden in the diocesan constitutions confirms this picture of a stubborn, combative laity that defended its own culture and religious customs against clerical intrusions.

In the reports there were also signs of a movement against the brotherhoods. As early as 1536 the constitutions of Toledo (repeated in 1566 and 1601) announced that henceforth new brotherhoods could not be established without license, because they have "multiplied and multiply in such numbers that they could bring harm."[42] In his first memorandum for Trent, Juan de Avila complained at length about brotherhoods: "In the brotherhoods there is great larceny and wrongdoing; and if the ordinary wishes to remedy it, the brothers oppose him by taking the case to Rome, with such harassment and disrespect for the bishop that they make him drop the case: more important, they litigate at the expense of the hospitals, while he litigates at his own expense. . . ." Avila advocated either abolishing the brotherhoods or placing them firmly under the jurisdiction of the Church—in either case consolidating the capital of the different brotherhoods toward the establishment of a few large, efficient hospitals, rather than many expensive small ones.[43]

The priest who wrote the Toledo report shared Avila's views.

> It remains for me to talk of the brotherhoods and their administrations and hospitals, which, unless I hear of a better plan, I would prefer to see combined into those of the Holy Sacrament and the souls in purgatory in the parishes in which they are based.[44]

He was tired of the brotherhoods and their intrusive, inefficient charity—"esta ya nuestra sensualidad enfadada de las cofradias y ynportunas demandas." He found that some forward beggars could receive help from several different brotherhoods, while "many honorable widows receive none on Easter or Christmas." Not surprisingly he favored letting the parish priest choose where the alms would go, presumably without favoritism or duplication. The matter of the social work of brotherhoods was more problematic for cities than for the countryside. The abolition of many brotherhoods and the concentration of their capital in large hospitals finally came about in the 1580s, under royal authority and with papal permission. After a trial run in the dioceses of Segovia, Palencia, and Cuenca, Philip II permitted each bishop to proceed as he saw fit. The consolidation of the hospitals of Daimiel was already approved at the time of the report (1575), but had not yet been put into effect. In Madrid it took place in 1580; and in Seville eighty-nine smaller hospitals were consolidated into two larger ones in 1587.[45]

The reports give no evidence for the control or suppression of hermits. From the diocesan constitutions it is known that the bishops were attempting to set up a system whereby they would, as it were, license lay hermits ("which permission we do not intend to give to persons who are married or to women," CS Toledo 1566). The most complete statement of the problem and a very detailed solution came in the 1626 constitutions of Cuenca:

> Many persons on their own authority, laymen not members of any religious order and sometimes married, dress in the habits of different devotions with the title or name of brothers so that they will seem to be religious. And to accredit themselves with the virtues they pretend to possess, they put themselves in charge of a hermitage and say they have to serve it and live in it, although they spend most of the year away from it asking for alms for said hermitage from place to place. In the process they ill serve our Lord, discredit the approved religious orders, and heavily burden the villages with their demands. Therefore, with the approval of the synod, we order and decree that nobody wear the habit of a hermit, nor dwell in a church or hermitage without our approval.[46]

Hermits were to be chosen, whether by priests or other persons by prerogative or custom, from persons well-known, "who will operate the chapels more out of devotion than self-interest." The bishop specified a dress code for the hermits—no habit, scapulary, or portable chapel, but rather lay clothes, or at most a plain smock with a layman's cape, hat, hairstyle, and shoes. The hermits were allowed to ask for alms only within a radius of two leagues, and only one hermit per town was permitted, "to put a stop to this species of lazy people in the villages" (*conque cessara un genero de gente holgazana enlos lugares*).

The reports do carry echoes of the efforts of bishops to regularize and enclose beatas. It was among such amateur religious, often under the supervision of a local priest, that the alumbrados found their adepts. For this kind of self-controlled consecration to God, through a simple vow, was a logical extension of a doctrine emphasizing direct communion with the divine without the discipline of monasticism.

The particular attraction of these movements for women has been insufficiently analyzed. The doctrine of a direct, personal, affective relation with Christ, open to lay as well as religious, must have appealed to women in part because it was the kind of relation that they knew already as the informal religious representatives of the family to the saints and God. Luis Vives's *Instruccion de la mujer christiana* (Spanish edition, 1529) and Pérez de Valdivia's *Aviso de gente recogida* (1585) were very different in content, but both were symptomatic of a new literacy and a renewed sense of spiritual equality among Spanish women of a certain standing. The numbers of women beatas in the sixteenth century (reportedly several thousand in the Jaén region alone) constituted a religious movement that can be seen, in part, as an alternative to the more practical devotions of peasant society.[47]

These loosely controlled amateur religious were perceived as a threat by a Church whose authority was already threatened on an unprecedented scale. Hence, throughout the century communities of beatas were encouraged to become regular convents or at least members of third orders.[48] The pressure became more intense as *beaterías* were found to be focal points of heresies. On May 29, 1566, Pius V issued a *motu proprio* ordering the regularization of the third orders, and various religious jurisdictions in Spain applied it to secular communities of beatas as well. The reports give two cases of third order Franciscan beatas changing over to cloistered nuns—in Daimiel (Ciudad Real) and in Villanueva de los Infantes (Ciudad Real), the latter in 1575. In both instances the beatas had been accustomed to go out when necessary. Those of Daimiel begged for alms, especially wheat, as far as seventy kilometers away in Almodóvar del Campo and Campo de Criptana.[49]

The tightening of controls on these independent women corresponded to proscriptions against women as hermits in isolated chapels and in general the careful segregation of sexes in matters religious. The priest-author of the Toledo city report decries the multitude of hermitages around the city: "And please God that they serve for devotion, and not as an occasion for liberty of women who should be enclosed [rrecogidas], or to the profit of certain devout vagabonds."[50]

The Council of Toledo in 1582 decided on measures that had already been taken by some of the military orders. Beatas who had made a solemn vow would be obliged to be cloistered; those who had not taken a solemn vow would be encouraged to take it; and those who refused would be allowed to continue in their communities, but not allowed to admit any new members, wear a habit, or swear obedience to any particular priest.[51]

Other "abuses" were to be controlled by strengthening the authority of the bishop over the clergy. Reformers inside and outside of Spain had continually complained of the proclamation of false miracles or the traffic in unverified relics. In Spain elementary measures of verification had been taken long before Trent, and these measures were merely more widely, though hardly more carefully, applied. We have seen that documents with testimony from witnesses in regard to apparitions and miracles were kept from at least the mid-fifteenth century. Certificates for relics did not generally exist until the mid-sixteenth century, but before then parish visitors did examine relics on their visits, and there is a case of insufficiently substantiated relics being sealed away into the wall of the church in Fuentelaencina (Guadalajara) around 1552. While the use of notarized statements from witnesses may have controlled some of the wilder claims of miracle cures, the certificates accompanying the relics flooding New Castile at this time were often made out in Rome on the flimsiest of evidence.[52]

One of the most practical reforms made in the sixteenth century was the reduction of the number of votive feast days. There is no mention in the reports of the towns and villages of the abolition or commutation of any of their vows not to work on given days. But in fact the bishops had taken some measures to ease a situation that was generally admitted to be intolerable. Alfonso de Valdés had pointed out that the excess of feast days was a burden to the poor and an occasion for vice. Juan de Avila argued that feast days need only be observed until mass, so people could work in the afternoon. The report of the city of Toledo, after listing thirteen days (!) observed in the city in addition to those ordered by Rome and the diocese, adds that others are not observed, "for the necessity of the poor."[53]

The community vows, by canon law, could only be commuted by the bishop, and in the constitutions we find what evidence there is of the burden that the vows meant to the people in the countryside. When the bishops of Palencia (in 1545) and Burgos (in 1575) allowed people to work after mass on vowed days, they claimed that their decisions were in response to popular appeals:

> In many places in our archdiocese, in addition to Sundays and holy days that the Holy Mother Church orders observed, there are many other days that the villages out of their devotions or council vows promise to keep; and afterwards, when they have to fulfill them and keep them they encounter many difficulties. For since many of these days fall at harvest time or grape-gathering time, when there is much necessity to bring in the wheat and wine and dig around the vines, and sow, many work and go against their vows; and other poor folk, because they,

their wives and children are unable to work, die of hunger
or go to work in other places thinking that there they do
not go against what they promised. And because the representatives of the villages of this archdiocese asked us to
order that those vows be relaxed or commuted to other
pious works, if the synod approves we order that the villages and the individual inhabitants that promised to keep
vows in council for days the church does not order to be
kept, once they have gathered in the morning in the
church and had mass celebrated or a procession held in
honor of the saint and by being there with devotion fulfilled their vows, they may freely go to work and get on
with their labors.[54]

In 1642 Urban VIII issued a sweeping decree allowing people to work on all but a limited number of feast days. Giving this decree as an excuse, some towns apparently tried to
avoid even the celebration of masses on their vowed days.
The Bishop of Sigüenza in 1655 reaffirmed the obligation of
parishioners to have mass said and pay the priest for it. He
permitted the priest to refuse divine offices to town authorities who did not pay up.[55]

This kind of reluctance to fulfill contractual obligations
with the saint is not evident in the reports. On the contrary
they strongly indicate that the people of New Castile took
their vows seriously. By the mid-seventeenth century the
vowed days were more of a burden than they had been in
1575, for the situation of the peasantry of New Castile
worsened considerably. But in the late sixteenth century it
was not necessarily the home-made feast days that people
were complaining about. In this the constitutions of Palencia (1545) and Burgos (1575), cited above, are almost certainly deceptive. For by 1530 in virtually all dioceses bishops had automatically commuted the vowed days of the
villagers, allowing them to work after mass. The diocese of
Burgos, for instance, had already relaxed vows for work in
harvest time in 1503. Indeed, in some dioceses (Segovia,

1478, Cuenca, 1531) bishops had flatly forbidden new village vows.[56] The villagers persisted in observing their vows in spite of the bishops.

Indeed, it seems the true reason the bishops were relaxing village vows, at times compulsorily, was that the villagers preferred their local vowed days to the obligatory feast days of the diocese and Rome. Following the line of the constitutions of Badajoz in 1501, the bishops of Segovia (1529) and Calahorra (1539) (reprinted in Segovia 1586 and Cuenca 1626) give the villagers' very tenacity in observing their vows as the reason for commuting them.[57] The fundamental problem is the same: too many fiestas at harvest time. But in addition, "the holy days that the holy Church orders kept are not as well celebrated or observed as they should be by the faithful, who consider holy days that they have chosen themselves to be more worthy of respect and celebration." The Cuenca text of 1626, after reprinting prohibitions and relaxations of vows dating back to 1531, complains, "what is contained in this constitution was ordained long ago and mandated by Synodal Constitution, and it has not sufficed, for the said fiestas are still observed by vow, devotion, and custom. . . ."[58]

Community vows were out of the control of the Church. The villagers set up a parallel but more restrained set of feast days, days of particular, significant helpers, as opposed to the (largely) biblical saints ordered by the Church, or the diocesan patron saints that bishops from time to time futilely tried to impose on the villages. Each village had its own calendar of sacred times, marked on the village memory by plagues and divine signs, part of solemn contracts with advocates in heaven. Many of the practices entailed in the vows clashed with what the Church considered decent standards of morality or mandated observance (as with charity feasts on fast days). When it was generally agreed that the excessive number of holy days was prejudicial to the poor and to the economy, the Church tried to eliminate these local vows, which it considered unimportant if not obnoxious. Naturally, it was unsuccessful. The Church could perhaps force people to observe a day, but it could not keep them from observing one. Witness how the towns, when ordered not to observe vowed bullfights, said they were no longer observing a vow, but merely doing what they pleased.

The average number of vows per village was about three. Only in episcopal cities was the number of specially vowed or locally mandated days significant. In the rest of the towns and villages the number of vowed days, compared with the number of diocesan-ordered holy days, was small indeed. In addition to about 52 Sundays and holy days that always fell on Sunday, Toledo (1582) required 40 additional holy days, Cuenca (1566) 42, and Sigüenza (1533) 36.[59] Of these additional holy days, one-seventh, or about five, would by chance fall on a Sunday. This means that in these dioceses, people would theoretically be unable to work about 85 days of the year. And in fact there were fewer holy days in New Castile than in many other dioceses. In 1553 Calahorra had ten more holy days than Toledo. But by the last quarter of the century, there were few diocesan holy days in New Castile that were not required by Rome. In a rare move, Archbishop Tavera of Toledo had cut nine diocesan holy days from the calendar.[60] The ultimate solution had to come from Rome, as it did in 1642. The issue of work on vowed days reveals the seriousness with which the peasantry regarded their contractual obligations with the saints, their own sacred times.

THE SURVIVAL OF LOCAL RELIGION

Those adjustments made by the bishops and the Councils in the sixteenth century left largely untouched the core of devotion: the vow and the patron. For at the root of these devotional acts and relationships is a defenselessness in regard to epidemic disease, plagues of locusts, vine blights, hail, and drought that remained unchanged. Religion in the form of bargains with the gods provided a means of control over these disasters. How was the *devotio moderna* to keep hail away? cure the crippled? bring back the dead? It made sense as a system of devotion of people buffered from these more mundane matters, who did not directly depend on the land for their livelihood. It made sense also for those not so intimately linked to their fellows in a sense of corporate responsibility before God as were most of the towns-people of New Castile.

What were seen as group afflictions required a group response. The emphasis of the Evangelical and Alumbrist reformers, first in the monasteries, then in the cities and countryside, was to internalize and individualize devotion. Susan Tax Freeman has shown the corporate nature of Castilian villages and hamlets in virtually all phases of work and leisure even in the twentieth century. It is natural that they should make a corporate response to outside threats. The humanists offered little in the way of solutions or even consolation for the group problems of these people, rural or urban.

The religion of most of the people of New Castile was rooted in a place, says Las Mesas, which was at once the Nazareth of the Marian shrine in the countryside and the Jerusalem of Holy Week in the town. The local landscape, urban and rural, had a sacred overlay; special places for contacting the divine were known to everyone.

Such a community had ongoing dealings with a number of saints who interceded for them with God. Some were specialized in protection from insects; others from plague; and others from hail or fire. In cities they might offer political protection as well. Still others, more venerated, were general protectors, especially consulted by individuals, and turned to by the town when all else failed. There would be a certain turnover of the specialist saints, but the general protectors would be more permanent.

Just as this local religious ambit had its sacred places and its sacred protectors, so it had its sacred calendar, marked by the supernatural interventions in its favor and the feast days of its protectors.

Occasionally one town's sacred place, saint, or time attracted the devotion of other towns. This made it a district or regional shrine. District shrines could serve groups of towns, who came in procession, the way a local shrine served a community of individuals. But the vast majority of sacred places and moments held meaning only for local citizens.

In each place a small band of people were professionally dedicated to maintaining and keeping holy the sacred places, and circulating the power of the saints. But everyone, especially town officials, knew that it was a collective responsibility going back in time and ahead into the future to observe the sacred contracts, and that dire consequences could follow lapses.

Local places, saints, and times differed from, but only occasionally conflicted with, the set proposed by Rome and the diocese. After all, they were to some extent modeled on Rome itself or the cathedral town, just as the ultimate model was Jerusalem and the Holy Land. That is, Rome proposed a sacred place—the parish church; a set of saints, especially Mary and the Apostles; and sacred times—Sundays, Lent, the obligatory liturgical feasts. The only conflicts came when the town celebrated one of its own saints at the expense of the exigencies of the Roman calendar. But essentially the two cycles, pantheons, and sacred geographies could be easily melded.

The Catholic Reformation, among other things, ensured that on those few occasions when the two systems came into conflict, the Roman one would win out. To do this it made sure that the lay operators of the local religious system were subject to the authority of the parish priest, and that lay religiosity, in its sight, was reputable—its saints and relics real, their powers genuine. The net effect was to strengthen local religion—which, as a result, has in Catholic countries largely survived to the present day.

I have tried to avoid the term *popular religion*, for the word *popular* has as many connotations as the Castilian word *pueblo*. Dario Rei, in an incisive article, has pointed out that *popular* for some scholars has come to connote *rural* as opposed to *urban*, *primitive* as opposed to *civilized, traditional* as opposed to *modern*, and *proletarian* as opposed to *capitalist* (not to mention *better* as opposed to *worse*, or the reverse). The kind of religion described in this study was rural and urban, lettered and unlettered, more or less modern, and even applied to the king. *Popular* does not fit.[61]

Although I agree with Rei that the only defensible distinction involved between *popular religion* and whatever else it is being compared with is that between religion as practiced and religion as prescribed, I believe that more can be said about the general characteristics of "religion as practiced." Religious customs may be similar or different, they may start by inspiration or arrive by diffusion, but by definition they all have one thing in common: they are tied to a specific place and a historical constituency. All practice takes place somewhere. Most western European life has been lived in historical communities over a particular terrain. Over time, practice becomes practices. As a result, religion-as-practice carries with it a conservative bias, a resistance to changes imposed on the terms of outsiders. This is part of the gap between prescribed and observed religion. So-called "little tradition" is often merely "great tradition" that has taken root in a particular place and lasted longer than its time.

In addition to its conservatism, local religiosity is localistic. Universal figures like Mary and Christ are particularized in specific shrine images and become Our Lady of Riansares or the Christ of Urda, and are valued above other Marys and Christs. There is a tension built into relations between the idea and the example, between the Church Universal as embodied in canon law and conciliar decree and the churches of Toledo, Tarancón, and Las Mesas.

Certain kinds of people did not think in local terms, and

their loyalties were only vestigially with their home place. Examples might include, for sixteenth-century Spain, humanists and Erasmians in the first decades, perhaps some circulating monastics, the alumbrados, and mystics like Teresa of Avila. These are precisely the people, because they were least local, because they were idea makers, literary as well as literate, who controlled the written culture and whose religiousness we know most about. After all, they are most like the translocal idea makers who write history. Our biases conforming with theirs, we systematically exclude information about the local, or look at it, from their view, as superstitious, whereas in fact the local-minded are by far in the majority in our culture as well as theirs.

The Catholic Reformation affirmed the local side of religion and merely tried to correct what it saw as its excesses. The history of Catholicism in practice, both before and after the sixteenth century, is a constant process of new agents and devotions creating a commonality across boundaries of place and nation, and a constant adaptation and cooptation of the general agents and devotions for local purposes. As long as religion was tied into the landscape, with specially prized images in specially sacred places; as long as true sources of grace were pieces of bone and specific bodies in graves; and as long as there was the notion that saints could have especially favored relations with particular communities—doctrines all reaffirmed at Trent—localism, regionalism, and nationalism would be with the Church.

In this sense the Catholic Reformation did not drastically suppress "popular" religion. The essential components of local religiosity remained the same in Spain, the heartland and model of the reform. In part the difference between New Castile and, say, France, has to do with the extent to which Castilian Catholicism was already under clerical control by the sixteenth century. The nuclear settlements of New Castile were more easily supervised than the dispersed habitat of Galicia, the Cantabrian coast, and much of France. When people did not live in the country, but rather apart from it, their potentially deviant relations with natural forces could be channeled more easily into orthodox waters. In much of France, as in Galicia, Asturias, and the Basque country, there was more for the Catholic Reformation to reform. And in Spain there was not, as in France, the long-term presence of Protestants to serve as an incentive for a particularly rigid diocesan supervision.

SIX

Christ Enshrined, 1580–1780

THERE is a two-way relation between local and universal religion. While the Catholic Reformation was reaffirming the subordination of the former to the latter, communities continued, as they always had, to adopt and domesticate the symbols and discourse of the Church Universal for local votive use. Devotion to the Passion of Christ from the fifteenth to the eighteenth century is a good example of this kind of localization. Three surveys mark this process in New Castile: the reports of 1575–1580; a questionnaire sent to parish priests in 1782–1789 by Cardinal Lorenzana of Toledo; and a catalog of village patron saints in the diocese of Cuenca in 1957.

Francisco Antonio Lorenzana was an enlightened prelate, knowledgeable in medicine and geography. Curious about his extensive see, he sent out to parish priests a printed set of questions, largely socio-economic. I have used the answers to the second question (out of fourteen):

If it is the head of a vicarate, district, annex, or of what parish; if it has convents of what order; and also if within the town or outside its walls there is any shrine and celebrated image, give its name and how far away it is; and also the name of the parish church.

The responses to Lorenzana's questionnaire cover 591 places in what are now the provinces of Badajoz, Cáceres, Toledo, Madrid, Guadalajara, Ciudad Real, Albacete, Jaén, and Granada. Of the towns, 525 were in the four provinces of Toledo, Madrid, Guadalajara, and Ciudad Real, and of these 314 were also covered by the 1575–1580 questionnaire of Philip II. For those 314 towns, then, it is possible to compare the saints revered in 1575–1580 with those revered two hundred years later. (See Tables 6.1–6.4.)

Devotion to the saints declined in the baroque period. Although the false chroniclers supplied local saints with extensive legends (among others Saint Blaise of Cifuentes and Saint Babiles of Boadilla del Monte), both the actual number and the percentage of saints' images especially revered declined.[1] Those that retained popularity were the local saints whose bodies were the basis for shrines.

Marian devotion remained at a high level. The proportion of Marian images of all images especially revered dropped slightly, from 65 to 55 percent. Devotion to the saints simply declined: half of the saints revered in 1580 were not even mentioned in 1780. In contrast, there was a kind of reshuffling of Marian devotion: old devotions declined, and less venerated images were accorded more attention. And a new echelon of Marian images was added; more than a third of those accorded special devotion in the 1780s were not even mentioned two hundred years earlier. Many of these new Marian devotions were advocations associated with the Passion, especially Our Lady of the Soledad.

Between 1580 and 1780 it was votive devotion to Christ that experienced the greatest growth, both absolute and relative. In 1580 these 314 towns reported only six images of Christ accorded special devotion. Two hundred years later, images of Christ, virtually all crucifixes or depictions of moments in Christ's last day, represented almost a third of the prime devotions.

What explains this popularity of images of the Passion, whether of Mary or Christ? Together they accounted for two-thirds (47 out of 73) of the new devotions. They were distributed throughout the region, with a special concentration in the towns around Madrid experiencing the greatest growth, and therefore most in need of new patrons.

These shrines represented the final stage of a slow process of localization that probably began in the fifteenth century. The cross had been an important symbol in Castilian devo-

Table 6.1. Towns Responding to Questionnaires, 1575–1580, 1782–1789

Present province	Reports to Philip II	Reports to Cardinal Lorenzana	Reports to both
Guadalajara	145	141	94
Madrid	91	187	77
Toledo	162	155	117
Ciudad Real	67	42	26
TOTAL	465	525	314

Don't know	9
Other provinces	57
TOTAL	591

Table 6.2. Images Drawing Special Devotion in Towns Responding to Both Questionnaires

	Number in 1580 (and % of total)	Number in 1780 (and % of total)
Mary	50 (65%)	75 (55%)
Saints	21 (27%)	19 (14%)
Christ	6 (8%)	43 (31%)
TOTAL	77	137

Table 6.3. Changes in Special Devotions, 1580–1780

	Abandoned[1]	Declined[2]	Maintained[3]	Increased[4]	New[5]
Mary	12	7	31	15	29
Saints	10	1	10	4	5
Christ	2	0	4	0	39

[1] Devotions of 1580 not mentioned in 1780.
[2] Devotions special in 1580 but merely listed in 1780.
[3] Devotions in both 1580 and 1780.
[4] Devotions special in 1780 but merely listed in 1580.
[5] Devotions of 1780 not mentioned in 1580.

Table 6.4. Location of New Devotions, 1780 (314 Towns, New Castile)

	Chapel	Parish church	Monastery	Hospital
Mary	23	3	3	0
Saints	3	2	0	0
Christ	16	19	3	1

tions throughout the reconquest—emblem of the Crusade worn by its military orders, insignia carried into the Battle of Navas de Tolosa in 1212 and posted on the heights of the Alhambra in 1492. But crucifixes were only exceptionally shrine images before 1600, and much less in Castile than in the kingdom of Aragon (the Christs of Burgos, Orense, Balaguer, and San Salvador de Valencia were the most important).

Each parish and brotherhood had a processional cross. These crosses, and relics of the True Cross in major cities, were used to conjure locusts and hail-bearing clouds, and in some places to dip in streams or the ocean for rain. In late medieval theology, the cross was a sign of great power to turn back the devil, and hail and locusts were as much of "the enemy" as Albigensians, Turks, and Moors.

It was perhaps this use of the cross as a weapon that led to its association with the Black Death. According to a legend included in the acts of the Second Council of Nicaea (787) and subsequently in the Roman martyrology, in 765 Jews of Beyrouth were supposed to have tortured a crucifix, which shed real blood. The blood worked miracles, and the Jews were converted. Blood from the crucifix was prized in relic collections. The legend in fact may have originated in Spain; it was particularly popular in Catalonia, where in 1348 Jews were blamed for the Black Death. It was in Catalonia that the devotional crucifixes were most popular; if the Black Death was caused by the enemy, then the crucifix would keep them at bay.[2]

Most of the Marian visions of villagers, in Castile and Catalonia alike, at the end of the fifteenth century included references to the cross. Mary supposedly handled real crosses during the visions—one at Cubas in 1449 made especially by villagers for the occasion; another at El Miracle, Lérida, in 1458 that was on an altar in a church; and a third at Escalona, Segovia, around 1490, that was standing out in the fields. Similar visions occurred in Italy in the same years, almost all in times of plagues, seeming to invite the people to penitential practices.[3]

In fifteenth-century Castile the response was village-wide processions, and additional penance took the form of fasting or pilgrimages. Penitents in Catalonia may have flagellated themselves in response to the visions, for there was already a tradition of flagellation during important crises or during missions like those of Vincent Ferrer. But not until the sixteenth century in Castile and Catalonia did flagellation become institutionalized in flagellant brotherhoods.

It has been claimed that brotherhoods of the True Cross existed in Toledo, Seville, and Zamora in the fifteenth century. But there is no indication that at that time they were flagellant brotherhoods. There may have been flagellant "companies" on the Italian model in Castile in the first years of the sixteenth century, but formal flagellant brotherhoods of the True Cross have not yet been documented before 1520. They were formed in Cáceres in 1521, Cabra in 1522, Villalpando in 1524, and formed or reformed in Toledo before 1536, Seville in 1538, Baeza in 1540, Jaén in 1541, and Jerez in 1542. Similar brotherhoods of the Blood of Christ were formed in Valencia in 1535 and were a regular part of penitential processions in Barcelona after 1544. No one has studied the beginnings of this most important movement systematically; in some form it may date from considerably earlier. By 1575 in the larger cities thousands of flagellant brothers participated in the Holy Thursday and Good Friday processions, were a regular component of petitionary processions, and operated hospitals, orphanages, and other social services.[4]

In the constitutions of the Cáceres brotherhood the parallel between flagellation and Christ's Passion is explicit: ". . . thinking and contemplating how the docile and humble lamb Our Lord, son of the true God, chose to be crucified on that most blessed tree and shed his precious blood; and deserving in memory of the Sacred Passion of Our Redeemer Jesus Christ and in remission of our faults and sins to shed our human blood. . . ." The flagellants shed their blood in imitation of Christ and for the remission of their sins.[5]

The new brotherhoods were immediately successful. They

represented a sharp break from past practice. Marie-Claude Gerbet's study of Cáceres demonstrates the difference. Older brotherhoods to saints had a limit on the number of members—30, 40, or 70. The newly founded Brotherhood of the True Cross had 850 members, noble or common, wives as well as husbands. The first Passion brotherhood of Jaén, that of the True Cross, was founded in 1541, and it too had a large number of members.[6]

Flagellation was not accepted quickly everywhere. The brothers of Seville had scruples, aware of criticism of flagellants by Jean Gerson at the Council of Constance, but they were reassured by a letter containing indulgences from Rome in 1538. After the brotherhoods of the True Cross, largely started by Franciscans, others followed quickly. By 1575 in Toledo there were four flagellant brotherhoods, ranging in size from six hundred to two thousand members (Santo Nombre de Jesús, Vera Cruz, Soledad, Angustias). In another, that of Santa Elena, brothers walked in Holy Week processions carrying heavy wooden crosses. In Jaén by the end of the century there were five flagellant brotherhoods (Vera Cruz, 1541; Angustias y Cinco Llagas, 1551; Soledad, 1556; Santo Sepulcro, 1580; and Santa Elena, between 1588 and 1594). Those of Soledad and Santo Sepulcro had over a thousand brothers when they were founded.

We can get an idea of the devotional spirit that accompanied the first years of these brotherhoods from a curious document in the archive of the Inquisition of Cuenca. On March 5, 1555, during Lent, many townspeople of Buendía (about nine hundred households) saw for the space of an hour a cross in the sky. Nineteen of them described what they saw to notaries public commissioned by the Brotherhood of the True Cross, and the testimony was sent to Cuenca.[7]

The cross was in the air next to a new *calbario* erected by the brotherhood half a kilometer out of town on the road to Villalba. At least eleven women saw it there. They apparently prayed at the calvary, alone or in small groups, daily during Lent. One was praying for a dying woman, most were simply praying "their devotions" on their knees, and one said she was "contemplating the Passion of Jesus Christ Our Redeemer."

Other women saw the cross from a spring about seven hundred yards from the calvary, and men saw it coming back from working in the fields. The men had not been praying, but rather pruning or digging around vines, cutting firewood, or preparing saffron patches.

For both women and men reactions ranged from praising God, the most common reaction ("Blessed are you Lord that the least miracle that you can do is this one," and "Glory to the Trinity for every day we see new and holy things"), to wondering what it was a sign of, whether the end of the world, or a personal lack of faith. It also provoked a special prayer for the sick woman, taking advantage of the unexpected proximity of the divine. The vision is an indication of the fervor of devotion to the Passion at the time, devotion that was expressed through the brotherhoods of the True Cross, their calvaries and their processions. Crosses were also seen in the sky in Peñas de San Pedro (Albacete) in 1517, in Griñón (Madrid) in 1569, in El Bonillo (Albacete) in 1638, and, according to village reports, in Santa Cruz de Mudela (Ciudad Real), Hueva (Guadalajara), and Bayona (Madrid).[8]

These brotherhoods were found throughout the countryside by the time of the 1575–1580 reports. Their presence can be deduced from information on chapels and vows and the occasional direct reference.

Towns with Brotherhood of True Cross	21
With chapels to the True Cross	10
With Brotherhood of Blood of Jesus	5
With chapel to Blood of Jesus	4
Other Passion brotherhoods	6
	46

Other chapels and brotherhoods may have been flagellant as well. The Brotherhood of the Rosary in Quer (Guadalajara) was a flagellant one. And the Brotherhood of the True Cross in El Cubillo (Guadalajara) was based on the chapel of "the Rosary of the Blood of Jesus" built in 1565. The Brotherhood of the Blood of Jesus of Ribatejada (Madrid) was also based on a Rosary chapel. It is therefore possible that the many chapels of the Rosary in the Guadalajara region were homes of flagellant brotherhoods. Similarly, in the district around Tarancón, the brotherhoods dedicated to the Holy Name of Jesus, which we speculated might have been founded by the Dominicans of Huete, may well have been flagellant brotherhoods like that based in the Dominican convent of Santa Catalina in Toledo.

Devotion to the Passion in 1575–1580 was active and growing. A number of chapels were new or under construction at the time of the reports. A disproportionate percentage of these were dedicated to the Passion. (See Table 6.5.)

The prolix respondents of Carrascosa del Campo (Cuenca), a town of 676 households, described their brotherhood in 1578: "There is another brotherhood of the holy True

Table 6.5. New Chapels, 1575–1580

True Cross	5
Rosary	5
Five Wounds	1
Conception	3
Saint Sebastian	3
Saint Roch	1
Saint John the Baptist	1

	All chapels	Chapels described as new or under construction
Percentage dedicated to Passion	3% (26/896)	32% (6/19)
Percentage dedicated to Passion or Rosary	7% (59/896)	58% (11/19)

Cross, in which there are more than five hundred brothers of candle [hacha] and discipline, with a few women. On the night of Holy Thursday a procession is held and the brothers go out, those of candles with their candles lit, and those of discipline flagellating themselves and shedding much blood. Clergy and monks who are in town go in the procession. It is very devout, and well-supplied with wax. They say sixty masses for each brother who dies."[9]

Some of these brotherhoods had life-size crucifixes, which became an important feature of general processions in their towns. The town register of Barcelona after 1544 mentions the "great crucifix of the Brotherhood of the Blood of Jesus" in town processions. In New Castile as the century progressed, the competing brotherhoods of Holy Week added more large images of scenes from the Passion, always including the Sorrowing Mother, carried in series over fixed routes, in imitation of Corpus processions. During the rest of the year these images would be stored in previously existing chapels, chapels specially built for the purpose, parish churches, or convents. Relations of brotherhoods with convents were unstable, and in the larger cities brotherhoods frequently moved from one base to another.

Here there is a pattern worth noting. Once a saint or a devotional procedure becomes popular, it is not the orders that spread it: rather, the orders move with it as it diffuses among the laity. In Jaén, for instance, flagellant brotherhoods were formed by Franciscans, Dominicans, Carmelites, Discalced Carmelites, and Trinitarians. Certainly some of the impetus for the founding of these brotherhoods in the cities was to make convents devotional centers and attract alms. But few convents controlled the brotherhoods for long. And devotion to the Passion was not only spread by orders and secular clergy, but also by lay apostles. One Francisco García, for instance, was known as Esclavo Luciano. He taught "the glories and mysteries of the Holy Cross" around 1616 in the villages of Alcarria and the mountains of Cuenca, reputedly "a second Saint Vincent Ferrer in his preaching, the conversion of souls, and continuous miracles."[10]

The Holy Week processions in which this kind of devotion found its ultimate expression were at once public ascetic disciplines and a kind of sacred theater, for which alms were collected along the route. The Passion was also evoked in stationary theater—in churches and convents. In the main square of Santa Cruz de la Zarza, a town of a thousand households, processions and a simulated crucifixion were held in 1567. In 1625 members of the Third Order of Saint Francis enacted "the passion of the Saviour and the dinner of Jesus in the house of the Pharisee" in Malagón (Ciudad Real). There are odd cases that came before the Inquisition, but there were many others that did not. Simulated passions are still enacted in many places in Spain (see Figure 10) and among the Penitentes of New Mexico.[11]

Another measure of the Christocentric nature of late-sixteenth- and seventeenth-century Spanish devotion is the unpleasant record of persecutions for sacrilege. Over the sixteenth century there was a shift in denunciations to the Inquisition of Cuenca from heretical propositions about Mary (her virginity above all) to propositions about Christ and the Eucharist. There was also a sharp increase in denunciations of assaults on crucifixes. Most of the denunciations were not substantiated, although it is possible that someone, somewhere, was whipping images for some reason, but the denunciations themselves are further evidence of a preoccupation with the Passion toward the end of the century. (See Table 6.6.)

A case in point took place in the Manchego town of Socuéllamos (seven hundred households) in 1569. There a sacristan carried a crucifix normally in the sacristy through the streets, claiming it had been whipped, showing the welts on it, and saying that he had found it face down in his vineyard outside of town. The crucifix was placed on a special altar, where people went to it with alms and prayers. A Dominican (who apparently had a grudge against the sacris-

tan, who did not let him preach in the church) denounced
the fraud six months after it happened. In a subsequent investigation the sacristan claimed a mysterious stranger had
taken the crucifix to the fields; the inquisitors were rather
inclined to believe that the sacristan himself took it out to
his vines to protect them from hail. Eventually the case pe-

Figure 10. Scene from a traditional representation of the Passion
in Riogordo (Málaga), Good Friday, 1977. Photograph by
Cristina García Rodero.

Table 6.6. Image Abuse from the Inquisition of Cuenca
up to 1650

Year	Town	Abuse	Expediente
1492	Canalejas	Jew whipped crucifix	252
1517	Cuenca	Priest stabbed crucifix	918
1523	Belmonte	Priest whipped San Sebastian	1199
1529	Molina de Aragón	Man whipped image of Mary because he did not sell merchandise	1503
1556	Huete	Crucifix stabbed	2305a
1569	Socuéllamos	Stranger supposedly whipped crucifix	3262
1575	Cuenca	Crucifix stabbed	3605
1580	Peñalén	Crucifix stabbed	3937
1583	Uclés	Crucifix knocked down with stone	4240
1584	Cuenca	Crucifix broken with sword	4292
1586	Leganiel	Crucifix touched with staff	750-244
1592	Socuéllamos	Crucifix thrown in fire	4753
1594	Motilla	Student whipped Baby Jesus	4811
1599	El Toboso	Crucifix profaned	4978
1610	La Alberca	Crucifix arm broken	5317
1610	San Clemente	Stone thrown at crossed staff of hermit	5328
1613	La Alberca	Cross broken	5444
1616	Cuenca	Crucifix whipped (hearsay)	726:1282
1616	Uclés	Crucifix stabbed	5584
1627	Quintanar de Marquesado	Christ image whipped	5937
1628	Tarancón	Crucifix stabbed	6020
1628	Paxaco	Crucifix fired on	6021
1640	Villanueva de Guadamajud	Crucifix stabbed	733:1422
1647	Villar de Cantos	Crucifix fired on	6434
1648	Pareja	Crucifix stoned	6462

tered out without a sentence. But the initial success of the sacristan in convincing the townspeople (although the welts were clearly painted on the image)—indeed, the very idea of the whipping of an image—illustrates a high level of attention to the Passion and its images.[12]

The obsession that Jews, especially, were whipping crucifixes or sacrificing children as if they were Jesus became a staple of urban "news." An early and influential instance was the supposedly ritual murder by Jews of a Christian child in La Guardia, near Ocaña, around 1490. Caro Baroja, who has studied the investigation records, believes that in this case there was a murder, a desperate recourse to magic by ignorant members of a rural Jewish community to avoid the first massive persecutions of the Inquisitions. By 1575, the caves where the murder supposedly occurred were well known, and two different towns reported the story. A shrine to the Niño de la Guardia was set up in 1560, and remains active today, just off the main highway from Madrid to Andalusia.[13]

Other reports of Christ-sacrilege, almost always vague in detail, were constantly cited in the *relaciones* or newsletters of the seventeenth century.[14] (See Table 6.7.) There was a

Table 6.7. Some Cases of Sacrilege Reported in Newsletters, 1630–1645

Year	Town	Sacrilege	Source
1632	Madrid	Jews abuse image of Christ	León Pinelo (1971) 292
1634	near Salamanca	Jews whip crucifix	MHE 13:71–72
1639	Madrid	Jews whip crucifix	Pellicer 1:104; LP 317
1640	Granada	Jews against Mary	Pellicer 1:165, 189
1641	Madrid	Portuguese priest whips child on Holy Thursday	Pellicer 2:22–23
1643	Yepes	Portuguese whip crucifix	MHE 17:112
1644	Madrid	Portuguese take *empanada* (meat pie) to be cooked with crucifix inside	Pellicer 3:202

rash of them in particular in regard to Portuguese *asentistas*, Jewish convert merchants protected by Olivares who in some measure served as scapegoats for Castile's beleaguered situation in the mid-seventeenth century. Since Protestants believed in the crucifixion as much as Catholics, Protestants' crimes were rather said to be directed against the Eucharist, and a number of miraculous hosts were enshrined throughout New Castile. In Madrid in 1700 there were at least three images thought to have been rescued from infidels or heretics. In the *humilladero* of Atocha was a crucifix that supposedly had been broken up by English heretics in 1564; the image of Our Lady of the Remedies in the Mercedarian convent had been saved from the fireplace of a heretic in Zeeland in 1572; and one of the most notable images in Madrid today, Jesus of Medinaceli, had been ransomed by Trinitarians in Africa in 1689.[15]

Starting gradually in the sixteenth century, but above all in the first decade of the seventeenth, images that had been profaned, images of the passion brotherhoods, and simple parish crosses began to work cures and be venerated in particular places. No longer merely players in the drama of Holy Week, they became the images of shrines, bringing to their brotherhoods, convents, and churches alms from votive offerings. The Marian image of the Soledad made in 1565 by Gaspar Becerro, disciple of Michelangelo, for the convent of Minims in Madrid, was immediately the focus for a large penitential brotherhood, which also operated a foundling hospital. Around 1611 the image became the center of a full-fledged shrine, stimulating cures and votive paintings.[16] Sometime between 1600 and 1617 the image of Christ carrying the Cross of the Brotherhood of the Nazarene, set up around 1590 in Jaén, began to work miracles. Gradually it became the de facto patron of the city, used in petitionary processions for rain and against plague. In 1703 sworn testimony was taken of its miracles. Throughout the peninsula separate chapels were constructed in parish churches and cathedrals for especially venerated images of Christ. (See Figure 11.)

This process of "fixing" had begun, of course, before the brotherhoods. That there was a receptiveness to devotion to the Passion in the sixteenth century can be seen in the alacrity with which crucifixes that were found or dug up were enshrined or venerated in Albalate de Zorita in 1514, Griñón in 1569, and Chiloeches in 1571. Often the new shrines sim-

Figure 11. A sacred crucifix, the Christ of Sauco, is returned to its shrine at Peñas de San Pedro (Albacete) after its annual visit to the parish church, August 28, 1974. Photograph by Cristina García Rodero.

ply started when images began to work miracles. In Zalamea de La Serena (Badajoz) an image obtained by Brothers of the True Cross from Seville in 1586 began working wonders in 1604. A crucifix in Tenerife began curing the sick at the end of the sixteenth century. Other instances occurred in Peñas de San Pedro (Albacete) preceded by lights and marvels in 1608; in Calatorao (Zaragoza) in 1612; in 1613 in Atienza (Guadalajara); and in Ribas del Jarama (a Christ tied to the column) in 1658.[17]

Other images first gave an extraordinary sign of their miraculousness, then worked miracles. The signs—the sweating or weeping of blood as Christ did in the Garden of Gethsemane or during the Passion—had been staples of medieval conventual religiosity. Indeed they were also known to the Greeks and Romans, who considered them portents.[18]

Such signs had been seen on occasion, but infrequently, in late-fifteenth- and early-sixteenth-century Aragon and Catalonia.[19] One of the first of the new series occurred on Good Friday in 1590, when a processional cross carried by a flagellant brotherhood in Igualada (Barcelona) had on it a blood-like substance. It is impossible in the twentieth century to know how this happened—in many instances the testimony of witnesses is there to be read; certainly there was some liquid on the images. Fraud is not to be ruled out.

I list cases of images giving off humors, a few condemned as fakes by the Inquisition, most of the others accepted at the time as true. (See Table 6.8.) Included are cases from beyond New Castile to show how widespread a phenomenon this was.[20]

Almost all of these images or paintings represented some phase of the Passion. The painting of Saint Francis that sweated twice in Traid depicted Francis receiving the stigmata, *his* passion. Many of the images went on to become the focus for local devotion, working miracles and becoming the formal or informal patrons of their communities.

Another way images of the Passion became shrine images was when they were "discovered" painted on walls. (See Table 6.9.) Some were found beneath layers of plaster, others were said to have been painted overnight by mysterious pilgrims. Such discoveries were particularly frequent toward the end of the seventeenth century in New Castile.[21]

For a number of the miraculous images and paintings special churches were built, predominantly in towns, at considerable expense, paid for by votive offerings (San Carlos, Tembleque, Sacedón, Honrubia, Miguelturra). For others new chapels were added onto parish churches, as had been done for the crucifixes found at Albalate de Zorita (Guadalajara) and Griñón (Madrid) in the sixteenth century (El Bonillo, Osa de la Vega, Alcobendas, Traid). But few of these shrines, after an initial wave of miracles, attracted devotion from beyond neighboring towns, and most remained local.

Table 6.8. Images Giving Off Humors

Year	Town and Circumstances
1590	Igualada (Bar.). crucifix, Good Friday procession
1621	Ismiquilpa (Mex.), crucifix
1621	Ocaña (T), Verónica (Inquisition)
1627	Barcelona, crucifix, Holy Thursday, Easter Monday
1627	Madrid, Marian image (Inquisition)
1629	Luna (Zar.), Christ of the Column, in Marian shrine
1634	Madrid, Christ in convent
1640	El Bonillo (Alb.), crucifix
1640	Riudarenes (Gir.). Marian painting
1641	Llers (Gir.), Marian image in procession
1644	Osa de la Vega (Cu), Verónica, Holy Thursday, Holy Saturday
1646	Parma (Italy), Christ, known in Spain
1646	Alcobendas (M), Christ of the Column in petitionary procession
1649	Seville, Christ carrying cross, in convent
1655	Huesca, crucifix
1655	Arén (Huesca), crucifix
1656	Seville, Christ carrying cross
1658	Toledo, Ecce Homo
16—	Honrubia (Cu), Verónica
16—	Madrid, crucifix (before 1629)
1706	Murcia, Mary of Sorrows
1710, 1713	Traid (G), Saint Francis
1713	Seville, crucifix
1728	Tarabilla (G), crucifix (Inquisition)
1755	La Guardia (Jaén), Marian image (Inquisition)
1764	Miguelturra (CR), mural of crucifixion
1765	Campo de Criptana (CR), painting of Christ (Inquisition)
17—	Manzanares de la Sierra (M), painting of Christ of the Sepulcher (before 1780)

The dramatic signs of the Passion demonstrate a new dialectic in the baroque period between the people and their images. With the signs the image literally came alive. Just as the people in processions and passion plays played Jesus and Mary, so the very realistic images they carried in processions were crafted to be as lifelike as possible. The people dressed and whipped themselves and wept so they looked

Table 6.9. Discovered Images

Year	Town	Image
ca. 1640	San Carlos del Valle, (CR)	Crucifix on wall discovered
1688	San Pablo (T)	Image of Christ beneath plaster
1689	Tembleque (T)	Crucifixion scene by pilgrim
1689	Sacedón (G)	Veronica beneath plaster
16(??)	Villalba del Rey (Cu)	Crucifix by pilgrim
1725	Villanueva de la Fuente (CR)	Miraculous drawing of crucifix on wall by a carpenter

like the images; and the images sweated blood and wept as if they were people.

Note the difference in wording between the questions in 1575 and 1782. The questionnaire in 1575 never mentioned images; it asked about relics and *ermitas*, about sacred places as opposed to sacred images. By 1780 the focus had widened: "if . . . there is any shrine or celebrated image . . ." Some of the replies of 1780 reflected this attention to realism and its effect on the senses. A Christ of the Column in the Madrid village of Humanes was "exquisite in artistry (*primorosa en arte*), and of an aspect that moves to reverence and devotion." An Ecce Homo in a Talavera parish church was "one of the most exquisite images in its effect on the senses"; and a crucifix in a Guadalajara village was "one of the most perfect that can be found." Two hundred years before images were noted for people's devotion toward them; they were *devota*, *milagrosa*, or *antigua*, but never, as in 1780, *primorosa*.[22]

The images that wept and bled, or that changed complexion and blinked, or whose eyes were seen to become brilliant and move, were participating in the tribulations of the people, and suffered for them, in the same way that the people participated vicariously in the Passion of Christ and the Sorrows of Mary. The signs, when believed, provoked mass processions, weeping, and all night vigils, as if the town or village was indeed Jerusalem, and the inhabitants were at once responsible for the crucifixion as well as beneficiaries of Christ's sacrifice. These activations of images, this "coming alive," are especially dramatic instances of what was probably a process occurring in most towns in the baroque period—images of the Passion affirming their membership or role in the community, their place in its particular pantheon. The emphasis on images signaled a shift away from holy sites in the countryside, at which the image was only secondary, to holy images miraculous in and of themselves—which, once their powers were manifest, could be placed in convenient and controllable places like in-town chapels, parish churches, cathedrals, and monasteries.

But these signal events did not merely have local significance. Many were reported in newsletters and their national and international significance weighed. Many were clustered at critical moments of the early modern era—the war between Castile and Catalonia in 1640 or the War of Succession (those of Traid and Murcia corresponded to the days of important battles). People at the time agreed that such events were signs, although usually they were unsure of what. But it was clear in this period of state-building that the saints were in some way participating in the political fortunes of Spain's kingdoms, and of Christendom as a whole.

New devotion to the Passion did not go unnoticed, and found a ready explanation. Some contemporary writers considered it a response to Protestantism.[23] In some part it may have been, but I doubt that on the whole these acts of devotion were intended as theological statements. The Passion, we have seen, was on people's minds fifty years before Protestantism appeared, and flagellant brotherhoods were probably active before the heresy was recognized. The Toledo priest who wrote the city's report in 1575 did mention the "Lutherans," but gave devotion to Mary, the Holy Sacrament, and the Souls in Purgatory, not devotion to the Passion, as ways of witnessing against them.[24]

Although there was considerable overlap, the most active

period of flagellation was in the sixteenth century, and the period of institutionalization of Passion images in shrines was in the seventeenth and early eighteenth century. Flagellation was well on the decline by 1650. The Brotherhood of the Soledad of Madrid had over two thousand flagellants and four hundred candle bearers in 1568. But around 1658, when it was still the largest procession in Holy Week, it had only eight hundred members, and a minority of these were flagellants.[25] Any explanation will have to account for the apparent paradox that the height of penitential behavior occurred during what was for Castile a period of prosperity relatively free from epidemics (1520–1590). It would be interesting to examine periods of extreme penitential behavior for Europe as a whole to see whether they were, in fact, times of precarious prosperity.

The transformation of passion devotions into local shrines corresponded with the subsequent disastrous decline of prosperity. Juan de la Portilla Duque, trying to explain the designs of God, wrote:[26]

For if we examine the twenty years from 1640 to the present 1661, it will be seen that we Spaniards have suffered all kinds of punishments, like bloody domestic and foreign wars, hatred and enmity with neighboring provinces, new tyrants of the Church armed against Spain, allying against her with other Christian nations, to which are added the ruins, fires, shipwrecks, the war, famine, and plague that ever-faithful Castile suffers and will always suffer.

He considered that these were not to be seen as punishments of God, but rather God's way of tempering Spaniards by adversity. And, in fact, he said, in spite of their trials Spaniards had expanded their devotions.

In this same time, in these last twenty years, we have built and consecrated to God, to his Most Holy Mother, and to his Saints, new temples, new altars, new chapels; rebuilt old churches, founded new congregations, and constructed different monasteries and hospitals with incredible outlays of new devotion and grandeur.

With hindsight we might say that it was in times of trial, from the epidemic of 1599 to the end of the seventeenth century, that direct divine help was most needed, and devotion to the Passion shifted from imitative expiation to vow and petition.

Lorenzana sent out his questionnaire in 1782 on his own initiative, and there was no equivalent questionnaire for the diocese of Cuenca. But one can compare the major advocates (rarely the same as the titular saints of the parish churches) of 1575–1580 with those of 1957, thanks to a book issued when each town sent its favorite saint to the coronation of Our Lady of Angustias, the patron of the diocese, in the city of Cuenca.[27] The ceremony itself, not infrequent in twentieth-century Spain, demonstrated the permanence of community devotions and an appreciation of their power by diocesan authorities. To the dominant city came the subordinate towns. Regional devotion to the patron saint, a canonical prerequisite for the coronation of images, was demonstrated by the fealty of the patron saints of the various towns.

Thirty-three towns were listed both in the reports to Philip II and the coronation book. A comparison of the prime devotions shows those that persisted and those that changed. The results largely correspond to the changes that occurred in the diocese of Toledo in the seventeenth and eighteenth centuries.

In eight of the towns, what was clearly the most popular image of the late sixteenth century remained so in 1957. In only two towns did what was then the most popular devotion change; that is, eight out of the ten clearly popular devotions remained the same. Six of the eight shrines were to Mary:

Na. Sra. de la Consolación—Iniesta
Na. Sra. de la Gracia—Belmonte

Na. Sra. de Rus—San Clemente
Na. Sra. de la Vega—Barajas de Melo
Na. Sra. de Riansares—Tarancón

The other two were shrines to Saint Anne in Carrascosa del Campo and El Pedernoso.

In the other two towns with clear patronage in the sixteenth century the devotions had changed as follows:

from San Silvestre to Na. Sra. del Villar—Villarrubio
from Na. Sra. de las Nieves to Na. Sra. del Rosario—Quintanar del Rey

In four towns the most popular images in 1957 were mentioned among others in the reports, but not in a way that would present them as special:

Santa Ana—Tribaldos
Na. Sra. de la Asunción—Vara de Rey (parish church)
Na. Sra. de la Concepción—Almendros
Na. Sra. de Manjavacas—La Mota del Cuervo

In the remaining nineteen towns, the 1957 patrons were not mentioned either as shrines or as objects of vows, or as the advocation of the parish church or chapels in the sixteenth-century reports. Probably most of them were devotions that arose in the towns since 1580. (See Tables 6.10 and 6.11.)

Mary

La Dolorosa—Enguídanos
Na. Sra. de las Augustias—Castillo de Garci Muñoz
Na. Sra. de la Misericordia—Puebla de Almenara (17th c.)
Na. Sra. de la Soledad—Fuente de Pedro Naharro
(17th c.)
Na. Sra. de las Angustias—Uclés
Na. Sra. de los Desamparados—Buendía
Na. Sra. del Rosario—Quintanar del Rey, Gabaldón, Huélamo
Na. Sra. de la Concepción—El Horcajo de Santiago

Na. Sra. del Remedio—Saelices
Virgen de la Cabeza—Palomares del Campo
Santa María del Espino—El Peral
Virgen del Valle—Torrubia del Campo
Santa María de la Cuesta—Huelves

Christ

Smo. Cristo de la Salud—Minglanilla
Sto. Niño de la Bola—Las Mesas (16th c.)
Santa Cruz—La Alberca
Smo. Cristo de la Viga—Villamayor de Santiago (c. 1680)

Table 6.10. Prime Devotions, 33 Towns of the
Diocese of Cuenca, 1580–1957

	1580	1957
Mary	7 (70%)	26 (89%)
Saints	3 (30%)	3 (9%)
Christ	0 —	4 (12%)

Table 6.11. Components of Change, Devotions 1580–1957,
Diocese of Cuenca

	Devotion maintained	Devotion increased	New devotions (not mentioned in 1575–1580 reports)
Mary	6	3	17 (6 Passion)
Saints	2 (Anne)	1 (Anne)	0
Christ	0	0	4 (3 Passion)

The number of towns is small, but the figures agree with the 1580–1780 trend and my own observations of present-day devotions in the region as a whole. The people of New Castile continued allotting less devotion to the saints through the nineteenth and twentieth centuries. Saints declined from a third of the devotions in 1580 to less than a tenth in 1957. In fact the only saint in these towns that served as a general advocate was Anne, the mother of Mary.

These figures register the wave of devotion to Christ. Las Mesas in 1957 was devoted to the child Jesus; La Alberca, where in 1610 and 1613 persons were accused by the Inquisition of breaking crucifixes, was appropriately dedicated to the Holy Cross. But indications are that by the end of the eighteenth century, devotion to images of Christ had played out. Special devotions to Christ were a third of those of the diocese of Toledo in 1780, but only an eighth of those of the adjacent diocese of Cuenca in 1957. Part of this decline corresponds to a decline in Passion brotherhoods. Although processions of Holy Week continued in many towns, public flagellation was prohibited in 1767 by Charles II. As far as I know, the only remaining town where a brotherhood of the True Cross performs flagellation is San Vicente de la Sonsierra (Logroño).[28] (See Figure 12.)

Few if any new shrines to Christ were founded in the entire region in the last two centuries, and some of the devotions new to the baroque period have disappeared. In Manzanares de la Sierra (Madrid), where a painting of Christ of the Sepulcher sweated sometimes in the eighteenth century, all memory of the event was lost by 1976. So, too, was lost the memory of a miraculous drawing of Christ on the wall of a chapel in Villanueva de la Fuente (Ciudad Real). The Christ of the Column that sweated in Alcobendas (Madrid) in 1646 is no longer accorded devotion. In the same town the shrine image of Our Lady of Peace had worked an "authenticated" miracle in 1677, supplying wine for a public feast, and thus Mary regained the preeminence she had temporarily lost. (The three hundredth anniversary of the miracle was celebrated in 1977.)[29] In many cases where devotion to miraculous images of Christ has survived, the images share the patronage of the town with Mary.

Today the very existence of the seventeenth- and eighteenth-century Christocentric devotion, shrines, and miracles is virtually unknown. Art historians following Emile Mâle have shown the Christ-centered nature of the imagery of the Catholic Reformation, but in general they are una-

Figure 12. Flagellants of the Brotherhood of the True Cross in the Holy Week procession of 1974 in San Vicente de la Sonsierra (Logroño). Photograph by Cristina García Rodero.

ware that this imagery corresponded to a wave of local piety and miraculism that resulted in a new stratum of community protectors. What began as penitential devotion at the end of the fifteenth century, an attempt to substitute personal suffering for prospective divine punishment, was converted by the end of the seventeenth century into a new set of sources of divine help, and in many cases gave way subsequently to devotion, once again, to Mary.

Major votive devotion, in Cuenca and throughout Spain with the exception of Galicia, rests today more than ever with Mary, both in images derived from the Passion like that of Our Lady of Angustias of Cuenca, and in the traditional shrines of the countryside. Doubtless this concentration on Mary in part reflects Church policy. Decisions to approve the dogma of the Immaculate Conception and to encourage attention to the visions of Rue de Bac (1830), La Salette (1847), Lourdes (1858), and Fatima (1917) seem in part to have been strategic choices to turn to the latent strength of local devotions in an effort to recoup losses from the French Revolution and the rise of secularization and socialism.[30]

Personal vows and shrines maintained by them remain today, as do many of the fiestas described in the reports to Philip II. Many of the shrines are filled with the same kind of ex-votos as four hundred years ago. Improvements in medicine have not eliminated the fear of death, and new sources of random danger, especially automobiles, have replaced some of the older ones. The nature of the personal vow has changed, however. It subsists less as a penance to avoid or commute a punishment, and more as a loving contract made in the hope of grace. For the major change in lay religion since 1580 is a philosophical one, connected with the concentration of devotion on Mary. The fear of God, the fear of the saints as punishers has largely been dissipated. This shift to the notion, already observed in the attitude toward Mary, of a positive, helping deity, accompanied the discontinuance, in the nineteenth century, of town vows in times of trouble. When and how it came about in Spain demands study.[31]

This great transformation of lay theology included, but is not explained by, an expansion of the notion of chance, which replaced a sense of collective responsibility for natural disasters. The notion of chance was already present in the sixteenth century. In many towns in La Mancha and Alcarria, alcaldes were chosen by lot, as, indeed, were the representatives of certain cities in the Cortes. The people also knew that even in some religious matters chance could be operative. We saw this in their efforts when reporting miracles or cases of dramatic responses to vows to demonstrate that the result was due to divine intervention. They were not blind believers in Providence as a rational, humanly explicable system of human cause and divine effects. The presence of *that* kind of providence had to be proven.

The idea of misfortune, as well as fortune, was also present. In the case of children's diseases or birth defects, there could be little moral responsibility on the part of the victim for its plight. It was mainly Mary who cared for these cases. Misfortune, at least in the form of the "unknown designs of God," as opposed to cause-and-effect punishment, was also operative with the weather. Only after a number of years was hail on a given day a signal for penance.

At some time between then and now, the idea of fortune and misfortune spread to major group situations. No longer were disasters viewed as the punishments of angry gods. Indeed, from clerical texts it seems that this notion had already begun to erode, if only temporarily, under the influence of the humanists at the beginning of the sixteenth century. Concomitantly, adult sickness over time was classed less as a punishment of a community and more as the misfortune of individuals. Here doubtless a reduction in the number and frequency of epidemics played an important role. And no doubt this shift reflected an erosion of local autonomy in all areas of life.

In any case, penance or the placation of saints was no longer an appropriate response. Collective religious solutions, as with group vows to epidemic saints, gave way to individual solutions, generally personal vows to the general patron saints. The benign mother saint was turned to more than ever. Corporate religion itself gave way, though by no means completely, to the religion of individuals.

The ultimate explanation for the shift to a benevolent God may be the obvious one. All-powerful gods are by definition responsible for one's situation on earth. If times are generally bad, if there is an ever-present threat of plague, devastation of crops, or famine, then that pain ultimately, for whatever reason, comes from God. The god is an angry one who punishes. There is no question that the economic lot of Spaniards has improved over the past three hundred years. It makes sense that when people are relatively well-off, when not only the fact of disaster, but the realistic potential for disaster is no longer present, they would find the old notion of an angry God more difficult to justify.

The other aspect of local religion that has largely disappeared is the sense of divine participation in the landscape, the search for signs in anomalous events or coincidences, the idea that the saints are always searching for their chosen towns. No longer is nature invested with the kind of sensitivity to the sacred that made the dove come and land in the transept during the petitionary mass to Saint Sebastian in Castillo de Garci Muñoz, or another dove land on the litter of a dead man in Pezuela during a funeral service; that led the dog in Albalate de Zorita to discover the buried cross, or the horse of the Knights of Saint John to shy before the image of Our Lady of Salceda; that led the eagle to roost with the image of Mary in Ventas con Peña Aguilera, or the bird to clean a street statue of Mary in Almonacid de Zorita; that made a certain cow separate from her herd and kneel each time she passed the chapel of Our Lady of the Vega in Morata. Or is it that these things still happen, and nobody, no devout and curious monarch, wants to know?

Text of Madrid Vow to Saint Anne and Saint Roch, 1597

Vow MADE by the cabildo of clergy, the Corregidor, the regidores, and the priors of all the convents of Madrid, with permission of the bishop, on their knees before the Holy Sacrament in the church of Saint Mary, July 25, 1597. This vow of a powerful city includes a promise to obtain a plenary indulgence that would have been extravagant for a smaller town.

Considering the grave ills and diseases that affect us, and attributing them, as well we should, to a chastisement and scourge of God angered by the sins of his people; and desiring to calm his wrath, we think that the most appropriate way to do this is to take his friends, the saints, as our advocates and defenders; and so, moved by the special trust and devotion we have for the glorious Saint Anne, mother of the Most Holy Virgin Mary Mother of God and Our Lady, and for the glorious Saint Roch, whose continued miracles have shown us how much his intercession before the Divine Majesty can obtain, we humbly beseech them to be our patrons and advocates in the presence of God, placating the wrath of God we have so justly merited. And so that they accede more easily to our humble supplication and the Divine Clemency sees fit to cede them to us as our special protectors, we make a vow to our Lord God in our name and that of this entire town, those absent as well as those present, and of all our successors to observe the feasts of the

SOURCE: Jeronimo de Quintana, *Historia de la Antiguedad, Nobleza, y Grandeza de la Villa de Madrid* (1629) (Madrid, Artes Gráficas Municipales, 1954) 863–864.

blessed Lady Saint Anne, our patron, and glorious Saint Roch, suspending all work, and to have said on their days every year their first vespers, and mass sung with solemnity, and to hold a general procession to the churches that we will indicate for the celebration of their feasts, attending personally at them, and our successors, unless we are legitimately impeded from doing so. And in addition we promise to build a chapel dedicated to Saint Roch. And to procure permission from His Holiness so that in all of Spain his mass is said and celebrated. And in order that these holy days are kept with devotion, we will also ask His Holiness to grant a plenary indulgence to those who having confessed and received communion on one of these holy days visit between the first vespers until sunset of the next day the churches that we will indicate for their celebration, praying to God for the health and conservation of this town; and this we promise, and vow, and we beseech that Our Lord receive these vows, and see fit to calm his anger against us, and we sign it with our names.

District and Regional Shrines, 1575–1580, New Castile

ALL are shrines to which at least one outside village goes.
Regional shrines are preceded by an asterisk.

SHRINES IN TOLEDO (PRESENT PROVINCE)

Town	Shrine	Villages That Go
	Marian	
Burguillos	Burguillos	Lugares de la comarca
Carriches	La Encina	Val Sto Domingo, 2 leguas
Casarrubios	Batres	La Cabeza, Zarzuela, Batres, El Alamo
El Espinoso	La Piedra Escrita	Lugares a la redonda, Robledo del Mazo
*Illescas (hospital)	La Caridad	De toda España (1562–)
Lominchar (Franciscans)	La Oliva	De otros que estan cerca; Recas
Orgaz	El Socorro	De la comarca
Pepino	Valdeencinas	Lugares de la ronda
Puente del Arzobispo	Bienvenida	Pueblos comarcanos; Valdeverdeja
San Martín de Valdepusa	La Bienvenida	Toda esta comarca
San Pablo (Augustinians)	La Fuensanta	Pueblos comarcanos en procesion
San Silvestre	La Fuensanta	Quismondo, Val S.D., Caudilla, Novés
Talavera la Reina	El Prado	Lugares comarcanos
El Toboso	Los Remedios	Gente de toda esta tierra
*Toledo	Cathedral	
*Toledo	La Estrella	Muchos lugares; de lexos tierras
Toledo (pc San Augustin)	La Gracia	
Velada	La Gracia	Eight villages in 11-km. radius
Villarrubia de Santiago (Biezma)	Castellar	Toda la comarca
	Saints	
Buzarabajo (despoblado)	S. Benito	Peromoro, Arcicollar
Cardiel	S. Benito	Cardiel, Nombela

Shrines in Toledo (present province)

Town	Shrine	Villages That Go
Escalonilla (parish church)	S. Germán relics	Cure forasteros dia S. Germán
Hurtado	S. Juan/Porta Latina	Caudilla, Gerindote
(*)La Guardia	Niño de la Guardia	Legend under Tembleque
*Maqueda (Frailes de la Sisla)	Sta. Ana	Novés, Alcabón, Maqueda, Val S.D. otros muchos
Rodillas (despoblado)	Santisteban	Caudilla, Huecas
?	la Magdalena	Huecas
	Unknown	
Argance	?	Huecas
Cubillete (pc, despoblado?)	?	Puebla de Montalbán

The following shrines may have had a regional devotion at the time, but the reports do not mention them as such: Na. Sra. del Sagrario in the Toledo Cathedral, San Eugenio in Toledo Cathedral, Niño de la Guardia.

The Talavera report lists the following shrines or chapels, with distance from the town:

Na. Sra. de Valdelonguo	4 l.	Na. Sra. de la Alcoba	1 l.	
Na. Sra. del Espino	5 l.	Santiago de Zarzuela	5 l.	
Na. Sra. de Piedra Escrita	3 l.	Santiago de la Dehesa	3 l.	
Na. Sra. de Gamonal	4 l.	San Simón	15 l.	
Na. Sra. de la Oliva	7 l.	San Bartolomé la Rana	16 l.	
Na. Sra. de Tortolas	3 l.	Santa Coloma	½ l.	

Shrines in Madrid (present province)

Town	Shrine	Villages That Go
	Marian	
Alcalá	El Val	Buges
Cubas	La Cruz	Forasteros de muchas y otras partes
*Fuencarral	Valverde	Madrid y otras muchas partes; novenas

Town	Shrine	Villages That Go
*Madrid	Atocha	Alameda, cures from region
Móstoles	Arroyo de Vinas	Arroyo de Molinos, Sacedón, Zarzuela, Odón, Navalcarnero
*Santorcaz	Ocalles	Una de las principales que haya en Castilla extramuros
*Talamanca	La Fuensanta	De toda la tierra; Madrid y otras partes
Paracuellos	Belvis	Villanueva de Fuente el Fresno
Villar del Olmo	La Antigua	El Olmeda
	Christ	
Torrejón de la Calzada (p. church)	Crucifijo	Muchas gentes de la comarca
	Saints	
Alcorcón	Sto. Domingo de la Ribota	Muchos lugares del contorno
*Boadilla del Monte	S. Babiles (tomb)	De muchas partes; Carabanchel de Arriba
Chamartín	La Magdalena	Fuencarral, Hortaleza, Canillas
Húmera	S. Pedro de Meaque	Carabanchel de Arriba
Lucero	S. Andrés	Móstoles, Odón, Sacedón
Morata (parish church)	S. Blas (dedo)	Pueblos comarcanos, dia S. Blas
Villarejo de Salvanés	S. Pedro de Salvanés	De toda esta comarca; Carabaña (agua)

Stos. Justo y Pastor may have had a regional cult at the time from their tombs in Alcalá, but the reports do not mention it. The classification of Atocha as regional is based on contemporary miracles in the shrine miracle books.

SHRINES IN GUADALAJARA (PRESENT PROVINCE)

Town	Shrine	Villages That Go
	Marian	
Auñón	El Madroñal	Comarca
Córcoles (Cistercians)	Monsalud	Comarca cures
Hontova (bel. to Sta. Ana of Tendilla)	Los Llanos	Cf. Renera
Pioz	La Mata	Pueblos comarcanos en tiempo de necesidad
*Tendilla (Franciscan Recollects)	La Salceda	De largas partes; Reyno de Toledo

SHRINES IN GUADALAJARA (PRESENT PROVINCE)

Town	Shrine	Villages That Go
Uceda (parish church)	La Varga	Reyno de Toledo
*Valdelloso	La Fuensanta	Infinita gente en toda tiempo
Zorita de los Canes	La Oliva	Almonacid
*Hita (Benedictines)	Sopetrán	Humanes, Robledillo (probably many more)
	Christ	
*Bustares (mountain top)	Sto. Rey de la Magestad	De muchas partes, grandisima devocion
	Saints	
Almoguera (parish church)	S. Xristobal (relics)	Comarcales for rain
Alvares	Sta. Ana	Formerly from as far as Seville
Azuqueca (convent)	S. Juan	Buges (M)
Cañizar	S. Vicente	Cofrades del cabildo . . . de diversas partes
Pioz	S. Roque	Pueblos comarcanos en tiempo de necesidad
Pozo de Guad. (parish church)	S. Mateo (stone)	Villa y comarca
Valdesaz (parish church)	S. Macario	De lejos
*Valtablado del Río (parish church)	S. Vicente (relic)	Nueve lugares voto; hasta 29 para agua
Peñamora	S. Miguel?	Robledillo (2 ½ l.)

Other strong devotions, possibly district shrines:

Almuña (parish church)		Cristo crucificado de gran devocion
Yebra	S. Bartolomé	De mucha devocion
Tendilla (monastery)	Sta. Ana	Previously regional; no indications in reports

SHRINES IN CUENCA (PRESENT PROVINCE)

Town	Shrine	Villages That Go
	Marian	
*El Cañavete	La Concepción de Trascastillo	Reinos de Valencia, Aragon, Murcia, Toledo, Sevilla y de casi toda Castilla le Vieja
Iniesta	La Consolación	De muchas partes
Loranca (Huete)	El Socorro	Carrascosa del Campo, Huete, Val de Paraiso, Langa

Town	Shrine	Villages That Go
Santa María de los Llanos (parish)		Comarca, Las Pedroñeras, Las Mesas
*Tarancón	Riansares	Villa, comarca, y de fuera lexos y de Burgos y otras partes
Tresjuncos	Atalaya	Villaescusa de Haro
	Saints	
Carrascosa del Campo	Sta. Ana	Lugares de la comarca
El Pedernoso	Sta. Ana	Toda esta comarca, novenas, velar
Villarrubio (parish church)	S. Silvestre (relic)	Mucha gente de muchas partidas Dec 31; and for storms

Other strong devotions, possibly district shrines:

Belmonte	N. Sa. de la Gracia	Capellan
Quintería de Sta. María de Poyos	N. Sa. la Soterrana	De gran devocion

SHRINES IN ALBACETE (PRESENT PROVINCE)

*La Roda	N. Sa. del Remedio de Fuensanta	De los lugares de su redondez de 15 a 20 leguas en su contorno; 10,000 personas, 900 carros la fiesta

SHRINES IN CIUDAD REAL (PRESENT PROVINCE)

Town	Shrine	Villages That Go
	Marian	
Alcubillas, Villahermosa	La Carrasca	Alhambra
Cabezarados	Finibus Terrae	Pozuelos, El Corral
Campo de Criptana	Criptana	Comarcanos, novenas
Ciudad Real	Alarcos	Alcolea de Almodóvar
Daimiel	Las Cruces	Daimiel, Torralba
Fuencaliente	Fuencaliente	
La Membrilla	El Castillo	Villa y comarca, capellan
Puertollano	La Gracia	Pueblos comarcanos, Almodóvar del Campo, Argamasilla
Sta. Cruz de Mudela	Las Virtudes	De toda la comarca, Torrenueva
Terrinches	Luciana	Pueblos comarcanos
Torre de Juan Abad	La Vega	Todos los pueblos comarcanos letanias, novenas
Villarrubia de los Ajos	La Sierra	Mucha gente de las comarcas

SHRINES IN CIUDAD REAL (PRESENT PROVINCE)

The shrine of Our Lady of Prado in Ciudad Real had a regional influence at the time, although there is no mention of it in the reports.

Town	Shrine	Villages That Go
	Christ	
Malagón	Santiespiritu	Muy frecuentada de pueblos comarcanos; clerigo
	Saints	
Cabezarados (parish church)	S. Juan	Tirteafuera (rogation)
Luciana	Sta. María Egipciaca	Villa y comarca; Aventoja, Piedrabuena

Locations and Sources of Relics, 1575–1580

RELICS FOR WHICH THERE IS SOME INDICATION OF ORIGIN

Town	Approximate time of arrival in village		Sources		Origin
			Direct	Indirect	
Toledo					
Almonacid	1567–1568	11,000 Virgins			
Cabañas (Sagra)	1575	Various	Pero Gonz. de Mendoza (benef. church, treasurer of Toledo cathedral)		Directly from Rome
Camarena	?	Various	Vecina from Italy		Directly from Rome
Camarena	?	Various	Vecino		Directly from Rome
Escalonilla	15th?	Germán et al.	Passing pilgrim died		
Lillo		Various	Bartolomé de la Isla (nat.) (capellan de S.M.)		Directly from Rome
Magán		Various			
Mocejón	ca. 1520	Various	Juan Alemán, sec. Emperador		
Puebla/Mont. (convent)	1530–?	2 of 11,000 Virgins			

RELICS FOR WHICH THERE IS SOME INDICATION OF ORIGIN

Town	Approximate time of arrival in village		Sources		Origin
			Direct	Indirect	
Talavera		Many different	"Un religioso"	Pius V	Catacombs of Rome
Villanueva/Alcardete (*ermita* Conc.)	1569–1570	Various			Rome
Cuenca					
Belmonte (Jes. coll.)	15??	Various	Jesuits		
Castillo de Garci Muñoz	16th c.	Bernardino	Francisco de Milán		
Palomares/Campo		Ursula et al.	Pedro de Salazar (de la capilla de S.M.)		
Mazarulleque	Not long before 1569	Various	Diego Pérez de Lerma (clerigo)		
		Various	Pedro del Castillo (ermitaño)		Directly from Rome
Ciudad Real					
Almodóvar/Campo	ca. 1577	Various	Juan Fernández, capellan de S.M. (nat.)		(Rome?)
Puertollano	1557	Various	Juan Fernández, capellan Emper. (nat.)		Rome
Madrid					
Arganda	Probably within 20–30 years	Various	Bartolomé de la Higuera (nat.) (clerigo)		"Letra francesa"

Place	Date	Relic	Source	Patron	Origin
Fuenlabrada	Recently	Various	ermitaño of Fregacedos		Directly from Rome
San Sebastián/Reyes	16th c.	Sebastián	Princess/Portugal		
San Sebastián/Reyes	Recently	Various	Lorenzo del Campo (tiniente de cura)		"Vocablos alemanes"
Santos/Humosa	16th?	Various			
Guadalajara					
Alcocer	14th c.	Various	Cardenal D. Gil de Albornoz		(Rome?)
Fuentelaencina	1575	Various	Valentín Josep (nat.) Jesuit	Reina María	Spira (Flanders) (1570)
Fuentelaencina	ca. 1552	Various	Alonso del Puey (beneficiado)		Directly from Rome
Almoguera	ca. 1460	Various Cristobal	Revelation to clerigo (buried under altar)		
Humanes	16th c.	Benedicta	Da. Mariana de Peralta (muger Fran. de Heraso, sec. de S.M.)		
Tendilla (pc)	1575	Various	Fr. Juan Baptista (nat.)	Reina Isabel	
(Mon. Sta. Ana)		Various	Tomás López (lizen.)	Pope	Directly from Rome
Uceda	1574	2 of 11,000 Virgins	Juan de Bolea (nat.) (asst. to Duque de Alba)	Carmelitas	Groeninga
Yebra	16th c.	Various	Fray Melchor de Yebra (Vic. Descalzas Madrid)	Princess Port. Da. Juana	
Fuentenovilla		Various	Passing clerigo who died		
Valtablado del Río		Vicente	From monastery Orden de Santiago?		From Rome

Relics With No Indication of Origin

Town	Relics	Bull? Certification?
Toledo		
Añover	Bartolomé, hair of Mary	
Estrella	Various	
Magán	Various	App. gobernador Arch. D. Gómez Tello Girón (recent)
Lominchar (Franciscans)	Various	
Olías	Blas	
Puebla/Montalbán	11,000 Virgins	Owned by Count
San Pablo (Augustinians)	Various	
Sta. Cruz/Zarza	Various	
Toledo	Various, esp. of patron saints of parish churches and cathedral	
Cuenca		
Belmonte (Domin. convent)	Espinas corona Cristo	
Villarrubio	Silvestre	
Uclés (Convent)	Many	
Ciudad Real		
Calzada	Quiteria	
Campo Criptana	Lignum Crucis	
Castellar/Stgo	Benito	
Fuencaliente	11,000 Virgins	
Tirteafuera	Lignum Crucis	
Valenzuela	Martín	
Madrid		
Batres	Various	
Boadilla del Monte	Babiles	
El Campo Real	Various	
Canillas	Blas	
Colmenar Viejo	Blas, 11,000 Virgins	
Daganzo	Blas	
Estremera	Zenón y compañeros	"Hay testimonio"

Town	Relics	Bull? Certification?
Loeches	Blas, Lorenzo	
Morata	Blas	
Santorcaz	Blas	"Aprobada por el Sumo Pontifice"
Talamanca	Blas, Lorenzo	
Valverde	Unidentified	
Villalbilla	Various	
Villar	Blas	
Guadalajara		
Atanzón	Blas	
Budia	Blas	
Pareja	Blas, Lignum Crucis	
Valdesaz	Macario	"Una bula de perdones de su Santidad"
Almonacid de Zorita	Various	
Cifuentes (Domin. convent)	Blas	
Cogolludo	Various	
Córcoles (Cistercians)	Various, 11,000 Virgins	
Pastrana	Over 3,000	
Uceda	Blas, Valentín, others	

Relics of Local Saints (See also Chap. 4, n. 11)

Uceda (in ermita)	"La cabeza de un hombre santo que se llamo Ysidro, hombre de santa vide que se dice fue alli hermitaño."
Cifuentes, et al.	San Blas (local?)
Valdesaz (G)	Macario
Santos/Humosa (M)	Bones of holy hermit Pedro (lived before 1491)
Cubas (M)	In Convent, body of María [Juana] de la Cruz
Boadilla del Monte (M)	San Babiles (local?)
Illán de Vacas (T)	Sant Illán
Uclés (Cuenca)	Pero Alonso de Valderacete
Ciruelos (Tol)	Burial place of Fray Reimundo; relic also in El Campo Real, Madrid
Toledo	Sta. Leocadia, San Eugenio, San Ildefonso
Toledo	Fray Reimundo, María de Ajofrín, Conde de Orgaz
Valenzuela (CR)	Relic of Fray Diego (who also lived in convent of Salceda)
Alcalá	Justo y Pastor, relics brought 1568
Alcalá	Fray Diego

Sources and Abbreviations

RELACIONES TOPOGRÁFICAS

There are few reports from the region now in the provinces of Cáceres, Badajoz, and Albacete. In this study only the reports from the five central provinces of New Castile are considered, with the exception of the shrine of Remedio de Fuensanta (La Roda, Alb.).
I have used the published editions of the reports. I cite them using the following abbreviations:

G I-VI Juan Catalina García, Manuel Pérez Villamil, *Relaciones topográficas de España* (*Memorial histórico español*, XLI, 1903; XLII, 1903; XLIII, 1905; XLV, 1912; XLVI, 1914; XLVII, 1915). While this transcription was made from an orthographically impure text, Noël Salomon (*La Campagne de Nouvelle Castille à la fin du XVIe siècle*, Paris, SEVPEN, 1964, p. 12), who has compared it with the original in the Escorial, avers that the changes do not affect the content. I have checked every quotation with the originals and found occasional misreadings and omissions, which I have corrected.

Cu I-II Eusebio Julián Zarco Bacas y Cuevas, *Relaciones de pueblos del obispado de Cuenca hechas por orden de Felipe II*, in *Biblioteca Diocesana conquense*, I, II, Cuenca, 1927. Includes some villages in the present provinces of Guadalajara and Albacete. Copies in BNM and at the University of California at Berkeley.

M Carmelo Viñas y Mey, Ramón Paz, *Relaciones histórico-geográfico-estadísticas de los pueblos de España hechas por iniciativa de Felipe II* (*Provincia de Madrid*), Madrid, CSIC, 1949.

These transcriptions and those of Zarco Bacas y Cuevas are excellent.

T I-III   Carmelo Viñas y Mey, Ramón Paz, *Relaciones histórico-geográfico-estadísticas de los pueblos de España hechas por iniciativa de Felipe II (Reino de Toledo)*, pt. 1, 1951; pt. 2 (2 vols.), 1963. The two volumes of part 2 have their pages numbered consecutively; I treat them as if they were three volumes.

CR   Carmelo Viñas y Mey, Ramón Paz, *Relaciones histórico-geográfico-estadísticas de los pueblos de España hechas por iniciativa de Felipe II (Provincia de Ciudad Real)*, 1971.

A word of caution to users of the above volumes: the editors assigned certain villages to provinces incorrectly; see Salomon for correct assignment.

See Figure 13 for a reproduction of the first of three pages of the 1578 questionnaire.

SYNODAL CONSTITUTIONS

The best list of Spanish synods and synodal constitutions, manuscript and in print, is that compiled by L. Ferrer in volume 4 of *Diccionario de historia eclesiástica de España*, pp. 2487–2494 (CSIC Madrid, 1976). Even in that compilation there are some errors and omissions. Locating copies of the constitutions is at least as difficult as finding whether or not they exist. José Simón Díaz, *Bibliografía regional y local de España I: Impresos localizados* (siglos XV-XVII) (CSIC Madrid, 1976, Cuadernos Bibliográficos 33) not only gives complete titles for most of those printed, but also lists libraries where they can be found as well as call numbers. The best collection is in the Biblioteca Nacional in Madrid, and additional copies are to be found in the libraries of the Real Academia Española, the Real Academia de la Historia, and the Palacio Real, not all of which are catalogued in Simón

❦INSTRVCCION Y MEMORIA
de las relaciones que se han de hazer y embiar a su Mageſtad para la deſcripcion y hiſtoria de los pueblos de Eſpaña, que manda ſe haga para honra y ennoblecimiento deſtos Reynos.

RIMERAMENTE los Comiſſarios y perſonas a quien a ſu Mageſtad diere cargo deſto, nombraran dos perſonas, o mas inteligentes y curioſas de los pueblos donde reſiden, que hagan la relacion dellos, lo mas cũplida y cierta que ſe pueda, por el tenor de los capitulos de ſta inſtruccion y memoria.

Y como Comiſſarios diputados para la dicha deſcripcion, embiaran a cada pueblo y Concejo, aſſi de los de ſu juridicion, como de los eximidos della, y hechos villas, y a todos los de ſeñorio qualeſquier que ſean, que cayeren dentro de los terminos de ſu juridicion, y fueren coterminos y vezinos a ella, vna inſtruccion y memoria impreſſa deſtas, mandando a los dichos Concejos en nõbre de ſu Mageſtad que luego nombren dos perſonas, o mas de las que mas noticia tuuieren de las coſas del pueblo, y ſu tierra, para que juntos hagan la relacion del, por el orden y tenor de los capitulos deſta inſtrucciõ y memoria. y queriendo he chaſe la embien ſin dilacion juntamente con la dicha inſtruccion.

Y porque no ſea neceſſario hazerſe en vn pueblo la dicha relacion mas de vna vez, ſi en alguno donde ya ſe uuiere hecho, ſe boluiere a pedir embiarſe ha al Comiſſario o Comiſſarios q̃ la pidierẽ, vna fe y teſtimonio de auerſe ya hecho y embiado a quien la uuiere pedido, y ſi dos Comiſſarios o mas cada vno por ſu parte pidieren relacion de alguno, o algunos pueblos donde no ſe uuiere hecho, embiarſe ha la relacion al primero q̃ la pidiere, y a los otros darſe les ha vna fe y teſtimonio de auerſe ya hecho y embiado al que primero la pidio.

Y como los dichos Comiſſarios fueren recogiendo las dichas relaciones, o las fees, y teſtimonios de auerſe hecho las yran embiando a ſu Mageſtad con las inſtrucciones impreſſas quando no ſean meneſter para embiarlas a otros pueblos.

LAS perſonas a quien en los pueblos ſe diere cargo de hazer la relacion dellos, reſponderan a los capitulos de la memoria que ſe ſigue, o a los que d'ellos uuiere que reſpõder por la orden y forma ſiguiente.

Primeramente en vn papel aparte pondran por cabeça de la relacion que ſe hiziere el dia, mes, y año de la fecha della, con los nombres de las perſonas que ſe hallaren a hazerla, y el nombre del Comiſſario, o perſona que les uuiere embiado eſta inſtruccion.

Y auiendo leydo atentamẽte el primer capitulo de la dicha memoria, y viſto lo que ay que dezir del dicho pueblo conforme a el, eſcriuirã lo que uuiere en vn capitulo a parte, y deſpues boluerã a leer el miſmo capitulo para verſi queda algo a que reſponder, y no lo auiendo paſſaran al ſegundo, y auiendole leydo como el primero, ſi uuiere algo que dezir, en el haran otro capitulo dello, y ſino dexarle han ſin hazer mencion del, y paſſaran al tercero, y por eſta orden al quarto, y a los demas, haſta acabar los de leer todos poniendo al principio de cada vno el numero que en la margen deſta memoria tuuiere, para que ſe entienda al que reſponde, ſin que ſea neceſſario referir lo contenido en el.

Reſpondiendo a todo breue y claramente, affirmando por cierto lo q̃ lo fuere, y por dudoſo lo que eſtuiere en duda, de manera que en todo aya la verdad que ſe requiere para la deſcripcion y hiſtoria de los pueblos, q̃ es lo que en eſta diligencia ſe pretende, ſin tener fin a otra coſa mas de ſolo a ſaber las coſas notables y ſeñaladas de que los pueblos ſe pueden honrar para la hiſtoria d'llos.

Figure 13. The first of three pages of the 1578 questionnaire. Biblioteca del Escorial.

Díaz's bibliography. Most of the constitutions are printed in Castilian. A few, especially the early ones from the Catalonian dioceses, are in Latin. Of particular interest are compilations like that of Burgos (1503? or 1511), which reprints all previous constitutions.

The use of the constitutions to deduce from their prohibitions aspects of religiosity in a given diocese is time-consuming. Constitutions were patched together from previous laws of the diocese, the constitutions of other dioceses, and chapters newly written. The dioceses from which constitutions are borrowed may be neighboring ones, especially within archdioceses (e.g., Cuenca may borrow from Toledo), but they are often dioceses in far corners of Andalusia or Galicia where the bishop previously served. The Constitutions of Segovia of 1586 were compiled from previous Segovian constitutions and those of Guadix, Salamanca, and Burgos. Hence before any particular wording of a prohibition of lay or clerical behavior can be taken as referring to customs in the diocese at a given time, one must consult virtually all previous printed constitutions, of that diocese and elsewhere, to see whether it has been borrowed. A borrowed constitution is weaker evidence than a newly written one for several reasons. In the first place, its specific wording refers to another diocese or another time. In the second place, a bishop might have included it in his constitutions not because a given problem had arisen, but because it might arise, or because it might have arisen.

One cannot always trust the marginal notations, common after 1580, which give the source of a particular chapter. Generally the marginal notations tell what bishop first proposed the text in the diocese, but not, as one might think, the author of the text, for they do not usually reveal borrowings from other dioceses.

I consulted the following constitutions, mostly of central Spain. Dates in parentheses are dates of publication (if different from year of synod). All are to be found in the Biblioteca Nacional, unless otherwise noted:

Astorga 1533
Avila 1481 (R. Ac. Esp.), 1533 (1534) (Bib. Pal.), 1549
 (1556)
Badajoz 1501, 1560
Burgos 1503? (Comp.), 1511, 1575 (1577)
Calahorra 1553 (1555)
Córdoba 1520 (1521), 1563
Cuenca 1531 (Arch. Dioc. Cuenca), 1566 (1571), 1602
 (1603), 1626
Guadix 1554 (1556) (R. Ac. Hist.)
Granada 1572 (1573)
Jaén 1511
Málaga 1572 (1573)
Osma 1536 (1538)
Palencia 1500 (1501) (Comp.) (Bib. Pal.), 1545 (1548)
Priorato de Santiago de Uclés 1578 (Arch. Hist. Nac.
 Cod. 307B, Ms. folios numbered in pencil) (Orden de
 Santiago)
Santiago 1576 (1579)
Segovia 1472 (repr. 1965), 1586
Sigüenza 1532 (1534) (R.A.H.), 1608 (1647) (R.A.H.),
 1655 (1660)
Toledo 1498, 1536, 1566 (1568), 1583, 1601

RELACIONES DEL CARDENAL LORENZANA

A *Legajo* with this title in the Diocesan Archive of Toledo
contains responses from about 370 priests, some reporting
on more than one town. The shortest is one side of a page;
the longest, that of Argamasilla de Calatrava, is eighty-four
pages. Lorenzana had the originals transcribed and—apparently—somewhat summarized. The manuscript résumés in
the Biblioteca Municipal de Toledo include 165 responses
for which the originals have been lost or mislaid. The résumés do not include the dates of the responses. They are
to be found in MS 84 (Vicaría General de Toledo), MS
85 (Vicaría General de Alcalá de Henares), and MS 86

(Vicarías Foráneas). A more detailed description of the résumé books can be read in Francisco Esteve Barba, *Catálogo de la colección de manuscritos Borbón-Lorenzana*, Biblioteca Pública de Toledo (Madrid, 1942). See Figure 14 for a reproduction of the 1782 questionnaire.

OTHER SOURCES

ADC	Archivo Diocesano de Cuenca
ADT	Archivo Diocesano de Toledo
AHN	Archivo Histórico Nacional
AIA	*Archivo Ibero-Americano*
BNM	Biblioteca Nacional Madrid
CS	Constituciones Sinodales
DHEE	*Diccionario de la historia eclesiástica de España*
MHE	*Memorial histórico español*

INTERROGATORIO,

A cuyos puntos deben responder los Señores Vicarios Jueces Eclesiásticos, y Curas Párrocos, cada uno en su distrito lo que comprehende.

I. Si es Ciudad, Villa, ó Lugar, á qué Vicaría pertenece, y si es Realengo, de Señorío, ó mixto, y el número de vecinos.

II. Si es cabeza de Vicaría, ó Partido, Anexo, y de qué Parroquia: si tiene Conventos, decir de qué Orden; como también si dentro de la población, ó extramuros hay algun Santuario, é Imagen célebre, declarar su nombre, y distancia: asimismo la advocacion de la Parroquial.

III. Se pondrá quántas leguas dista de la Metrópoli Toledo, quántas de la cabeza de la Vicaría, y quántos quartos de legua de los Lugares confinantes; expresando en este último particular los que están al Norte, al Mediodia, Levante, ó Poniente respecto del Lugar que responde, y quántas leguas ocupa su jurisdicion.

IV. Dirá si está orilla de algun rio, arroyo, ó laguna, si á la derecha, ó la izquierda de él baxando agua abaxo: dónde nacen estas aguas, en donde y con qué se juntan, y cómo se llaman: si tienen Puentes de piedra, de madera, ó Barcas, con sus nombres, y por qué Lugares pasan.

V. Expresarán los nombres de las Sierras dónde empiezan á subir, dónde á baxar, con un juicio razonable del tiempo para pasarlas, ó de su magnitud; declarando los nombres de sus Puertos,

tos, y en dónde se ligan, y pierden, ó conservan sus nombres estas cordilleras con otras.

VI. Qué Montes, Bosques y Florestas tiene el Lugar, de qué matas poblados; cómo se llaman, á qué ayre caen, y quánto se extienden.

VII. Quándo, y por quién se fundó el Lugar: qué armas tiene, y con qué motivo: los sucesos notables de su historia, hombres ilustres que ha tenido, y los edificios, ó castillos que aún conserva.

VIII. Quáles son los frutos mas singulares de su terreno; los que carece: quál la cantidad á que ascienden cada año.

IX. Manufacturas y Fábricas que tiene, de qué especie, y por quién establecidas: qué cantidad elaboran cada año: qué artífices sobresalientes en ellas: qué inventos, instrumentos, ó máquinas ha encontrado la industria para facilitar los trabajos.

X. Quales son las Ferias, ó Mercados, y los dias en que se celebran: qué géneros se comercian, extraen y reciben en cambio: de dónde, y para dónde: sus pesos y medidas, Compañias, y Casas de cambio.

XI. Si tiene Estudios generales, particulares, sus fundaciones, método, y tiempo en que se abren: qué Facultades enseñan, y quales con mas adelantamiento, y los que en ellas se han distinguido.

XII. Qual es su gobierno político, y económico: si tiene privilegios, y si erigió en favor de la enseñanza pública algun Seminario, Colegio,

gio, Hospital, Casa de Recoleccion y Piedad.

XIII. Las enfermedades que comunmente se padecen, y cómo se curan: número de muertos y nacidos, para poder hacer juicio de la salubridad del Pueblo.

XIV. Si tiene aguas minerales, medicinales, ó de algun beneficio para las fábricas: salinas de piedra, ó agua, canteras, piedras preciosas, minas, de qué metales, árboles, y yerbas extraordinarias.

Finalmente todo quanto pueda conducir á ilustrar el Pueblo, y que no se haya prevenido en este Interrogatorio.

NOTA.

Procurarán los Señores Vicarios formar unas especies de Mapas, ó Planos de sus respectivas Vicarías, donde pondrán las Ciudades, Villas, Lugares, Aldeas, Granjas, Caserías, Ermitas, Ventas, Molinos, Despoblados, Rios, Arroyos, Sierras, Bosques, Caminos, &c. que aunque no están hechos como de mano de un Profesor, nos contentamos con sola una idea, ó borron del terreno, porque lo arreglarémos dándole aquí la última mano.

Esta misma prevencion se hace á los Señores Curas Párrocos, porque me consta hay muchos aficionados á Geografía, y cada uno de estos puede demostrar muy bien lo que hay al contorno de dos leguas de sus Iglesias.

Figure 14. The questionnaire sent out by Cardinal Lorenzana in 1782. Archivo Diocesano de Toledo.

Notes

CHAPTER 1. INTRODUCTION.

1. Marcel Bataillon, *Erasmo y España: Estudios sobre la historia espiritual del siglo XVI* (Mexico, Fondo de Cultura Económica, 1966); Augustin Redondo, *Antonio de Guevara et l'Espagne de son temps* (Geneva, Librairie Droz, 1976); Luis Salas Ballust, introductions to *Obras completas* of Juan de Avila (Madrid, Biblioteca de Autores Cristianos, 1952–1953); Tomás Marín, various studies on Bishop Díaz de Luco, DHEE 2:750–753; J. I. Tellechea, *El Arzobispo Carranza y su tiempo* (2 vols., Madrid, 1968); Melquiades Andrés Martín, *Los recogidos* (Madrid, Fundación Universitaria, 1976); additional bibliography in II Congreso de Espiritualidad de Salamanca, *Corrientes espirituales en la España del siglo XVI* (Barcelona, Juan Flors, 1963). Before completing this manuscript I had not been able to consult Julio Caro Baroja, *Las formas complejas de la vida religiosa: Religión, sociedad y caracter en la España de los siglos XVI y XVII* (Madrid, Akal, 1978).

2. Mary R. O'Neil, "Religion versus Superstition: An Examination of Historical Interpretations of Popular Religion" (unpublished manuscript).

3. For the Spanish Inquisition in general, Bartolomé Bennassar, *L'Inquisition espagnole (xve–xvie siècles)* (Paris, Hachette, 1979) gives a bibliography of the most recent works. A. Domínguez Ortiz, *La clase social de los conversos en Castilla en la edad moderna* (Madrid, CSIC, 1955); Julio Caro Baroja, *Los Judíos en la España moderna y contemporánea* (3 vols., Madrid, Arión, 1962); Haim Beinart, ed., *Records of the Trials of the Spanish Inquisition in Ciudad Real* (Jerusalem, National Academy of Sciences and Humanities, 1974–); Carlo Ginzburg, *I Benandanti: Stregoneria e culti agrari tra Cinquecento e Seicento* (Torino, Einaudi, 1966), and *Il formaggio e i vermi: Il cosmo di un mugnaio del '500* (Torino, Einaudi, 1976) .

4. Michel Vovelle, *Piété baroque et déchristianisation en Pro-

vence au XVIIIe siècle (Paris, Plon, 1973), and (with Gaby Vovelle) *Vision de la mort et de l'au-delà en Provence du XVe au XXe siècle* (Cahier des Annales, 29, Paris, A. Colin, 1970); Jeanne Ferté, *La Vie religieuse dans les campagnes parisiennes, 1622–1695* (Paris, Vrin, 1962); Louis Pérouas, *Le Diocèse de La Rochelle de 1648 à 1724; sociologie et pastorale* (Paris, S.E.V.P.E.N., 1964); Jean Delumeau et al., *La Mort des pays de Cocagne* (Serie Études, 12, Paris, University of Paris, 1976).

5. Emanuel Le Roy Ladurie, *Montaillou, village occitain de 1294 à 1324* (Paris, Gallimard, 1975); Richard Trexler, "Florentine Religious Experience: The Sacred Image," *Studies in the Renaissance* 19 (1972) 7–41, and *Florence in Formal Array: The Public Life of a Renaissance City* (New York, Academic Press, 1980).

6. Fermín Caballero, *Discursos leídos ante la Real Academia de la Historia* (Madrid, 1866), 12–13.

7. In the revised questionnaire of 1578 the same questions with minor changes were numbered 40 and 41; CR xix, xxiv.

8. T III 492.

9. Fundamental works for the rural history of this area: Noël Salomon, *La Campagne de Nouvelle Castille à la fin du XVIe siècle* (Paris, S.E.V.P.E.N., 1964); Julio González, *Repoblación de Castilla la Nueva* (2 vols., Madrid, Univ. Complutense, 1975, 1976); Modesto Ulloa, *La hacienda real de Castilla en el reinado de Felipe II* (rev. ed., Madrid, Fund. Univ. Esp., 1977); Bartolomé Bennassar, *Valladolid au siècle d'or* (Paris, Mouton, 1967). Unless otherwise noted, sources for information that follows on individual towns are their responses to the questionnaire.

10. T III 506.

11. T III 525. Linda Martz, Julio Porres, *Toledo y los toledanos en 1561* (Toledo, CSIC, 1974).

12. C. J. Bishko, "The Castilian as Plainsman: The Medieval Ranching Frontier in La Mancha and Extremadura," in A. Lewis and T. F. McGann, *The New World Looks at Its History* (Austin, University of Texas Press, 1963) 47–69; Michael R. Weisser, *The Peasants of the Montes* (Chicago, University of Chicago Press, 1976).

13. Cu II 41; Carla Rahn Phillips, *Ciudad Real 1500–1750:*

Growth, Crisis, and Readjustment in the Spanish Economy (Cambridge, Harvard University Press, 1979).

14. Salomon, *Campagne*, 97–102, 130–132, 279ff.; Weisser, *Peasants*, 61; Paulino Iradiel Murugarren, *Evolución de la industria textil castellana XIII–XVI* (Acta Salamanticensia, filosofía y letras, 84, Salamanca, 1974).

15. Salomon, *Campagne*, 258, 268; his analysis substantially agrees with that of Carmelo Viñas y Mey, *El problema de la tierra en la España de los siglos XVI–XVII* (Madrid, CSIC, 1941).

16. These figures and Table 1.2 are adapted from Annie Molinié-Bertrand, "Le Clergé dans le royaume de Castille à la fin du XVIe siècle," *Revue d'histoire économique et sociale* 51 (1973) 5–53 (table 1, p. 12). Many clergy, of course, were not parish priests. See A. Domínguez Ortiz, *La sociedad española en el siglo XVII*, vol. 2, *El estamento eclesiástico* (Madrid, CSIC, 1970).

17. Rogelio Duocastella, *Análisis sociológico del catolicismo español* (Barcelona, Nova Terra, 1967) 24.

18. For Madrid, Jeronimo de Quintana, *Historia de la antiguedad, nobleza, y grandeza de la villa de Madrid* (Madrid, Imprenta del Reyno, 1629); I have used the 1954 edition of E. Varela Hervías (Madrid, Artes Gráficas Municipales) 871–944. For Alcalá, Huete, Almagro, and Yepes, see Molinié-Bertrand; for Ciudad Real, see Phillips.

19. A. Redondo, *Antonio de Guevara*, 94–99.

20. CR 611; cf. Pedro de Alcoçer, *Historia de Toledo* (1554) cxvii: "que aunque militan debaxo de regla y orden voluntaria, sin clausura, biuen vida honesta y recogida."

21. Communities: Camarena, Talavera, El Toboso (T); Villamayor de Santiago, Uclés, Villaescusa de Haro (Cu); La Solana (CR); Griñón (M); Guadalajara.

22. B. Velasco, "Fundación del convento de terciarias franciscanas de Santa Isabel en Cuellar," AIA 31 (1971) 475–483.

23. T III 547–550, 558.

24. M 299–300, Cu II 28–29, G II 56.

25. M 300.

26. Compiled from Otilio Gómez Parente, *Crónicas franciscanas de España* (vol. 1, Madrid, Editorial Cisneros, 1976) introduction.

27. B. Bennassar, *L'Inquisition espagnole*, 25.
28. William A. Christian, "De los santos a María: Panorama de las devociones a santuarios españoles desde el principio de la Edad Media hasta nuestros días," in C. Lisón Tolosana, ed., *Temas de antropología española* (Madrid, Akal, 1976) 49–106.

CHAPTER 2. VOWS

1. Bandits: La Despernada, M 240; La Roda (Alb.), Cu I 85. Rebels: various references to *comuneros* and fighting at accession of Isabella. Raids from Torija on villages of Guadalajara and Madrid in mid-fifteenth century: Fuencarral, M 258; Berniches, G I 30; Jadraque, G I 266–267; Tendilla, G III 71; Esquivias, T I 401. Aggressions of nobles on peasant communities: Auñón, G I 410; Carrascosa, Cu II 26.
2. G I 221, G I 198; T I 174, M 373, CR 397, CR 83, 86; in Totanés (T III 637) many of the children under eight died until the villagers filled in a swamp.
3. CR 133–134, CR 300, M 126.
4. Juan de Pineda, *Diálogos familiares de la agricultura Cristiana*, ed. Juan Meseguer Fernández (5 vols., Madrid, 1963–1964) 4:253 (written ca. 1578).
5. Alcorcón (1576), M 42. In nearby Getafe they remembered a plague around 1492 preceded by a famine in which they too ate bread made from weeds, and they thought that this plague was worse than that of 1507 (M 291).
6. Plague of 1506–1507: Daimiel, Saceruela, CR; Las Mesas, Torrubia del Campo, Cu; El Cubillo, G; Getafe, Meco, Santorcaz, M; Mesegar, Puebla del Almoradiel, Puebla de Montalbán, Seseña, Totanés, T; and probably Ballesteros, CR (1508) and El Campo Real, M (ca. 1510). The places that reported the dates of these epidemics and invasions are only a small sample of the total number of places affected. Hundreds of villages and towns reported vows to saints because of epidemics and locusts, but gave no dates. The imprecision of these samples of dated vows means that not only were many more places experiencing these same disasters (perhaps ten times as many for recent years, twenty times as many in 1507), but also that the areas in which

they occurred were wider than can be deduced from the samples. Sometimes the respondents gave an exact date for disasters and vows, but most of the time they gave it approximately, usually in even decades, e.g., *habra treinta años*. The dates preceded with "ca." have been calculated from the villagers' estimates of years elapsed and the date of their report. They are probably correct within five years, assuming the villagers were rounding off to the nearest decade.

For the plague of 1506–1507: Charles Gibson, "An Historical Event and Its Interpretation: The Castilian Grain Crisis of 1506–1507," *Social Science History* 2:2, 230–247; Joaquín de Villalba, *Epidemiología Española* (2 vols., Madrid, Mateo Repullés, 1802) 1:129–130. Jordi Nadal, *La población española en los siglos XVI–XX* (Barcelona, Ariel, 1966) 53.

7. Villalba, *Epidemiología*, 1:129–130.

8. In Totanés the disease, dated 1506, was called "pestilencia . . . por otro nombre commun parpellotas" (T III 637).

9. G VI 361.

10. G IV 166.

11. Villalba, *Epidemiología*, 1:154.

12. G IV 323.

13. Cu I 113, 305.

14. Cu I 113; Iuan de Quiñones, *Tratado de las langostas mvy vtil y necessario . . .* (Madrid, Luis Sanchez, 1620) (BNM R-31178); Extremadura, New Castile, and Andalusia still experienced invasions of grasshoppers in the twentieth century—*Enciclopedia universal ilustrada* (Barcelona, 1915) 29:656–662; Z. Waloff, *The Upsurges and Recessions of the Desert Locust Plague: An Historical Survey* (London, Anti-Locust Memoir no. 8, 1966).

15. Villalba, *Epidemiología*, 1:109, 163, 183; Lopez de Corella, *De morbo postulato, vulgo tabardillo* (Zaragoza, 1574); Luis de Toro, *De febris epidemiae et novae quae latine puntularis, vulgo tabardillo et pintas dicitur . . .* (Burgos, 1574). P. Laín Entralgo, *Historia de la medecina moderna y contemporánea* (Barcelona, 1963) 35; G IV 55.

16. Villalba, *Epidemiología*, 1:196; Juan de San Gerónimo, *Memorias 1562–1591* (Colección de Documentos Inéditos

para la Historia de España, 7: 5–442) 335; [Consell de Cents Jurats] *Manual de novells ardits* 5 (Barcelona, Henrich, 1896) 248-249; M 615.

17. For typical examples of terminology, see Valdilecha, M 653; Móstoles, M 397; Valverde, M 659; Cobeña, M 191; and Getafe, M 298. Alonso de Herrera, *Libro de agricultura, que tracta de la labrança y de muchas otras particularidades y prouechos del campo. Nuevamente corregido y añadido por el mesmo* (Medina del campo, Francisco del Canto, 1569) (BNM R/11674) 47v–48r. The book was first issued in 1513 and went through 27 editions, the most recent in 1970 in the Biblioteca de Autores Españoles. I have also used Silverio Planes, *Plagas del campo* (Madrid, 1949).

18. ADC 2050, clérigo de Sevilla, conjuros contra la langosta, 1547; 2340-A-B, clérigo nigromántico, 1557; also 2604 Abia 1559. For priests-magicians in England, see Keith Thomas, *Religion and the Decline of Magic* (New York, Scribners, 1966) 274–275.

19. Martín de Castañega, *Tratado de las supersticiones y hechicerias* (1529) (Madrid, Sociedad de Bibliófilos Españoles, 1946) 91; Pedro Ciruelo, *Reprobacion delas supersticiones y hechizerias* (1538) (Madrid, Colección Joyas Bibliográficas, 1952), Pt. III, Chap. 10; Martín de Azpilcueta Navarro, *Manual de confesores y penitentes* (Estella, Adrian de Anuers, 1566) 628; Gaspar Navarro, *Tribunal de supersticion ladina* (Huesca, 1631) disputa xxxii.

20. Castañega, *Tratado de supersticiones*, chaps. 19 and 22; and Ciruelo, *Reprobacion*, Pt. III, Chap. 9.

21. CS Toledo 1566 (1568) De Sortilegis 73v–74r. In the *Siete partidas*, Alfonso el Sabio encouraged enchantments with good intentions, including "to turn aside a cloud from which hail or fog is descending that it may not injure the crops; or to kill locusts or insects which destroy grain or vines" (pt. 7, title 23, law 3, trans. Samuel Parsons Scott, Chicago, Commerce Clearing House, 1931, p. 1432).

22. The text of the trial is in Julián Zarco Cuevas, *Pleito que se puso en la Abadía de Párraces para el exterminio de la langosta* (Madrid, Archivos, 1932).

23. T III 773–776. They operated at the end of the fifteenth century.

24. Azpilcueta, *Manual* (1566) 90. His exposition is entirely orthodox (cf. Aquinas, *Summa theologica*, pt. 2, quest. 88, *De voti; Siete partidas*, pt. 1, title 8).
25. William A. Christian Jr., *Person and God in a Spanish Valley* (New York, Academic Press, 1972) chap. 3, *passim*.
26. Commutation of vows: *Joannis Maldonati, opuscula quaedam docta simul et elegantia* (Burgos, 1549) 31r-32v; cited in Bataillon, *Erasmo y España*, 616–617. J. Goñi Gaztambide, *Historia de la Bula de la Cruzada en España* (Vitoria, Seminario, 1958). Vows of wives that involved expenditure of their time or money could be abrogated by their husbands. Antonio, archbishop of Florence, *Summa de confessione llamada defecerunt* (Burgos, Fadrique de Basilea, 1499) 62r.
27. Azpilcueta, *Manual*, 105.
28. Ibid., 115.
29. This fear of saints is lampooned by Alfonso de Valdés in his *Diálogo de las cosas ocurridas en Roma* (ed. 1928, 136), who has his retrograde archdeacon say, "No vedes que los sanctos cuyas fiestas quitassedes se indignarian, podria ser que nos viniesse algun gran mal?" Similarly, 197; K. Thomas, *Religion*, 27.
30. M 116, M 123.
31. G I 60, T I 5, G VI 190, T I 301, T II 18, M 253, G VI 354, Cu I 12, CR 144, G I 256.
32. T I 301, T II 87 (ca. 1548).
33. G I 60, G II 479.
34. G I 420, G I 333.
35. T II 385, M 299.
36. G IV 265. Vow was to "Dia santo de Jesus," and Jan. 1 as well as May 10 was observed.
37. G II 244–245.
38. Cu I 363.
39. G III 369.
40. C. M. Abad, "Antiguedad de la fiesta de la Inmaculada Concepción en las iglesias de España," *Miscelánea Comillas* 22: 27–87 (Comillas, 1954); Nazario Pérez, *La Inmaculada y España* (Santander, Sal Terrae, 1954).
41. E. Amann, *Le Protoevangile de Saint Jacques et ses remaniements latins* (Paris, Letouzey et Ane, 1910); J. Dani-

go, "Le Culte de Sainte Anne," *Sanctuaires et Pèlerinages* 9 (1963) 31:49–64.

42. The feast of Saint Anne was observed in the following dioceses. The date given is that of the synod in whose constitutions the feast is listed as obligatory.

Observed	Not observed
Avila 1549	Badajoz 1501
Sigüenza 1532 (but not 1608)	Jaén 1511
	Córdoba 1520
Calahorra 1539 (date instituted)	Cuenca 1531, 1566, 1602, 1626
	Granada 1572
Astorga 1553	Málaga 1573
Guadix 1554 (must attend mass where said, but work is permitted)	Toledo 1583, 1601
	Sigüenza 1608
Segovia 1586	
Santiago 1576 (city only; half day)	
Burgos 1411–1412, 1443 (but not 1399–1404)	

Juan de Robles, *La vida y excelencias r miraglos de santa Anna y dela gloriosa nuestra señora santa Maria fasta la edad de quatorze años: muy deuota y contemplatiuamente copilada* (Seville, Jacobo Cromberger, 1511) BNM R/31. 388, gives several Spanish miracles of Saint Anne, and mentions the shrines of Saint Anne of Tendilla and a chapel operated by the monastery of Saint Ysidro of León, where he was a canon.

43. Pedro Gonçalez de Mendoça, *Historia del Monte Celia de Nuestra Señora de Salceda* (Granada, 1616, 882p) 14–16.

44. CR 106–107.

45. Juan de Avila, "Memorial 1º para Trento," 1551; ed. C. M. Abad in *Miscelánea Comillas* 3 (1945) 37: "Parece que la muchedumbre de las fiestas de holgar se debe restringir; y que, sacados los domingos, no dure la obligacion de las fiestas, sino hasta ser oida Misa maior. Y sera bien dispensar con los arrieros, para que, sin pecado, puedan caminar con sus cargas en el dia de la fiesta, y sin oir Misa; porque todos asi lo hacen."

46. Luis de Zapata, *Miscelánea*, written ca. 1592, *Memorial histórico español* 11 (Madrid, 1856) 472–473.
47. Cu I 270–271; Zapata, *Miscelánea*, 470–472.
48. G II 137.
49. G IV 323.
50. CR 144.
51. Azpilcueta, *Manual*, 121ff.
52. M 578–579.
53. CR 419.
54. Cu I 305.
55. Roch: W. Telfer, *The Treasure of São Roque* (London, Society for Promoting Christian Knowledge, 1932) 11–12; Ricardo Conejo Ramilo, *Historia de Archidona* (Granada, 1973) 496-499; Agustí Duran i Sanpere, *Barcelona i la seva història* (Barcelona, 1973) 520-521. See also n. 78 below.
56. Ciruelo, *Reprobacion*, Pt. III, Chap. 10; Andres de Salazar, *Vida y milagros de San Gregorio Obispo de Ostia* (Pamplona, Juan Otoyza, 1624); CR 77.
57. D. Ortiz y Zuñiga, et al., *Anales eclesiásticos y seculares de la ciudad de Sevilla*, bk. 20, vol. 4 (1795 ed.) 141–142; the town of Alcoy (Alicante) kept water from the Navarre shrine in the church sacristy for use against locusts, and this may have been a common practice. It was used there in 1513–1515 and 1547–1548. José Vilaplana Gisbert, *Historia religiosa de Alcoy* (1903) (Alicante, Dip. Prov., 1977) 319–320.
58. Hieronymo Roman, *Chronica de la orden de los ermitaños del Glorioso Padre Sancto Agustin . . .* (Salamanca, Ioan Baptista de Terranova, 1569) (BNM R-30177) 52v, 53r, 130r; Francisco de Ribera, *Vida de San Augustin* (Madrid, 1684); Fernando Rubio Alvarez, "Devoción popular a San Agustín en Andalucía en tiempos pasados," *Archivo Hispalense* (Seville) 30 (1959) 95, 197–207.
59. CR 477; Cu I 305, 289; see n. 22 above.
60. G I 198. On threat of hail in region CS Sigüenza 1655 (1660) 110.
61. [Barcelona, Consell de Cents Jurats] *Manual de novells ardits, passim.* Barcelona petitionary procedures for 64 droughts from 1521 to 1631 included bringing relics of Santa Madrona to the cathedral from Montjuich (51 times);

making processions on 7 different days to 7 monasteries or churches dedicated to Mary, known as the *set goigs* or *set cambres* (46 times, 283 processions); making 5 processions on 5 days in honor of the 5 wounds of Christ, known as the *cinch nafres* or *plagues de Jesu* (23 times); taking the body of Saint Sever to the monastery of Santa Clara (13 times); taking the relic of the True Cross to the harbor and bathing it, last time in 1584 (12 times). Additional procedures included a set of processions known as *les hermites*, begun in the early seventeenth century; observance of a given day as if it were All Souls Day in order to obtain the intercession of the souls in purgatory (1566, 1628, 1629, 1631); the dispatch of pilgrims to Montserrat (in 1556); and starting in 1628, the exposure of the Holy Sacrament.

62. Christian, "Santos a María," 73.

63. According to Augustine and Aquinas it was lawful to seek to know God's will by casting lots if there was urgent necessity—provided it was done with reverence *Summa theologica* Q 95, art. 8; the procedure was time-honored in the West. Ronald Finucane, *Miracles and Pilgrims: Popular Beliefs in Medieval England* (London, Dent, 1977) 63, 85; Ciruelo, *Reprobacion*, Pt. II, Chap. 1.

64. La Solana, CR 484. Lots were used to select alcaldes in Daimiel, CR 234-235; El Toboso, T III 582; Leganés, M 345; and the towns in the district of Almoguera, G II 181, including Moratilla, G IV 245, Alvares, G VI 291, and Brea, M 45.

65. Caesarius of Heisterbach, *The Dialogue on Miracles* (London, Routledge and Sons, 1929) 2:58. Jaime I of Aragon received his name from a candle lottery. Juan de Robles, *Vida de Santa Anna* (n. 42 above), chap. 12, cites as a miracle the outcome of a candle lottery in Burgos. There a woman who had endowed both the feast of Saint Anne and that of Our Lady of the Snows could no longer afford both. She assigned to each saint a candle, choosing to maintain the feast to the saint whose candle lasted longest. That of Saint Anne lasted much longer, and it was concluded that Mary was deferring to her mother.

66. T II 371.

67. G I 107–108; cf. also Balconete, G II 86.
68. G I 211, G III 270 (El Cubillo, 1507).
69. G II 138.
70. M 641. Other cases of lotteries: locusts, G VI 437, T I 45, T III 706; vine pests, T III 779, M 79; water, T II 153.
71. M 144, T II 269–270.
72. Cu I 338.
73. T I 335, 270.
74. T II 12.
75. G II 137, CR 188.
76. CR 135. For other aspects of the cult of Saint Joseph in sixteenth-century Spain, see *Estudios Josefinos* 18 (1964) *San José y Santa Teresa.*
77. CR 161–162, 328, 554, 420.
78. "Coplas hechas por un religioso de la orden de sant Augustin de el bien aventurado sant Roch . . . en tiempo de pestilencia" (Toledo, Juan de Villaquiran, 1513–1520), no. 814 in A. Rodriguez-Moñino, *Diccionario Bibliog. de Pliegos Sueltos Poéticos* (Madrid, Castalia, 1970); Vincent Sorribes, "La devoció valenciana a Sant Roc," *Analecta Sacra Tarraconensia* 28 (1955) 321–337.
79. Primitivo Gutiérrez Chimeno, "Villalpando y su tierra por la Inmaculada, 1466–1966" (Zamora, 1966), pamphlet, p. 16. Quintana, *Historia de Madrid,* 863–864, full text.
80. Salomon, *Campagne,* 151–154, 297. M. Weisser, *Peasants,* 107, found that in 1628 in one village of around a hundred households about a third of the households were involved in legal proceedings. For the legal problems of Perales, see M 438–439.
81. Quer, G V 304.
82. Description of funeral *caridad* in Juan Antonio Gaya Nuño, *Tratado de mendicidad* (Madrid, Taurus, 1961); for a present-day *caridad* in Soria, see Susan Tax Freeman, *Neighbors* (Chicago, University of Chicago Press, 1970) 112–113. Zapata, *Miscelánea,* 427–428.
83. *Siete partidas,* pt. 1, title 23, law v–vi; M 444.
84. CR 106.
85. Valdeconcha, G IV 307; Puebla de Almoradiel, T II 251; Cobeña, M 191.
86. Azpilcueta, *Manual,* 126.

87. M 472.
88. CS Sigüenza 1655 (1660) 109.
89. M 298–299, G V 220.
90. T I 403.
91. M 397.
92. Cu II 105.
93. CR 23.
94. CR 122.
95. Cu I 56.
96. G II 137.
97. CR 207.
98. Trexler, "Florentine Religious Experience" (n. 5 above), p. 17.
99. Cu I 305.

CHAPTER 3. CHAPELS AND SHRINES

1. Albalate, G II 113; Chiloeches, G IV 55; Griñón, M 313; Santa María/Llanos, Cu I 131, 218; Ventas/Peña Aguilera, T II 213; Luciana, CR 283; Santa Cruz/Mudela, CR 463; Fuencarral, M 260; Puertollano, CR 418–419; Brugel, T I 153; Cazalegas, T I 294.
2. Catalonia: Narciso Camós, Iardin de Maria (Barcelona, 1657). Cristobal de Granados, Historia de la Fuen-santa (Madrid, 1648) fol. 85, writing in reference to the legends of Fuensanta and Our Lady of Castellar (Villarrubia, T).
3. Montiel, CR 350; Auñón, G I 415–416; Tendilla, G III 86–87; Peñalver, G I 256–257; Fuencaliente, CR 252; San Pablo, T II 392–393; Iniesta, Cu I 32; Puerto San Vicente, T II 299.
4. Other versions in Gonçalez Mendoça, Historia del Monte Celia, and Pedro de Salazar, Cronica y historia de la fundacion y progresso de la provincia de Castilla, de la orden del bienaventurado padre San Francisco (Madrid, Imprenta Real, 1612) 234.
5. Toledo Descención, T III 496, 525, 540; Daimiel Crosses, CR 238ff.; Daimiel Peace, CR 237; Belmonte, Cu I 270; Cubas Cross, M 212–213; Hontova, G IV 143; Almonacid de Toledo, T I 64–65; Cubas Blas, M 212; Ventas Peña Aguilera, T II 218–219; Fuenlabrada, M 269; Toledo Stephen and Augustine, T III 541.

6. Cf. Mario Martins, "Narrativas de apariçoes de Nossa Senhora ate ao sec. xii," *Acta Salamanticensia* (1958) 703–722.

7. AHN Inq. Leg. 114², exp. 7, Juan Garcia.

8. M 212–213.

9. Gonçalez de Mendoça, *Historia del Monte Celia*, 77–88, attempts to explain why Our Lady of Salceda appeared to knights instead of the powerless.

10. T II 464; Francisco de Pisa, *Apuntamientos para la segunda parte de la "Descripcion de la imperial ciudad de Toledo"* (1612) (Toledo, Diputación Provincial, 1976) 53, 82.

11. Cu I 84–85.

12. T I 497–498. Pedro de Herrera, *Descripcion de la capilla de Na. Sa. del Sagrario* . . . (Madrid, Luis Sanchez, 1617) (Harv. Span 3225.5).

13. Gonçalez de Mendoça, *Historia del Monte Celia*, 394–399; also Pedro de Salazar, *Cronica*, 240.

14. G I 418.

15. Gonçalez de Mendoça, *Historia del Monte Celia*, 69–70.

16. CR 243.

17. Cu II 38–40.

18. What has survived in the parish archive of Griñón is an eighteenth-century copy, undated, of the original investigation and miracles. It consists of 43 numbered *pliegos* (182 pages) of depositions. The first 110 pages contain reports of sixteen miracles taken by the Alcalde ordinario Thome de Coca from July 16, 1569, to April 3, 1570. The last 72 pages contain the "Informazion" of the finding of the crucifix, testimony taken June 21 to July 3, 1569, from fourteen witnesses by Juan de Villorrex before the lord of the town, Alonso de Mendoza y Toledo, at the request of Christoval Hernandez, "Prior general del Concejo, justicia y regimiento" of Griñón. Much of the material is faithfully resumed in Antonio Bernardo Campò y Melgarejo, *Historia y explicacion de la informacion que se hizo del aparecimiento del santissimo christo aparecido en el termino de la villa de Griñon en el dia viernes 17. de Junio año de 1569* . . . (Madrid, Antonio Sanz, 1737).

19. The Pérez de Valdivia book (Barcelona, Casa de Hieronymo Genoues, 1585) is in Houghton Library, Harvard Uni-

versity. J. M. Sánchez Gómez, "Un discípulo del P. Mtro. Avila en la Inquisición de Córdoba. El Dr. Diego Pérez de Valdivia, catedrático de Baeza," *Hispania* 9 (Madrid, 1949) 104–134.

20. CS Cuenca 1602 (1603) 244; similarly, a late sixteenth-century proclamation of the Inquisition in the district of Toledo warned against alumbrados who said that "certain feverishness, tremblings, pains and spells that they suffer are signs of the love of God, whence they know that they are in grace and have the holy spirit" (sig. Aiii r; see below, n. 41 to chap. 5).

21. Lope Paez, *Espejo de virtudes, en la vida, y mverte de la V. M. Francisca Ines de la Concepcion, Abadesa del Convento de N. Señora de Belen de Cifventes* . . . (Toledo, Iuan Ruiz de Toledo, 1653).

22. A copy of this investigation was graciously obtained for me by Fr. Gaspar Calvo Moralejo, author of "Santa María de la Cruz," *Antonianum* 50 (1975) 561–576. Excerpts of the investigation were printed by Antonio Daça in *Historia, vida, y milagros, extasis, y revelaciones de la bienaventurada Virgen Santa Iuana de la Cruz* . . . (Madrid, Luis Sanchez, 1610) fol. 103, and discussed by Pedro Navarro in *Favores de el rey de el cielo hechos a su esposa la Santa Juana de la Cruz* . . . (Madrid, Thomas Iunti, 1622) 3–26.

23. Cebrià Baraut, *Santa María del Miracle* (Montserrat, Abadia de Monserrat, 1962); Lluís G. Constans, *Història de Santa María del Collel* (Malgrat, Emilio Canet, 1954); Francisco Sanz de Frutos, *Historia de Nuestra Señora de la Cruz* (Vitoria, Hijos de Pujol, 1887). The Escalona (Seg.) parish archives contain a contemporary, certified copy of the 1617–1618 retrospective investigation of these apparitions, in 95 folios, with testimony of 12 witnesses giving hearsay evidence of the apparitions and direct evidence of cures in the previous 20 years. I treat these and other visions in *Apparitions in Late Medieval and Renaissance Spain* (Princeton, Princeton University Press, 1981).

24. Steven Sharbrough, "The Cult of the Mother in Europe: The Transformation of the Symbolism of Woman" (unpublished Ph.D. dissertation, Dept. of History, University of California, Los Angeles, 1977).

25. Christian, "De los Santos a María" (see above, n. 28 to chap. 1).

26. From other sources it is known that Saint Anne of Tendilla rendered sterile women fertile; that the Niño de la Guardia cured babies with hernias, cripples, the sick, and "trabajados," and that the shrine of Monsalud cured the possessed and prevented rabies. Juan de Robles, *Vida de Santa Anna*, chap. 12; Rodrigo de Yepes, *Historia de la muerte y glorioso martyrio del Sancto Innocente, que llaman de la Guardia, natural de la ciudad de Toledo* . . . (Madrid, Juan Iñiguez de Lequerica, 1583) 53v; Antonio de Yepes, *Crónica general de la orden de San Benito* (Madrid, 1960) 3:333–336, included a report of a monk of the abbey of Monsalud written in 1617.

27. Geronimo de Quintana, *Historia del origen y antiguedad de la venerable y milagrosa imagen de Nuestra Sra de Atocha* (Madrid, 1637) 71-84; Alfonso de Valdés, *Diálogo de Mercurio y Carón* (1528), ed. José F. Montesinos (Madrid, Clásicos Castellanos, 1929) 21; G II 490; Cu I 270.

28. Antonio Ares, *Discurso del ilustre origen y grandes excelencias de la misteriosa Imagen de nuestra Señora de la Soledad del conuento de la Victoria de Madrid.* . . . (Madrid, Pedro Taço, 1640) art. 8:1.

29. This finding is not typical of all major Marian shrines, at least according to their own propaganda; miracle books generally include cures of illnesses, including the plague. The miracle most common at Notre Dame de Rochefort in the seventeenth century was the cure of fevers; see Robert Sauzet, "Pèlerinage panique et pèlerinage de dévotion: Notre-Dame de Rochefort au XVIIe siècle," *Anales du Midi* 77:74 (Oct. 1965) 375–399. The point here is that the villagers do not seem to view Mary as critical, either in vows or miracles, for this purpose.

30. (Pedro de Burgos) *Libro de la historia y milagros, hechos a inuocacion de nuestra Señora de Montserrate* (1550) ed. 1605, miracles no. 162 (1523), 235 (1542) also (new series) 11 (1592), among others. Cebrià Baraut has identified the earliest extant copy of this work as published in Barcelona in 1536 or 1537, possibly by Pedro Montpezat. The work was apparently written in 1514, and there may have been

editions earlier than 1536. C. Baraut, "Un ejemplar desconocido de la historia y milagros de nuestra Señora de Montserrat de Pedro de Burgos," *Gutenberg-Jahrbuch* (1958) 139–142.

31. *Historia de como fue hallada la ymagē de Santo Crucifixo q̃ esta en el monasterio de sancto Agustin de Burgos* (1554) miracles 23, 24 (ca. 1454).

32. Gabriel de Talauera, *Historia de Nuestra Señora de Guadalupe* (Toledo, Thomas de Guzman, 1597) 322.

33. Iayme Prades, *Historia de la adoracion y uso de las santas imagenes, y de la imagen de la fuente de la salud* [in Traiguera, C.P.] (Valencia, Felipe Mey, 1597) 463. A fascinating book. Besides giving the history of the shrine, it discusses other major shrines, to Christ as well as Mary, and relates devotions to struggle against Protestantism. There is a copy in the Marian Library, Dayton. The Council of Valencia (1565) prohibited the use of *medidas*: "That nobody measures the images of saints with threads or anything else, in order to take the measure to the sick, nor let there be given to the sick hosts on which there are things written, as all this smells of superstition." Tejada y Remiro, *Colección de cánones y de todos los concilios de la iglesia de España y de América*, 2d ed., 5 vols. (Madrid, Imp. de Sta. Coloma, 1861) 5:300. The measuring of images and the use of these ribbons or threads as talismans continues in many parts of Spain today.

34. G III 367–368; Joaquín de la Jara, *Historia de la Imagen de Nuestra Señora del Prado* (Ciudad Real, 1880) 450.

35. CR 254–255; Cu I 84–85; T II 392–393; T II 218–219; Christ of Burgos, *Historia* (1554) 20, 47; G II 187; CR 419; T II 52.

36. The *estampa* in Bernardo de Cartes, *Historia de la milagrosa Imagen de Nuestra Señora de Monsalud* (Alcalá, Joseph Espartosa, 1721) bears the title "abogada de la rabia mal de ojo melancolias y aflicciones de corazon." Seventy-three miracles are included in the book, some from the sixteenth century.

37. CR 143–144.

38. Peñalver, G I 256; Loranca, Cu II 23; Auñón, G I 417; Cañavete, Cu I 247; Almonacid de Toledo, T I 65.

39. For Montserrat, Burgos, and Niño de la Guardia, see above,

nn. 26 and 30. Lucas de Tuy, *Libro de los miraglos de sant Isidro, arçobispo de Seuilla* . . . (Salamanca, 1525); Felipe de Guimerán, *Breve historia de la orden de Nuestra Señora de la Merced* . . . *Tratase mas en particular de la benditissima casa de la Madre de Dios del Puche de Valencia, de sus milagros* . . . (Valencia, Hered. Juan Nauarro, 1591). "Dos historias, la vna dela sancta casa de Nuestra Señora de Guadalupe, y su principio y fundacion y cosas notables della. Y la otra del principio y fundacion dela casa del Señor Sanctiago de Galizia, patron de España: y de las cosas notables desta sancta casa" (Seuilla, Impresa en casa de B. Gonçalez y H. de Chaues, 1575) [Valencia, Artes Gráficas Soler, 1965].

40. Christ of Burgos, *Historia* (1554) 27v–33r. Gonçalez de Mendoça, *Historia del Monte Celia*, 390–393.

41. Azpilcueta, *Manual*, 75. Similarly, in a 1622 biography of Juana de la Cruz, of Cubas, Fr. Pedro Navarro sought to explain why certain images of Mary no longer work miracles: "Finally, I hold that some images of Our Lady that worked many miracles in the past do so no longer in punishment for our inordinate self-interest and avarice; for hardly has a holy image begun to be known for a miracle or two when within two days the walls are covered with shrouds, crutches, and hands and feet of wax, without any more justification or legal testimony than the avarice of those who commit that misdeed, converting to interest and lucrative commerce that which should be used to incite the devotion of the faithful. The holy council of Trent was well aware of this danger, which it sought to preclude by so justly ordaining that no new miracle be admitted in any church without a judicial and rigorous episcopal investigation." [In *Favores de el Rey de el Cielo, hechos a su esposa la Santa Juana de la Cruz, Religiosa de la Orden tercera de Penitencia de N.P.S. Francisco* (Madrid, Thomas Iunti, 1622), p. 39.]

42. CS Toledo 1536 8r; 1566 (1568) 74r–v; Uclés 1578 88v.

43. *Nueva Recopilacion* (Alcala, 1598) bk. 2, tit. 10, law 26; Burgos *Historia* (1554), miracle 33.

44. G I 416–417.

45. Juan de San Gerónimo, *Memorias* CDIHE 7 (1845) 148, hermit of la Herrería de Fuente Lámparas.
45. Miguel de Cervantes, *Persiles y Segismunda* (Madrid, Clásicos Castalia, 1969) 265.
47. CS Toledo 1566 (1568) 52r; 1583 48v; 1601 11v–12r; CS Cuenca 1531 46r–v; 1602 (1603) 196, 304–306; 1626 356–357. See also CS Santiago 1576 82v; Uclés 1578 65v. The problem was raised earlier in CS Jaén 1511 19v: ". . . algunas personas seglares diziendo que tienen confradias las tales hermitas se entremeten a poner en ellas hermitaños r mayordomos r administrar los bienes r rentas r limosnas dellas . . ." The synod approved a system of licensing.
48. T I 488.
49. M 600–601.
50. M 268; Cu II 96; Gonçalez de Mendoça, *Historia del Monte Celia*, 18–20.
51. CS Cuenca 1602 (1603) 196.
52. DHEE I 352; Cu I 106 (Vara de Rey).
53. CR 252.
54. Nieves de Hoyo Sancho, "Fiestas patronales y principales devociones de la Mancha," *Revista de dialectología y tradiciones populares* 3 (1947) 113–144; CR 309.
55. Cu II 21.
56. Terrinches, CR 500; M 45–46; the report of Uceda (G III 367–368) has a similar miracle.
57. CS Sigüenza 1584, cited in 1655 (1660) 38.
58. Alfonso de Valdés, *Diálogo de las cosas ocurridas en Roma* (1529), ed. José F. Montesinos (Madrid, Clásicos Castellanos, 1928) 206; Huecas, T I 485.
59. CS Sigüenza 1532 (1534) 15r; CS Cuenca 1566 (1571) 72v; 1531 12r; 1602 (1603) 126, cites 1592.
60. Basilio Arce, *Historia del origen, fundacion, progresso y milagros de la casa y monasterio de Nuestra Señora de Sopetran* (Madrid, Vda. Alonso Martin, 1615) 93r–v.
61. CS Burgos 1498–1511, 1575 (1577), 276; Toledo 1583 56v–57r; T I 264–265; CR 238; T III 567.
62. M 396.
63. See description for the present day in Jesús García Perdices, *Cual aurora naciente* (Guadalajara, 1974) 44, a survey of Marian shrines in the province of Guadalajara.

64. Valtablado (G), Cu II 155; Villarrubio, Cu I 381; Villarejo, M 174; Cardiel, T I 226, T II 153.

65. Damián Iguacén Borau, *Vida de San Urbez, Sol de la Montaña* (Zaragoza, El Noticiero, 1969); Joan Segura, "Història del santuari de Sant Magí," in *Certamen catalanista de la joventut catòlica de Barcelona* (Junta de 1887) 139–304; Sanç Capdevila, *Història compendiada del santuari de Sant Magí de la Brufaganya* (Tarragona, 1924). CS Segovia 1586 87v–88r forbade the practice of bathing images or relics in times of drought: "Otro si ordenamos, y mandamos, que ningunas personas desta ciudad, ni Obispado, de aqui adelante no usen de bañar en fuentes, ni rios, ni pozos, y otras partes cuerpos, o reliquias de sanctos (de lo qual tienen supersticion en algunas partes) diziendo ques causa, que llueua en tiempo de seca: ni hagan otras semejantes ceremonias, so pena de excomunion, y de cincuenta ducados aplicados para obras pias, fabrica, y gastos de justicia por yguales partes."
For Barcelona, see above, n. 61 to chap. 2. The Inquisition of Cuenca condemned as superstitious the bathing for rainfall of the ancient relics of San Tuy in Taranquena (G) in 1655 . . . but discreetly, for the bishopric of Sigüenza had permitted the ritual (ADC, Inq., Leg 497, Exp 6602). Well into the twentieth century inhabitants of Tahull (Lérida), where I revised this essay, put the feet of the image of Saint Quirs in a stream when asking for rain.

66. C. Lisón Tolosana, "Aspectos de 'Pathos' y 'Ethos' de la comunidad rural," *Expresiones actuales de la cultura del pueblo* [Anales de Moral Social y Económica XLI] (Madrid, Centro de Estudios Sociales del Valle de los Caidos, 1976).

67. CR 610.

68. CR 77; M 96; Cu II 38–40; M 590; Cervantes, *Persiles y Segismunda*, 314; CR 66; T III 532.

69. Christ of Burgos, *Historia* (1554), miracle 40.

70. Luis de la Cuadra, *Catálogo-inventario de los documentos del monasterio de Guadalupe* (Madrid, 1973) 209. Royal edict in 1564 against Chinchón and Colmenar for impeding questors.

71. J. de la Jara, *Nuestra Señora del Prado*, 448: ". . . habiendo

corrido muchas tierras y santuarios buscando quien le remediesse . . ."; Cervantes, *Persiles y Segismunda*, 313–315.

72. See also maps of chapels in Christian, "De los santos a María," 63, 69.

73. On castles, Nieves de Hoyo Sancho, "Fiestas patronales," 122.

CHAPTER 4. RELICS AND INDULGENCES

1. Christian, "De los santos a María," *passim*.
2. CR 253–254, G I 219.
3. Cu I 381, CR 171.
4. Cu II 155, G VI 203; see also above, n. 65 to chap. 3.
5. G II 187.
6. Cu I 304.
7. T I 382–383, G VI 133.
8. Macarius, Valdesaz, G I 182; Matthew, Pozo de Guadalajara, G VI 224–225.
9. Roch, CR 77; Ysidro, G III 368–369, 283, and note.
10. Saint Eugene: T III 540, 543–544; *Compilacion de los despachos tocantes a la translacion del bendicto cuerpo de Sant Eugenio martyr primer arcobispo de Toledo, hecha de la Abbadia de Sandonis en Francia a esta sancta Yglesia* (Toledo, Miguel Ferrer, 1566); J. F. Rivera Recio, *San Eugenio de Toledo y su culto* (Toledo, Diputación Provincial, 1963). Saint Leocadia: T III 541; Miguel Hernandez, *Vida, martyrio y translacion de la gloriosa virgen, y martyr Santa Leocadia . . . Con la relacion de lo que passo en la ultima translacion, que se hizo de las santas reliquias de Flandes a Toledo* (Toledo, Pedro Rodriguez, 1591); Francisco de Pisa, *Historia de la gloriosa virgen y martyr Santa Leocadia, Patrona de Toledo* (Madrid, Diego Rodriguez, 1617). Saints Justo and Pastor: Ambrosio de Morales, *La vida, el martyrio, la inuencion, las grandezas, y las translaciones de los gloriosos niños martyres san Iusto y Pastor. Y el solenne triumpho con que fueron recibidas sus santas reliquias en Alcala de Henares en su postrera translacion* (Alcala, Andres de Angulo, 1568). The towns of Los San-

tos de la Humosa and Tielmes (M) claimed Justo and Pastor as their own (M 594).

11. M 108, G I 187. The replies of village priests to a questionnaire of Cardinal Lorenzana in the 1780s include some traditions of "local" saints that may have been extant in 1575: that Macarius of Valdesaz (G) had been a hermit; that Quiteria was martyred at Marjaliza (T) (the 1576 report mentions a chapel to her there); that Saints Germain and Servando were hermits near Villarrubia de los Ojos (the 1575 report lists a chapel to "San Serbante"); and that a holy shepherd, Remondo, different from Fray Reimundo the Cistercian, was buried at Ciruelos (T) (there was a chapel to Remondo in 1576). Some of these stories may be based on the false chronicles of the seventeenth century, like the 1780s report of Boadilla del Monte that San Babiles was an eighth-century bishop of Pamplona martyred near Boadilla while teaching catechism, or that the chapel of Zucueca in Granátula (CR) had been the cathedral of the Saint Blaise buried in Cifuentes. By 1780 there was at least one new holy body, that of Juan de Buena Vida, a hermit who was buried in a chapel near Sayatón (G).

12. T I 310–311. In his latter days he, too, is supposed to have been a hermit. Toledo city, T III 540–541; Cu II 40.

13. T II 454, T II 299.

14. CR 554; Gonçalez de Mendoça, *Historia del Monte Celia*, 450–461; Diego also at Valdeflores near Pastrana, G III 194.

15. Known as San Blas de Otero for cave outside Cifuentes, G II 366–367, notes.

16. G II 368, G II 345, Cubas M 212, Camarena T I 200–201.

17. M 213; Salazar, *Cronica*, 545; see also above, n. 22 to chap. 3.

18. T III 540–541. In vol. 2, pp. 912–913 of his *Compendio historial de las chronicas y universal historia de todos los reynos d'España* (Anvers, 1571), Esteban de Garibay listed Spaniards venerated as saints in New Castile but not yet canonized. In addition to Fray Diego de Alcalá and María de Ajofrín "por cuyos meritos cada dia obra nuestro señor maravillas," he named Fray Martín, a disciple of Saint Francis, and Beatriz de Silva, founder of the Conceptionist order, both in Franciscan monasteries in Toledo.

19. G II 344; see also above, n. 21 to chap. 3.

20. G I 144.

21. J. de la Jara, *Nuestra Señora del Prado*, 381.

22. See description of arrival of relics in Pareja (G) in 1599, G I 120–121, note of J. Catalina García.

23. M 578; G III 85–87; G II 54–55; G IV 322–323; Salazar, *Cronica*, gives relics and their sources donated at the founding of the Clarisas Descalzas of Madrid, 352–356; T II 119; G III 321.

24. Juan Manuel de Estal, "Felipe II y su archivo hagiográfico de el Escorial," *Hispania Sacra* 23 (1970) 193–333; W. Telfer; see also above, n. 55 to chap. 2.

25. Maurice Boyd, *Cardinal Quiroga; Inquisitor General of Spain* (Dubuque, William C. Brown, 1954) 35.

26. G III 365–366. Bolea also gave a holy thorn to the convent of the Piedad of Guadalajara, where his sister was a nun (Salazar, *Cronica*, 469).

27. Cu I 269. On the role of Jesuits in education, see Richard L. Kagan, *Students and Society in Early Modern Spain* (Baltimore, Johns Hopkins University Press, 1974).

28. G I 120–121. The fomenting of popular devotion to saints and relics is prescribed in Loyola's *Spiritual Exercises* (pt. 2, "Rules for Thinking with the Church," 6). Jesuits were holding missions in the region in the early 1580s (J. de la Jara, *Nuestra Señora del Prado*, 450).

29. Miguel Hernández was the priest. On relics in the context of controversy see Alfonso de Valdés, *Diálogo de Roma*, 192–197, and Margharita Morreale, "Comentario de una página de Alfonso de Valdés: El tema de las Reliquias," *Revista de Literatura* 21 (1960) 67–77.

30. [Barcelona Consell de Cents Jurats], *Manual de Novells Ardits* 9 (1900) 20–21 (June 3, 1611).

31. T III 700–741.

32. Tejada, *Canones*, 5:435.

33. José Godoy Alcántara, *Historia crítica de los falsos cronicones* (Madrid, Rivadeneyra, 1868); T. D. Kendrick, *Saint James in Spain* (London, Methuen, 1960).

34. From Inquisition interrogations; Bennassar, *Inquisition espagnole*, 258.

35. J. de Avila, "Causas y remedios de las herejias" (Memorial

2° para Trento), ed. C. M. Abad, op. cit., 109–111. Very important text from a man who knew the countryside.

36. F. Farfan, *Regimiento de castos: Y remedio de torpes* (Salamanca, Cornelio Bonardo, 1590) 77. Already completed when his *Tres Libros contra el peccado de la simple fornicacion* was published in 1585.

37. Rodrigo de Santaella, *Manual d' doctrina necessaria para los visitadores y clerigos de las yglesias* (Universidad de Alcala, 1530) BNM R 6559², f. 34v. Capitulo lxiii como a de oyr las mugeres. Iten enseñeles q̃ no han de cōfesar las mugeres en secreto sino en publico: ni las han de hazer assentar haz a haz sino al lado porq̃ no les mirē las caras. O facies mulieres vetus vres. Ni se tarde mucho cō ellas: ni muy amenudo las oygā: ni al varō han de mirar porq̃ no lo turbē ni lo agan auergōçar. y como han de tratar mas dulcemēte los letrados y nobles r virtuosos que se traē consigo gran verguença y confusion que los rusticos r ydiotas/ que si no son asperamente reprehendidos ni han verguença ni conoscen la graueza del peccado.

38. CR 256.

39. M 188.

40. G III 85.

41. Bernuy, T II 385; Auñón, G I 406; Magán, T II 12; Sta María del Campo, Cu I 238; Auñón, G I 419; Ribas, M 528; El Peral, Cu I 55–56; La Membrilla, CR 309; Cobeña, M 188–191; Daimiel, CR 244; La Despernada, M 243; Toledo, T III 560–561; Mazarulleque, Cu II 96; Villanueva de Alcardete, T III 740–741; Fuentelaencina, G II 54–55; Lillo, T I 512; Valdesaz, G I 182.

42. José A. Tapia, *Historia de la Baja Alpujarra* (Almería, 1966) 266–275.

CHAPTER 5. LOCAL RELIGION: VARIATIONS, ALTERNATIVES, AND REFORM

1. Weisser, *Peasants*, 49–50.

2. ADC Inq. Exp 1411, 3825, 4170.

3. T III 560–567.

4. T III 567.

5. There were only two chapels to La Soledad listed in the

countryside—one in Santa María del Campo (Cu) that had been converted from a chapel to San Sebastián, and another in Colmenar Viejo (M). There was also a hospital in Pastrana.

6. Pisa, *Apuntamientos* (see above, n. 10 to chap. 3) 41–43; Ramón Molina y Nieto, *Toledo y su Reina, crónica de la coronación de la Virgen del Sagrario* (Toledo, Ed. Cat. Toledana, 1926) 34–35, 90–91.

7. T III 562.

8. Pisa, *Apuntamientos*, 44–49; Quintana, *Historia de Madrid*, 991ff.

9. Alameda de la Sagra to Atocha M 18; T III 540.

10. Quintana, *Historia de Madrid*, 173–174. Other Madrid images obtained more or less legally from the countryside: ibid., 890, 911, 927, 995, 148–149, 158.

11. Cu I 131–132.

12. See Julian Pitt-Rivers's analysis of the word *pueblo* in *People of the Sierra* (Chicago, University of Chicago Press, 1961) 7–33, and Julio Caro Baroja, "El sociocentrismo del pueblo español," in *Razas, pueblos y linajes* (Madrid, Revista de Occidente, 1957).

13. The letter is printed in José Miguel Velaus, *Epítome historial de la Sta. Cruz que se venera en la hermita del castillo de las Peñas de San Pedro* (Madrid, 1767).

14. Albalate, G II 113; in the parish archive is an eighteenth-century transcription of the 23–26 May 1555 investigation, with testimony from 13 witnesses and one of the discoverers of the cross. Relaciones Lorenzana MS 85, 342v–344r mention Philip III's visit.

15. Illescas T I 497.

16. T III 529.

17. Pisa, *Apuntamientos*, 41–43.

18. Quintana, *Historia de Madrid*, 329.

19. Eugenio Alberi, *Le relazioni degli ambasciatori veneti al senato durante el secolo decimosesto*, Ser. 1, vol. 5 (Firenze, 1861) 62, 423.

20. D. Erasmus, *Enchiridion* (Sp. ed.) 257–259, cited in Bataillon, *Erasmo y España*, 201.

21. V. Beltrán de Heredia, "El Edicto contra los Alumbrados

del Reino de Toledo," in *Miscelánea Beltrán de Heredia* 3 (1972) Biblioteca de Teólogos Españoles, 27, 217–220.

22. CS Cadiz 1594.
23. See above, n. 19 to chap. 2; Mondas, T II 446; Julio Caro Baroja, *Ritos y Mitos Equívocos* (Madrid, Istmo, 1974) 31–76.
24. Tejada, *Cánones*, V 257–258; CS Toledo 1566 (1568) 51, repeated CS Cuenca 1602 (1603) 191–192; also CS Toledo 1583 29v, CS Uclés 1578 64v; CS Cuenca 1602 (1603) 139–140.
25. Mascaraque, T II 67; El Toboso, T III 583; Alhambra, CR 45; Fuentelaencina, G II 56; Getafe, M 299; Santorcaz, M 589. This may not be a bullfight. "El dia de San Pedro y San Pablo se mataban tres reses vacunas, y se daban en caridad; esta se quito en tiempo del christianisimo Cardenal Siliceo."
26. Carrascosa del Campo, Cu II 21; Tarancón, Cu II 60; Auñón, G I 420; Ocaña, T II 186; Talavera, T II 464; Boyd, *Cardinal Quiroga*, 35–36.
27. Indecent images and dressing of images in profane clothes: Council of Trent, Session 25, Dec. 3, 1563, and Council of Toledo 1565, Papal Decree 1642. Crescenciano Saravia, "Repercusión en España del Decreto del Concilio de Trento sobre las imágenes," *Boletín del Seminario de Estudios de Arte y Arqueología* (Valladolid, 1960) 26:129–143.
28. G I 220–221; also in report of Centenera, G II 436.
29. John Bossey, "The Counter-Reformation and the People of Catholic Europe," *Past and Present* 47 (May, 1970) 51–70.
30. T I 485.
31. *Veladas:*
    CS Burgos 1411 (1503) 32r, 1498 (1503) 69r, forbidden except Holy Week; 1500 (1503) 72v, excommunication. For lack of effect, see miracles of Christ of Burgos during vigils.
    CS Segovia 1472 (repr. 1965), 1586, no mention.
    CS Avila 1481 Tit. II, pt. 2, chap. 5, forbidden. Reprinted 1556.
    CS Toledo 1498, no mention; 1536 6v–7r, permitted with authority present and lights; 1566 (1568), forbidden; 1583

48r–v, 1601 51, permitted in town churches with supervision.

CS Badajoz 1501 IX:2, CS Córdoba 1520 (1521) 45r–v, permitted except eves of holy days, or on holy days. Both by Alonso Manrique.

CS Jaén 1511 41v–42r, forbidden.

CS Sigüenza 1532 (1534) 8r, permitted with supervision; 1566 (1571) repeated 1608 (1647) 33–34, forbidden.

CS Palencia 1440–1460 (1501) sig. di–dii; 1545 (1548) 61v, forbidden.

CS Calahorra 1553 (1555) 65r, forbidden.

CS Astorga 1553 35v, forbidden after Ave Maria.

CS Guadix 1554 (1556), encouraged Christmas, Maundy Thursday, Easter Morn, with supervision; at other times cause for excommunication.

CS Cuenca 1531, permitted only in cathedral on eves of Our Lady and Saint Julian, 48r; 1566 (1571) 64v, 1602 (1603) 192–193, 231, forbidden.

CS Granada 1572 (1573) 93v–94r permitted Christmas, Maundy Thursday, Easter Morn, with priest patrolling with candle.

CS Santiago 1576 (1579) 71r, forbidden.

CS Uclés 1578 65r, permitted with lights and supervision, men and women separate, no disguises.

Forbidden by Councils of Toledo, Valencia, and Santiago in 1565 (Tejada 5:236–237, 300, 345).

32. CS Sigüenza 1532 (1534) 15r, must go and return in one day; 1608 (1647) 34, ½ league.

CS Osma 1536 (1538) 46r, not more than 1 league beyond town limits; must return to eat in their houses; exceptions: cathedral and Na. Sra. del Espino of Soria.

CS Palencia 1545 (1548) 55r, "so color de processiones r ledanias se hazen embriaguezes y deshonestidades comiendo y beuiendo en ellas y andando burlando/ y parlando los clerigos con los legos y los hombres con las mugeres . . . "; not more than 1 league from town; eat at home.

CS Toledo 1566 (1568) 59r, not more than 1 league from town.

CS Uclés 1578 69v, 1 league limit.

CS Segovia 1586 47v, copied from Salamanca, Const 56, 1 league limit. Cf. also CS Jaén 1511 24r, criticizing lack of seriousness in processions: ". . . las dichas processiones se fazē con poca devociō r oraciō r poco recogimiēto yendo enellas los legos entre los clerigos y los clerigos entre los legos: y las mugeres entre los hombres reyēdo r parlando r cō poca atēcion sin rezar ni dezir oracion alguna para alcançar de nuestro Señor aquello por que la tal procession se haze. Demanera q̄ ni los clerigos pueden dezir ni cantar los oficios r oraciones que en semejātes processiones se suele fazer y dezir ni los legos ni las mugeres rezan ni dizen oracion alguna."

33. Arce, *Historia de Sopetran*, 101.
34. CS Osma 1536 (1538) 30r, 65v.
   CS Astorga 1553 52v–53v, text of royal edict.
   CS Segovia 1472, chap. 16, sought to limit to one the customary funeral *caridades* of bread, wine, and cheese at burial, end of novena, and anniversary.
35. CS Toledo 1566 (1568) 69r.
   CS Uclés 1578 77rv–78r.
   CS Cuenca 1602 (1603) 311–312.
   CS Sigüenza 1608 (1647) 140–141.
36. CR 545, 591; Cu I 355; M 299, 444; M 189 "por ser vigilia el dicho dia y estar vedado por el santo concilio Tridentino que en semejantes dias de vigilia de ayuno no se diesen caridades . . ."
37. Badajoz, personal experience; Benito Nuñez Martín, *Un recuerdo. Historia de la milagrosa imagen de Nuestra Señora de Chilla, patrona de Candeleda* (Madrid, Escuela Gráfica Salesiana, 1967) 57–58.
38. T III 560.
39. CS Astorga 1553 64v–65r, CS Cuenca 1566 (1571) 82r–v, CS Burgos 1575 (1577) 237.
40. See above, nn. 35–37 to chap. 4.
41. For an excellent discussion of the campaign against fornication, Bennassar, *L'Inquisition espagnole*, 327ff. Francisco Farfan, *Tres libros contra el peccado de la simple fornicacion: donde se averigua, que la torpeza entre solteros es peccado mortal, segun ley diuina, natural, y humana: y se responde a los engaños de los que dizen que no es peccado*

(Salamanca, Hered. Matthias Gast, 1585) BNM R/4.696, Brit. Museum, bk. 1, chap. 9: "Reprehende el autor a los vulgares, Que temerariamente se entremeten a escudriñar y aueriguar questiones de Theologia," pp. 109–123. Bound with other sixteenth-century material relating to the Inquisition is a late sixteenth-century proclamation of the Inquisition of Toledo, five printed folios, in the Biblioteca Nacional. It is a kind of syllabus of errors in five parts: "judaismos," "Masometanas," "Luthero," "alumbrados," and a fifth part, without a name, which we might label "doubt" or "paganism." This latter part is another indication of the kind of independent thinking going on in New Castile in regard to Church doctrine: ". . . Or who have said, or affirmed that there is no heaven for the good nor hell for the bad and that there is nothing more than birth and death, and that have said, in this world you won't see me suffer and in the next you won't see me punished or that have said heretical blasphemies like "I do not believe," "I cease to believe," "I reject God our Lord and the virginity and purity of Our Lady the Virgin Mary, or who denied her virginity saying that Our Lady the Virgin Mary was not a virgin before, during, or after giving birth, or that she did not conceive by the Holy Spirit or who said heretical blasphemies against the heavenly saints. . . . And if they know of anyone who claimed that simple fornication, or usury, or perjury is not a sin, or that said that the soul of man is no more than a breath, and that blood is the soul, and that insulted or ill-treated images or crosses, or that anyone did not believe in the creed or doubted any one of the articles of faith. . . ." Sig A4r–v of proclamation beginning, "Nos los Inquisidores contra la heretica prauedad y apostasia en la Ciudad y Reyno de Toledo, Obispados de Auila y Segouia, de los Puertos aca, por Autoridad Apostolica" bound with "Copilacion delas Instructiones del Officio dela sancta Inquisicion" (Granada, 1537) and other similar instructions, BN R/15114. On similar skepticism of common people in England, see Keith Thomas, op. cit., 166–173.

42. CS Toledo 1536 12; similarly, CS Cuenca 1602 (1603) 193–194.

43. Juan de Avila, First *Memorial* (1551), 32.

44. T III 560, 564.

45. Daimiel CR 245; Quintana, *Historia de Madrid*, 229–230; Ortiz y Zuñiga, *Anales*, 4:125–129.

46. CS Toledo 1566 (1568) 52r = CS Toledo 1583 48v; CS Burgos 1575 (1577) 208; CS Uclés 1578 65v; CS Cuenca 1626 356–357; also CS Cuenca 1531 46r–v, no new hermitages; 1602 (1603) 196, against hermit entrepreneurs; CS Toledo 1601 11v-12r and CS Cuenca 1602 (1603) 304–6, against peddlers of religious objects; and CS Jaén 1511 19v, cited above, n. 47 to chap. 3.

47. V. Beltrán de Heredia, "Los Alumbrados de la diócesis de Jaén," *Miscelánea* 3, 294; Donald Howard Marshall, "Frequent and Daily Communion in the Catholic Church of Spain in the sixteenth and seventeenth Centuries." (unpublished Ph.D. thesis, Harvard University, 1952) 280.

48. For pressure on communities to regularize, Salazar, *Cronica*, 493 (Talavera 1515) and 489 (Escalona 1527).

49. Tejada, *Cánones*, 5:409; Daimiel, CR 244; Villanueva de los Infantes, CR 591.

50. T III 541.

51. Tejada, *Cánones*, 5:475–476; CS Cuenca 1602 (1603) 230.

52. Trent, Session 25, Dec. 3, 1563; M 601–602; G II 55.

53. A. Valdés, *Diálogo Roma*, 136–137; Juan de Avila, see above, n. 45 to chap 2; T III 545. For an analysis of French fêtes, see Yves-Marie Bercé, *Fête et revolte: Des mentalités populaires du XVIᵉ au XVIIIᵉ siècle* (Paris, Hachette, 1976) 152ff.

54. CS Palencia 1545 (1548 49r); CS Burgos 1575 (1577) 201.

55. CS Sigüenza 1655 (1660) 109.

56. CS Burgos 1503 78r; CS Segovia 1478 cited in CS 1586 44v; CS Cuenca 1531 cited in CS 1602 (1603) 124–125.

57. CS Calahorra 1539, cited in 1553 (1555) 26r–v; Segovia, 1586 43r, cites 1529. Similarly, CS Badajoz 1501 I:10 "occasion para que todas las fiestas se guarden mal."

58. CS Cuenca 1626 212–213; first text is that of Calahorra rephrased for emphasis.

59. CS Toledo 1583 58v–59r; CS Cuenca 1566 (1571) 21r–v; CS Sigüenza 1532 (1534) 6v.

60. CS Calahorra 1553 (1555) 25r–v, CS Toledo 1536 13v–14r.

61. Dario Rei, "Note sul concetto de 'Religione Populare,' "

Lares 40 (1974) 264–280; also J. C. Schmitt, "'Religion populaire' et culture folklorique: Note critique," *Annales* 31:5 (1976) 941–953.

CHAPTER 6. CHRIST ENSHRINED, 1580–1780

1. See above, nn. 11, 15, 33 to chap. 4. The priest of Boadilla del Monte (Relaciones Lorenzana ADT 15-VI-1785) cites Tamayo de Bargas on Saint Babiles.
2. C. Korolevskij, "Beyrouth," *Dict. d'hist. & Geog. Eccles.* 8: 1305–6; Manuel Trens, *Les majestats catalanes* (Monumenta Cataloniae, vol. 13, Barcelona, Ed. Alpha, 1966) 50–52; Fortià Solà, *La santa majestat de Caldes de Montbui* (Barcelona, La Bona Parla, 1934) 102–103.
3. William A. Christian, Jr., *Apparitions in Late Medieval and Renaissance Spain* (Princeton, Princeton University Press, 1981).
4. Marie-Claude Gerbet, "Les confréries religieuses à Cáceres de 1467 à 1523," *Mélanges de la casa de Velazquez* 7 (1971) 75–105; J. Meseguer, "Las Cofradías de la Vera Cruz. Documentos y notas para su historia," AIA 28 (1968) 109–110, 199–213; Gabriel Llompart, "Penitencias y penitentes en la pintura y en la piedad catalanas bajomedievales," *Revista de dialectología y tradiciones populares* 28 (1972) 229–249; T III 561–565; Rafael Ortega Sagrista, "Historia de las cofradías de la Pasión de Semana Santa," *Boletín del Instituto de Estudios Giennenses* 3:10 (1956) 9–71; [Barcelona] *Manual de Novells Ardits* 4 (1895) 147.
5. Marie-Claude Gerbet, "Les confréries," 96n.
6. Ibid., 85–6.
7. ADC Inq. Leg. 202, Exp. 2292, 23 sides. "toca a la cruz ꝗ dize q viero en el cielo; Ynformaçion de los cofadres de la Santa bera +"
8. Velaus (see above, n. 13 to chap. 5); Sta Cruz Mudela, CR 457; Hueva Relaciones Lorenzana MS 85 293r–294r; Griñón, by neighboring villagers when cross found (see above, n. 18 to chap. 3); El Bonillo, woman recalled cross in sky as foreshadowing sweating of image; Información, parish archive.
9. Cu II 27.

10. Juan de la Portilla Duque, *España restaurada por la Cruz* (Madrid, Domingo García Morras, 1661) 367–368.
11. ADC Inq. Leg. 242bis:3218; 181:2067. AHN Inq. Leg. 309. See also Juan de San Gerónimo, *Memorias*, CDIHE 7 (1845) 263–265; Dorothy Woodward, "The Penitentes of New Mexico" (1935) in collection of same title (New York, Arno Press, 1974).
12. ADC Inq. 244:3262.
13. Julio Caro Baroja, *Los Judíos*, 1:165–176.
14. Jerónimo de Barrionuevo, *Avisos* (1654–1658), ed. A. Paz y Melia (2 vols., Biblioteca de Autores Españoles, Madrid, Atlas, 1968, 221–222); *Cartas de Algunos Jesuitas* (1634–1648), MHE vols. 13 (1861) 14, 15, 16 (1862), 17 (1863), 18 (1864), and 19 (1865); José Pellicer, *Avisos* (1639–1644), in Antonio Valladares, *Semanario erudito*, vols. 31–33 (Madrid, 1790); Luis Cabrera de Córdoba, *Relaciones de las cosas sucedidas en la corte de España, desde 1599 hasta 1614* (Madrid, J. Martín Alegria, 1857); Antonio Rodríguez de León Pinelo, *Anales de Madrid de León Pinelo (1598–1621)* (Madrid, E. Maestre, 1931); León Pinelo, *Anales de Madrid, 447–1658*, ed. Pedro Fernández Martín (Madrid, Instituto de Estudios Madrileños, 1971).
15. Madrid images mistreated from Quintana, *Historia de Madrid* (1629, 1954): Marian statue carried in unholy way 1602 (871–872); Ecce Homo stabbed in convent (903); streetcorner image of Mary stabbed by heretics (178–179).
16. A. Ares, *Discurso . . . Soledad* (1640) (see above, n. 28 to chap. 3).
17. Francisco Barrantes Maldonado, abito de Alcantara, *Relacion de la calificacion, y milagros del Santo Cruzifixo de Çalamea, desde treze de setiembre del año de seyscientos y quatro, hasta el de seyscientos y diez y seys, ciuidida en dos libros* (Madrid, Vda Alonso Martin, 1617) BNM 2/69178. Antonio de San Felipe, *Origen y milagros . . . del Ssmo Christo de Zalamea . . .* (Madrid, por Antonio Martin, 1745) BNM 3/19903. Luis de Quiros, *Breve sumario de los milagros que el Santo Crucifijo de San Miguel de las victorias de la ciudad de La Laguna de la isla de Tenerife ha obrado hasta el año 1590 . . .* (Zaragoza, Juan de Lanaja, 1612; La Laguna, 1907). "Milagros de la Sta Cruz de la Va

de las Peñas de S Pedro," manuscript book, Parish Archive, 129 folios 1608–1609; Summary in AHN Clero Libro 31. Calatorao: Roque Alberto Faci, *Aragon, Reyno de Christo y Dote de Maria SSma* (Zaragoza, Joseph Fort, 1739) pt. 1:64. Atienza, Libro de Milagros ordered by Pedro de Salazar, visitor. Francisco de Iesus Maria (Merced. Desc.), *La Flor del Campo y Azuzena de los Valles Carpetanos: Historia del Santo Christo de los Afligidos. Venerado en el convento de Santa Cecilia de la villa de Ribas* . . . (Madrid, Roque Rico de Miranda, 1686) BNM 3/18239. See description of reception by 16 towns when image arrived, 112.

18. Caesarius of Heisterbach, *Dialogue on Miracles*, 1:455; 2: 188–189; P. Saintyves, *Les Reliques et les images legendaires* (Paris, Mercure de France, 1912) 85–106; Charly Clerc, *Les Théories relatives au culte des images chez les auteurs grecs, IIme siècle après J.-C.* (Paris, Fontemoing, 1915) 44–49.

19. Francisco Diego de Ainsa y Iriarte, *Fundacion, excelencias, grandezas y cosas memorables de la* . . . *ciudad de Huesca* (Huesca, 1619) 511–512 (Christ sweated in procession 1497); S. Garcias Palou, *El Santo Cristo de Alcudia* (Palma, Graf. San Cayetano, 1974) (Christ sweated blood in drought, 1507); Agustín de Arques Jover, *Breve historia de Nuestra Señora del Milagro de Cocentayna* (Madrid, Cano, 1805) (image wept blood 1520); other sixteenth-century cases in Aragon in Faci, *Aragon*, 1:41–42, 70–71.

20. (1) Romuald Díaz, *El Sant Crist d'Igualada* (Montserrat, 1965); (2) Cristobal de los Santos, *Tesoro del cielo* . . . (Madrid, 1695, BNM 3/68762) 138; (3) AHN Inq. Leg. 113^{1}: 4; (4) *Manual Novells Ardits* 10 (1902) 144; (5) AHN Inq. Leg. 114^{1}: 5; (6) Joseph Ant. de Herrera, *Descripción Histórico-Panegírica* . . . *de N. Señora de Monlora* (Zaragoza, Domingo Gascón, 1700 BNM 2/8944); (7) MHE 13 (1861) 52; (8) Transcription of investigation in parish archive; (9) J. H. Elliot, *The Revolt of the Catalans* (Cambridge University Press, 1963) 426; (10) Camós, *Iardin de Maria*, 166–167; (11) (number 2 above); (12) MHE 18:299; (13) "Infformacion de la milagrosa Imagen del Sto Christo de la Columna cuya Sta efigie . . . ," 98 folios, 1646 parish archive; (14) Ortiz y Zuñiga, *Anales*, 4:398; (15) Barrionuevo, *Avisos*, 1:196; (16) Faci, *Aragon*,

1:139; (17) Barrionuevo, *Avisos*, 2:2; (18) Ibid., 2:183; (19) Pablo Manuel Ortega, *Tratado Historial de los su-dores de la Santa Cara de Dios* (Murcia, 1725) cited in his *Chronica de la Santa Provincia de Cartagena . . . de S Francisco* (pt. 2, Murcia, Mesnier, 1746) 142–143; (20) Quintana, *Historia de Madrid*, 891; (21) Arch. Catedral de Murcia, Leg. 271, "Toda la Historia dela Milagrosa Imagen de Na Sa de las Lágrimas," Luis Belluga y Moncada, *Carta* (1706) *Sermon* (1707); (22) pamphlets BNM V.E. cᵃ 644 no. 5, BRAH Papeles Varios 4-1-8 1062 no. 7; (23) Matute, *Anales*, I 99–100; (24) ADC Inq. Leg. 591:7178 29 pp.; (25) Montuno Morente, *Nuestra Señora de la Capilla* (Madrid, 1950) 394; (26) Rel Lorenzana ADT 2-IV-1785, 1776 print of medida with summary of investigation; (27) ADC Inq. Leg. 613:7412; (28) Rel. Lorenzana ADT 27-X-1784.

21. San Carlos del Valle: Rel. Lorenzana La Membrilla ADT 18-X-1788; San Pablo Rel. Lorenzana ADT 1788; Tembleque: "Historia delo ocurrido enla Pintura del Ssmo Xpto de Santiago de la Palma que se venera en el Valle deesta Villa de Tembleque, pintado por dos Peregrinos no conocidos, el Viernes 25 de junio de 1688," by Fray Eugenio Fernandez de Miñano y Mora (1689) MS 11 pliegos held by Cofradía; Sacedón: Francisco Corona, *Historia de la maravillosa aparición del divino rostro de Nuestro Señor Jesu-Christo en el antiguo hospital de Sacedón en el año 1689* (Madrid, R. Velasco, 1881) (pamphlet, 56 p); Villalba del Rey: image is in private house, shown to visitors, oral legend; Villanueva de la Fuente: Rel. Lorenzana ADT 14-VI-1782.

22. All quotes from Rel. Lorenzana: Humanes, "primorosa en arte, y de aspecto que mueve a reverencia, y devocion," ADT 31-V-1788; Monasterio, "cuia santa ymagen es de las mas perfectas que se pueden encontrar," MS 85 329r; Talavera, "efigia la mas primorosa en sentir de facultativos," ADT 18-V-1782.

23. R. Ortega Sagrista, "Historia Cofradías Jaén," 12 (see above, n. 4) gives references.

24. T III 566–567.

25. León Pinelo, *Anales* (1971) 99.

26. Portilla Duque, *España restaurada por la Cruz*, 370–371.

27. [Martín Chirveches], *Crónica oficial de la coronación de Nuestra Señora de Angustias* (Cuenca, 1957).

28. Roberto Saénz Sierra, *Los picados de San Vicente de la Sonsierra* (Barcelona, 1977).

29. The records of the investigation of this miracle are in the parish archive.

30. Thomas A. Kselman, "Miracles and Prophecies: Popular Religion and the Church in Nineteenth-Century France," unpublished Ph.D. thesis, University of Michigan, 1978.

31. D. P. Walker, in *The Decline of the Doctrine of Hell* (London, Routledge, 1964) considered the origins of the notion of a friendly God in eighteenth-century England, and found that its first proponents were mystical eccentrics. But we do not learn why their inspirations should have found acceptance. Michel Vovelle has charted the progress of a decline in spiritual attention to the afterlife in eighteenth-century Provence; he found it occurred first among the urban bourgeoisie of Marseilles, but he tells most about a decline of religiosity, rather than a reorientation in religious sensibility. For Italy, see Carlo Ginzburg's thoughtful essay, "Religione, Folklore, Magica," in the Einaudi *Storia di Italia*, vol. 1 (Milan, 1967).

The matter is largely unstudied in Spain. A certain clerical moderation of the notion of divine punishment was under way at the end of the century (Lorenzana himself is an example), but missionaries like Antonio María Claret in the mid-nineteenth century strongly reaffirmed traditional doctrines. My impression is that as in France a more humane God was first to be found in bourgeois milieux; that as in France a unified concept of God broke down first in the cities, while the notion of a stern God subsisted in that part of rural Spain which remained Catholic, nursed by missions, well into the twentieth century. Indeed, in the depths of the post–Civil War period it was once again dominant.

Index

Aside from accents (added to all names to conform to modern usage) most town names are as given in the reports. Modern forms are in brackets. In parentheses are the present-day province, the date of the report, and the population at that date in households. Most shrines are indexed under town names (see Appendix B).

Library of Congress Cataloging in Publication Data

Christian, William A.   1944-
    Local religion in sixteenth-century Spain.

    Includes bibliographical references and index.
        1.   Spain—Religious life and customs.
    2.   Catholic Church in Spain—History.
    I.   Title.
BX1584.C49   282'.46   80-7513
ISBN 0-691-05306-5